ROMMEL'S DESERT WAR

ROMMEL'S DESERT WAR

The Life and Death of the Afrika Korps

Samuel W. Mitcham, Jr.

STEIN AND DAY/*Publishers*/New York

STEIN AND DAY PAPERBACK EDITION 1984

Rommel's Desert War was originally published in hardcover in
1982 by Stein and Day/*Publishers*.

Copyright © 1982 by Samuel W. Mitcham, Jr.
All rights reserved, Stein and Day, Incorporated
Designed by L. A. Ditizio
Printed in the United States of America
STEIN AND DAY/*Publishers*
Scarborough House
Braircliff Manor, N.Y. 10510

ISBN 0-8128-8045-5

For Terrie Knox

Photos courtesy of the National Archives.

Maps by M. Hwang.

Selected quotations from *The Trail of the Fox: The Search for the True Field Marshal Rommel* by David Irving, copyright © 1977 by David Irving, are reprinted by permission of the publisher, E. P. Dutton.

Selections from *The Foxes of the Desert* by Paul Carell, translated by Mervyn Savitt, copyright © 1960 in the British translation by E. P. Dutton & Co., Inc., in the United States and by Macdonald & Co. in the United Kingdom, is reprinted by permission of the publisher in the United States, E. P. Dutton.

Excerpts of approximately 1,000 words from *Rommel: The Desert Fox* by Desmond Young, copyright 1950 by Desmond Young, are reprinted by permission of Harper & Row, Publishers, Inc.

Excerpts of approximately 900 words from *The Rommel Papers*, copyright 1953 by B. H. Liddell Hart. Reprinted by permission of Harcourt Brace Jovanovich, Inc.

ACKNOWLEDGMENTS

Special thanks go to my former professor Dr. John C. Lewis and my good friend Dr. Lorraine Heartfield for all their assistance and encouragement along the way. Further thanks go to Dr. Edwin H. Hammond, without whose informal writing class this book would never have been published; to Dr. Charles S. Aiken, who taught me to be critical of my own typewritten work and helped me sharpen my analytical skills; to Major Everette Roper, Major Donald Jolly, Colonel Ernest Bruce, and Ted Cattron for teaching me the military trade; to Nina Helfert, Janet Williams, John Morgan, Robert O. Bass, and Captain Tom Maertens for proofreading and advice; to Connie Powell, who typed an earlier version of this manuscript; and to Manik Hwang for constructing the maps.

Gratitude is also extended to all those who assisted, directly or indirectly, in this endeavor. These include (but are not limited to) Colonel William J. Lyles, Major Dolan Watson, Fred Lindsey, Hinton Leonard, Harvey Hudnall, Ricky Fife, Bob Gildersleeve, Jane Bennett, Dr. Glenn Greene, Robert Wyatt, Joy Medford, Pat Bing, Melissa North Higgs, Pam Sharpe, and Marilyn Osterlund. Special appreciation goes to Mike Guidry, Calton Yeager, and Dr. Sidney R. Jumper for all their kind assistance at critical times.

Last, but certainly not least, I wish to express my deep appreciation to my parents, Mr. and Mrs. Wayne Mitcham of Bastrop, Louisiana, and to my brothers, Steve and Marq, for all their help and encouragement throughout this project.

CONTENTS

Maps

TABLES

PHOTOGRAPHS

(photos between pages 90 and 91)

The Desert Fox in field uniform
Rommel's panzer troops in action in France
The Desert Generals
Italian troops at an oasis
Italian troops digging in
The 5th Panzer Regiment moves out
A heavy howitzer battery changes position
A reconnaissance battalion faces a *ghibli*
Rommel's communications and command vehicles
Field Marshal Albert Kesselring
Field Marshal Erwin Rommel
The High Command
Rommel at Fuehrer Headquarters
An improvised 150-millimeter self-propelled gun
Tanks of both armies burning
The Afrika Korps in action
A desert in flames
A German graveyard

Introduction

World War II holds a special interest for Americans because it is the last war the United States won, or even tried very hard to win, for that matter. As the generation that fought that war grows older, one listens with fascination to the GIs' tales—perhaps a little enlarged over the years—of night bombings and commando raids, kamakazi attacks and parachute assaults, daring escapes and desperate jungle fighting. If you listen to a British veteran, and show any interest at all, sooner or later the talk will come round to Erwin Rommel. The aging veteran's eyes will become just a little misty as he dwells on the accomplishments of this warrior and, if you didn't know better, you couldn't tell from the Englishman's tone of voice that he was talking about the enemy. This isn't the case with the current, younger set of Patton enthusiasts in the United States. They are painfully aware that their hero failed to realize only two of his great ambitions and objectives: He did not capture Berlin and he never got the chance to decisively engage and defeat Field Marshal Erwin Rommel, the Desert Fox. The seriousness of this latter failure is intensified by the knowledge that Patton was obsessed with defeating Rommel and that Field Marshal Montgomery, Patton's archrival, actually won victories over this great German commander. The Patton partisans fervently, and sometimes loudly, proclaim that their idol would have smashed Rommel had the chance arisen, and perhaps they are right, for Patton was an undeniably brilliant leader of armored forces. The point, however, is that large numbers of people on both sides of the Atlantic are fascinated by this man Rommel, even though he has been dead for more than 35 years. In the minds of millions he seems still alive, through his accomplishments and through his legend. This book deals with his accomplishments. It focuses on that desperate and decisive period from January to December 1942, when the outcome of the Desert War was in doubt and then was finally decided. That the outcome was ever in question is the true measure of Rommel's genius, for his German forces were always so badly outnumbered that there should never have been a contest, but there was. The battles in the Western Desert in 1942 constitute one of the toughest and most hard-fought campaigns in military history. This book presents them largely from the viewpoint of Erwin Rommel, one of the few great captains of our century.

ROMMEL'S DESERT WAR

Low Tide

It was December 7, 1941, and the German Afrika Korps was beaten. This was an incredible fact, for it had never happened before, but now even General of Panzer Troops Erwin Rommel had to admit it. Of the 412 tanks and armored vehicles with which he entered the "Crusader" battles over two weeks before, only 26 remained in operation.[1] That 814 enemy tanks and armored vehicles had been knocked out was of little consequence at the moment, because the British Eighth Army could afford the losses, but Panzer Group Afrika could not.[2] The Siege of Tobruk had been broken after 242 days, the Panzer Group's Italian units were incapable of further resistance, and now word came that Major General* Walter Neumann-Silkow, the popular leader of the 15th Panzer Division, had been killed by a shell burst. Major General Johannes von Ravenstein of the 21st Panzer had been captured by New Zealanders several days before, so the Afrika Korps had lost both of its divisional commanders in one campaign. The Allies were now capable of threatening the Panzer Group from the south and east simultaneously, and Rommel could no longer deal with a coordinated pincer attack. The German victory at Bir el Gobi, in which Neumann-Silkow had died, would buy only a 24-hour respite, and now the last reserves had been used, and supplies were practically exhausted. Erwin Rommel was at the end of his resources. British reserves, on the other hand, were already regrouping in assembly areas, and Rommel knew that he could not stop another all-out attack. Realistically facing the facts, he gave the order for the retreat to begin that night. It was a bitter decision. He decided to make one final stand at Gazala, 120 miles west of Tobruk, but if it failed all of Cyrenaica (northeastern Libya) would have to be abandoned.

---

*Appendix 1 shows the relative importance of German ranks, and the size and type of unit each grade normally commanded.

The First Battle of Gazala began on December 11. All Allied attacks were repulsed, but by December 15 the Germans were almost out of ammunition. Major General Summermann, the commander of the newly formed 90th Light Division, was killed in one of the fire fights.† Now all three German divisions in Africa had lost their commanders.ʹ The stand at Gazala had failed; the Cyrenaican capital would fall. The retreat continued.

A retreat is always hard on the rank and file, especially when casualties have been very heavy. The 15th Motorized Infantry Battalion of the 15th Panzer Division, for example, had started "Crusader" with 480 officers and men. Now they had only five officers, 14 NCOs, and 58 enlisted men left, along with three support guns, 10 Volkswagen field vehicles, five heavy trucks, and six motorcycles.ʹ As high as these losses were, they were not unusual. Nevertheless, German morale did not sag. Rommel, ever-present in victory, was even more visible now, constantly making his presence felt among the men. Unlike the British, he realized that holding terrain in North Africa meant nothing. What good was 300 miles of desert to Germany? What mattered was keeping the Panzer Group, and particularly the Afrika Korps, intact.

The British might have overtaken and destroyed the bulk of Panzer Group Afrika, but they did not, for Rommel's name itself was a potent weapon in retreat. "Nobody can see any escape," the new commander of the 90th Light told his staff on December 20. "The British outnumber us enormously. The puzzle is, why are they following us so slowly? Time and again they have enabled us to dodge encirclement. There is only one explanation: their awe of General Rommel, and his capacity for surprise— that's why they're following so hesitantly."ʹ

Northeastern Libya extends into the Mediterranean Sea like a gigantic bulge. The Coastal Road, the only decent, paved highway in the country, followed the edge of the bulge from the Egyptian border through Cyrenaica to Rommel's main base at Tripoli and on into Tunisia. If the British were to trap Rommel, the easiest course would be to cut the road between Benghazi on the northwestern tip of the bulge and Mersa el Brega, a village on its western base (see Map 1). From December 23 through December 30 they tried to do just that near Agedabia, but they had waited too long. On December 17, a shipment of 40 panzers had arrived from Europe, and

---

† The 90th Light was an independent division directly under the control of Panzer Group Headquarters. It was never a part of the Afrika Korps.

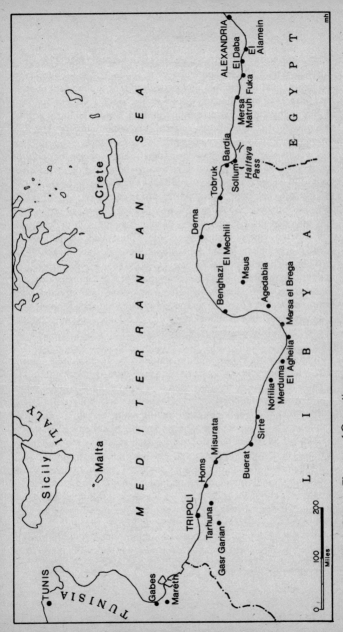

Map 1. The North African Theater of Operations.

German mechanics had repaired several more disabled tanks. The Afrika Korps now had 70 operational panzers, and was able to turn on its tormentors with a series of unexpectedly furious counterattacks from December 27 to 30. In the running tank battles west of Agedabia a number of small Allied pursuit columns were wiped out; the British lost at least 65 tanks, while the Afrika Korps suffered only minor damage.[6] The Axis infantry successfully evacuated Benghazi, while the panzer troops kept the escape route open. By the first week in January the retreat was over, and the survivors of the Panzer Group were resting and rebuilding their formations at El Agheila. The first year of the Desert War between the British and Germans had ended almost where it had begun.

The British, who had not yet grasped the insignificance of occupying a few million acres of barren desert, thought they had won the battle for North Africa. One newspaper reported: "The remains of the German Afrika Korps and the Italian Army are retreating along the Coastal Road on the Bay of Sirte to Tripoli. The main objective, the destruction of enemy forces in the Western Desert, has been achieved. The German armor has been defeated. Only a handful of German tanks have survived and they are fleeing in panic to Tripoli."[7] Obviously they had not studied Rommel's life and career, or they would have known that he did not panic; if fact, he was already thinking of resuming the offensive.

Erwin Johannes Eugen Rommel was born at Heidenheim, Swabia, a district in Wuerttemberg, southern Germany, on November 15, 1891. His father, who had the same name, was a schoolteacher, like his father before him. There was no military tradition in the Rommel family, although the elder Erwin had served briefly as a lieutenant in the artillery. Nevertheless, at a very early age and strictly on his own, young Erwin decided to become an army officer. His father tried to dissuade him, and for some very good reasons. The Prussian aristocrats dominated the German military hierarchy under the Kaisers; they always had and it seemed that they always would. The best Rommel could look forward to was 30 years or more of service and retirement at the relatively low rank of major, with a modest pension.[8] Despite parental opposition, Erwin entered the army as a member of the 124th Infantry Regiment on July 19, 1910.

Private Rommel had all the traits of a typical Wuerttemberger: toughness, self-reliance, thrift, and a stubbornness that sometimes bordered on pigheadedness. He was an uncomplicated, down-to-earth person and remained so until the day he died. With the characteristic single-mindedness of purpose that was to become the hallmark of all his future activities, young Rommel devoted himself to his new career. Within four months he was promoted to corporal, and by January 1911 he was a sergeant.[9] That spring he was sent to the War Academy at Danzig, to attend Imperial Germany's equivalent of Officers' Candidate School.

While stationed in Danzig, Rommel was introduced to a young lady named Lucie Maria Mollin, the cousin of a fellow officer candidate. Lucie was an attractive, slim, dark-haired girl whose olive complexion revealed some Italian blood in her ancestry. She was the daughter of a West Prussian landowner and was in Danzig studying languages. Young Lucie was also an accomplished dancer who had already won several dance contests. The young Swabian cadet fell in love with her almost immediately. The couple soon considered themselves informally engaged, although they were not married until November 1916.

Lucie was the only woman in Rommel's life. Fidelity and loyalty were characteristics inbred in him, and strengthened by years of practice. These characteristics in large measure explain why it took him so long and so much soul-searching before he decided to act against Adolf Hitler three decades later.

Rommel graduated from the War Academy and was commissioned a second lieutenant in January 1912. He returned to his regiment, and spent most of the next two years drilling recruits and serving as a platoon leader in the 7th Company. In 1914 the regimental staff decided he needed broader experience, and attached him to the 49th Field Artillery Regiment at Ulm. He was commanding a horse-drawn artillery platoon in this unit when World War I broke out.[10]

Up to this point, Rommel's career was about average and absolutely undistinguished. To many people, his existence would seem quite boring. He was a minor subaltern in a "non-elite" infantry regiment in an isolated post in southern Germany. He had almost no social life. He neither drank nor smoked, and, since he was engaged, he refused to take part in the after-dark escapades of the other bachelor officers. On the job, he was all business. His strong will grew even stronger. He had a tough streak in him, and it frequently showed itself.[11] Rommel never exhibited the slightest tolerance or consideration for anyone he thought lazy, inefficient, or disloyal.

The battlefield transformed this serious young man into a warrior of the first class. Desmond Young wrote: "From the moment that he first came under fire he stood out as the perfect fighting animal: cold, cunning, ruthless, untiring, quick of decision [and] incredibly brave."[12] "He was the body and soul of war," one of his fellow officers commented later.[13]

During World War I, Rommel was successively a platoon, company, and battalion-size detachment commander. He was wounded several times, and was almost killed in September 1914 while attacking three French soldiers with an empty rifle. "A bullet, entering sideways . . . shattered my upper left leg, and blood spurted from a wound as large as my fist," he recalled later. He passed out in no-man's-land, but was rescued, and woke up in a field hospital.[14]

Rommel was given a company in the elite Wuerttemberg Mountain Battalion (later Regiment) in 1915, and remained with it until January 1918. This new unit was not organized to fight as an entity, but was designed to give company commanders maximum scope for initiative and independent operations. Rommel excelled at both. One of his lieutenants wrote: "Anyone who once came under the spell of his personality turned into a real soldier. However tough the strain he seemed inexhaustible. He seemed to know just what the enemy were like and how they would probably react. His plans were often startling, instinctive, obscure. He had an exceptional imagination, and it enabled him to hit on the most unexpected solutions to tough situations. When there was danger, he was always out in front, calling on us to follow. He seemed to know no fear whatever. His men idolized him and had boundless faith in him."[15]

His exploits became legends in the regiment. Operating against Italians in the Alps in October 1917, Rommel infiltrated through enemy lines, and in 50 hours of almost continuous movement captured 150 officers, 9,000 men, 81 pieces of field artillery, and the pivotal position of Monte Matajur. Two entire brigades had surrendered to him.[16] For this brilliant string of victories, Rommel was promoted to captain and awarded the Pour le Mérite, a decoration roughly equivalent to the American Congressional Medal of Honor when awarded to someone of such relatively low rank. He wore this medal with the greatest pride until the day he died. Virtually every available photograph of Rommel in uniform shows his "Blue Max" dangling at his throat. In contrast, photos rarely show him carrying his field marshal's baton, except those taken the day Hitler gave it to him.

As one of Germany's most decorated and brilliant young officers, Rommel was allowed to remain in the post-World War I Army, restricted by the

Treaty of Versailles to 100,000 men. His first command was a "Red" Naval Company, which was considered unreliable due to its Communist sympathies. Rommel turned it into a reliable security force. With it he prevented Communist revolutionaries from storming the town hall at Gmuend in 1920.[17] Later Rommel was given command of a company in the 13th Infantry Regiment at Stuttgart, where he remained, very happily, until 1929. Due to slow promotions, typical of a small army, he did not reach the rank of major until after 1930.[18]

At home, the daring warrior enjoyed the quiet life. Here, Lucie was the center of his world. He did not care for the movies, the theater, or parties, but preferred to stay around the house with Frau Rommel and the family dog. He must have been an easy husband to live with. When he went home, he left his job outside. None of the strife or tension of the barracks, parade ground, or battlefield ever entered there. Rommel was a good-natured person at home, unconcerned with food, and an excellent fix-it man. Once he disassembled and reassembled a motorcycle in the living room, just to see what made it run. He liked stamp collecting and later became quite a camera buff, but enjoyed outings in the country even more. He and Lucie frequently went skiing together, or on canoe trips, or horseback riding. He enjoyed dancing with his wife and taking trips when on leave. Once he even visited his old battlefields in Italy, with Lucie hanging on the back of his motorcycle. Erwin Rommel the husband had only one major failing: He attempted to play the violin, apparently without a great deal of success.[19] In short, their life together was rather simple and perhaps colorless, but certainly peaceful, comfortable, and happy.

The Rommels had only one child: a son named Manfred, who was born on Christmas Eve 1928. Their family life, however, remained essentially unchanged. Rommel wanted his son to become a mathematician; somewhat surprisingly, he went into politics, and was mayor of Stuttgart (a city of 625,000) in 1979.

In October 1929 Captain Rommel was transferred to the Infantry School at Dresden, where he temporarily took up his father's profession of teaching. He became an extremely popular instructor. His commandant wrote: "His tactical battle lectures, in which he describes his own war experiences, offer the cadets not only tactical but also a lot of ideological food for thought . . . [they] are always a delight to hear." A year later the school's senior instructor described him as "a towering personality even in a milieu of hand-picked officers . . . A genuine leader, inspiring and arousing cheerful confidence in others. A first-rate infantry and combat instructor, constantly making suggestions and above all building up cadets' characters . . . Respected by his colleagues, worshipped by his cadets."[20]

While teaching at Dresden, Rommel had time to write his World War I memoirs, which were published as a book in 1936. *Infantry in the Attack* soon became a best seller in Nazi Germany and, more importantly for Erwin Rommel, was read by Adolf Hitler. The dictator was impressed and decided to meet the author. He had Rommel attached to his security forces for the Nazi Party rally at Nuremberg. When the rally was ending and it came time for Hitler to leave, he told Rommel to allow no more than half a dozen cars to follow him. This meant having to stop an entire convoy of generals, cabinet ministers, and high-ranking officials. Rommel did exactly as he had been instructed, and even blocked the road with two tanks, despite the curses of some of the most powerful men in Nazi Germany. "This is monstrous, Colonel!" one of them roared. "I intend to report this to the Fuehrer!" Apparently he did, too, for Hitler called Rommel in that night and thanked him for executing the order so well.[21]

Two years later, in 1938, Colonel Rommel received a choice assignment. He assumed command of the Infantry School at Wiener Neustadt, in the Austrian Alps. Later he wrote that this was the happiest period of his military career. The countryside was beautiful and the duty both challenging and rewarding. Under other circumstances, Rommel might have retired here. However, a summons came from Berlin, and the 47-year-old infantryman reported to his commander-in-chief. He was given command of the Fuehrerbegleitbataillon, Hitler's personal bodyguard, which he commanded as the German Army entered the Sudetenland. This ad hoc force consisted of about two companies of infantry, armed with machine guns, rifles, antitank guns, and anti-aircraft weapons. It looked as if they would be needed. War clouds hung low on the horizon until the Allies backed down at Munich and abandoned their Czechoslovak friends. A few months later, Hitler finished off the helpless Czechoslovakian state. As he was about to enter the capital city of Prague, Hitler turned to the commander of his bodyguard and asked the officer how he would enter the government sector if he were Hitler.

"I should get into an open car and drive through the streets to the Hradschin without an escort," Rommel replied.

Hitler followed this bold advice. There were no incidents.[22]

During his three periods of temporary duty as the commander of the Fuehrer Guard Battalion, Rommel's admiration for Hitler grew. Rommel witnessed none of the adverse reactions Hitler would later show to bad news. There were no temper tantrums, no unreasonable behavior, no fits. In 1939, Adolf Hitler still maintained control of all his faculties. He impressed Rommel with his actions under stress, his incredible memory, and his physical courage. The two liked and respected each other. Now Rommel was even closing his private letters with "Heil Hitler! Yours, E. Rommel."[23] He came closer to being a Nazi during this period than at any other in his life. Nevertheless, he still nourished a healthy suspicion for some of Hitler's paladins.

Erwin Rommel was never politically adroit; he was, in fact, politically naïve. Like many idealistic German officers of the day, he could not imagine a German chancellor betraying his oath to the nation. It was 1943 before Rommel learned that the Nazis were systematically pursuing a policy of genocide against the Jewish people. Who told him is still a mystery. Rommel was apparently sworn to secrecy and carried the secret to his grave. Even in late 1943 he was not sure that Hitler was personally involved in the Holocaust. Only when Rommel was completely convinced of Hitler's personal guilt did he decide to join the conspiracy against him, but by then the Thousand-Year Reich had only about a year to live.

Between his additional duty trips and leaves, Rommel and his family enjoyed life at Wiener Neustadt, in the mountains southwest of Vienna. The family went on many excursions and hiking trips into the Alps. They lived in a charming little house, surrounded by a flower garden. Rommel often remembered this period with great pleasure. At home, he enjoyed playing with his son and dabbling in photography. However, in mid-1939 the good times ended. The international situation took a serious turn for the worse. Rommel again joined Hitler's entourage as the commander of the bodyguard. On August 23, Hitler promoted him to major general.[24] Nine days later the panzers crossed the Polish frontier. World War II had begun.

Adolf Hitler in Poland in 1939 was far different from the shell of a man who died, cringing and almost completely mad, in a subterranean bunker in 1945. Rommel had a great deal of trouble with him. "He was always wanting to be right up with the forward troops," the future Desert Fox complained. The Fuehrer went so far as to expose himself to Polish sniper fire, and to observe the storming of a river line by German infantry. "He seemed to enjoy being under fire," Rommel remarked.[25]

In Poland, Rommel had a chance to observe the effects of a Blitzkrieg firsthand. He saw the importance of pushing forward in mechanized warfare, even if points of resistance had to be bypassed at the risk of being cut off. He learned the value of Heinz Guderian's maxim that masses of tanks, not dribbles, should be employed against the enemy. Rommel also recognized the importance of leading tank formations from the front, and the value of close air-ground coordination. Although he had been in the infantry for 29 years and probably had not seen the inside of a tank before 1936, he decided his future lay in the armored branch.

On their return from Poland, Rommel approached Hitler and requested a command of his own.

Hitler took a personal interest in his new general. "What do you want?" he asked.

"Command of a panzer division," replied Rommel, without batting an eye.

Much later, Rommel commented to Major General Alfred Gause: "That was an immoderate request on my part; I did not belong to the armored branch of the service, and there were many generals who had a much stronger claim to a command of this nature."[26] Nevertheless, in February 1940, Rommel arrived at Godesberg, on the Rhine, to succeed Lieutenant General Georg Stumme as commander of the 7th Panzer Division.

The panzer division that Rommel took over in February 1940 hardly fit the standard propaganda description of an elite armored force. It was one of the four light divisions that Hitler had ordered converted into panzer units in the winter of 1939-40. It boasted only one tank regiment of three battalions, instead of the normal contingent of two regiments of two battalions each, an organizational arrangement that left Rommel with 218 tanks, or about 75 percent of the armor of a normal panzer division. To make matters worse (much worse, in fact), over half of Rommel's tanks were of the captured Czechoslovakian variety.[27] They had simply been incorporated into the German Army in 1938. These T-38 tanks weighed only about nine tons, and would be of little use against the British and the French.

Some of the German-made tanks proved of hardly greater value. The

Panzer Mark I (PzKw I) had originally been built as a training tank and as a carrier for a 20-millimeter anti-aircraft gun. However, nothing larger than a machine gun could be mounted on its small chassis. It was, in short, a small assault vehicle of dubious value. General Guderian, the creator of the German Armored Corps and father of the Blitzkrieg, explained that it was designed strictly as a training vehicle. "Nobody in 1932 could have guessed that one day we should have to go into action with this little tank."[28]

The Panzer Mark II (PzKw II) was somewhat of an improvement, but not much. The J Model (PzKw IIj) weighed only 10.5 tons and had very thin armored protection. It could be penetrated by even the smallest enemy antitank gun.

The most important tank in Rommel's arsenal, although certainly not the most numerous, was the Panzer Mark III (PzKw III). The H Model (PzKw IIIh) weighed 23 tons and carried a full five-man crew, as compared to three in the earlier models of the PzKw III, which weighed only 20 tons. All the PzKw III's carried a 50-millimeter main battle gun and two MG-34 machine guns, which made them a very dangerous weapon in both tank and combined arms battles. The maximum armored thickness of the PzKw III was 60 to 77 millimeters, depending on the model. This made them safer than the Mark I or II, or the Czech tanks, but hardly rendered them invulnerable to British antitank guns. Perhaps the greatest asset of the Mark III was its speed, which averaged 25 miles per hour on the road. This was much better than the British main battle tank, the Matilda, which had a maximum road speed of 15 miles per hour.

The fastest tank Rommel commanded in the French campaign was the Panzer Mark IV (PzKw IV), which could cover 26 miles per hour on the road. It weighed about the same as the PzKw III, but unfortunately was armed with a very short 75-millimeter main battle gun, which rendered it next to useless in a tank battle. German panzer leaders liked to use it as an infantry support vehicle, instead of pitting it head to head against the longer-ranged Allied tanks, although this sometimes proved unavoidable. However, it did have another redeeming feature: it could bombard enemy positions up to 3,000 meters away with high-explosive ammunition, even when on the move. This capacity made it an effective type of mobile artillery. Later models of the Mark IV had a longer-barreled 75-millimeter main battle gun, and were more feared by the enemy than even the Mark III. Unfortunately for Rommel, these models would not appear in great numbers until 1944, too late to help him in France or North Africa.

The men of the 7th Panzer were in no better shape than their panzers. They were from the province of Thuringia, which was not noted for producing good soldiers. Rommel promptly set about bringing them up to his standards. He arrived on February 10, and immediately ordered a divisional inspection, brushing aside his officers' protests that it was Sunday. After touring his new command, the Swabian sent all his regimental commanders on leave. "I won't be needing you until I've learned the ropes myself," he snapped.[29]

Rommel himself was up before 6:00 A.M. every morning. His first chore was to run a mile every morning before breakfast. He had grown overweight during his six months of relatively soft duty at Fuehrer Headquarters, and found it hard "To fight back the inner Schweinehund in me that pleads, 'Stay in bed—just another fifteen minutes.'"[30]

"I don't suppose I'll find many men anxious to follow my example," he wrote Lucie. "Most of my officers are very comfortably inclined. And some are downright flabby."[31]

Rommel immediately set about correcting the situation. Training intensified almost as soon as he set up shop. Soon discipline improved; the ineffective and lazy officer was sent packing, while those of higher caliber were given greater responsibility. The men quickly responded to their new leader, who made them feel like elite shock troops, even though they were not; however, soldiers who think they are the best frequently become the best, as Rommel was well aware. Morale soared as proficiency increased among soldiers and junior commanders. Rommel's program paid off. When the order was given to invade France in May 1940, the 7th Panzer was ready. It barreled through the Ardennes, broke the Meuse River line at Dinart, and raced through northern France and Belgium. At Celfontaine it destroyed the 1st French Armored and 4th French North African divisions before punching through the Maginot Line extension near Sivry. After the main German armored forces under Heinz Guderian broke through to the sea, the Ghost Division (as the 7th was now nicknamed) helped cover his northern flank, and faced the largest Allied armored attack of the campaign at Arras on May 21. The last British tank was knocked out within 50 yards of Rommel's position, but when the enemy finally fell back the only major Allied attempt to relieve the Dunkirk Pocket had failed, and France was doomed. After this, the 7th took part in mopping-up operations around Lille, stormed across the Somme and Seine, and captured St. Valery and

Cherbourg in heavy fighting and almost without assistance. It was within 200 miles of the Spanish border when France surrendered.[32]

During the French campaign the Ghost Division suffered 2,594 casualties, including 682 killed, 1,646 wounded, and 266 missing. This represented 20 percent of the entire force. Rommel himself had been slightly wounded when his tank was knocked out just after crossing the Meuse. However, during these six weeks the 7th Panzer had taken 97,468 prisoners, shot down 52 aircraft, destroyed another 15 on the ground, and captured a dozen more. They had captured the commander of the French Atlantic Fleet and four of his admirals, a French corps commander, and 15 to 20 other generals, including the commander of the 51st British Highlander Division and many of his men. They had bagged 277 field guns, 64 antitank guns, 458 tanks and armored vehicles, 4,000 to 5,000 trucks, and tons of other military equipment, in addition to cutting off the retreat of thousands of Allied soldiers who surrendered to other units.[33] In short, the 7th Panzer had distinguished itself in every way, and proven that its commander was capable of even greater things.

In early February 1941 Erwin Rommel arrived home on a well-earned leave, but on his second evening at Wiener Neustadt Berlin called. Rommel was ordered to report to Fuehrer Headquarters at Staaken immediately. Almost as soon as he arrived senior staff officers began briefing him on the situation in North Africa. Rommel already knew that the Italian army in North Africa had been defeated by the British, but now he learned the true extent of the disaster. In less than two months 10 Italian divisions had been destroyed. Graziani's army in Libya and Egypt had lost 130,000 men, 1,300 guns, 400 tanks, and 150 aircraft, while inflicting only 2,000 casualties on an enemy they outnumbered at least three to one. All that was left of Mussolini's Italian Empire was an artillery regiment at Sirte and a makeshift garrison that held a 12-mile perimeter around Tripoli.[34] Hitler told his officers, "The loss of North Africa could be withstood in a military sense but have a strong psychological effect on Italy. Britain could hold a pistol at Italy's head. . . . The British forces in the Mediterranean would not be tied down. The British would have the free use of a dozen divisions and could employ them most dangerously. . . . We must make every effort to prevent this. . . ."[35] The action he had in mind was direct military intervention. The force he decided to send would include the 15th Panzer and 5th Light (later redesignated 21st Panzer) divisions. They would be controlled by a newly formed headquarters, the Afrika Korps. Its first commander would be Erwin Rommel, who received his promotion to lieutenant general along with the new post.

The decisions Hitler and the General Staff made at Staaken set in motion a whole series of events that profoundly affected the course of the war in North Africa, and to a greater degree than even they expected. Blatantly ignoring orders to conduct a defensive war, Rommel shocked the Allies and Nazis alike by launching a surprise offensive before disembarkation of the Afrika Korps was even half completed. For the next six months the tide of battle ebbed and flowed as Rommel overran Cyrenaica, only to be bogged down before the key port of Tobruk. The Royal Air Force and Navy, operating out of their tiny island-base of Malta, played such havoc with Rommel's rear areas that he was receiving less than 60 percent of his supply requirements by May 1941.[36] Despite serious odds against him (British tanks frequently outnumbered his panzers more than two to one), Rommel turned back two major attempts to relieve Tobruk (Operations "Brevity" and "Battleaxe") while simultaneously keeping the garrison bottled up. These victories, along with his successes in France and the conquest of Cyrenaica, made Rommel a hero in the Third Reich. The legend of the Desert Fox was born. Soon the legend crossed the battle lines and he became the most admired and respected soldier on either side. Equally important, Rommel had developed his theories of mobile warfare that would carry his outnumbered army nearly to the Suez Canal. He advocated and insisted upon a high level of tactical coordination among the tanks, infantry, and antitank gunners. In a typical battle, the antitank gunners, using the terrain to the best advantage and covered by the panzers, would attack the British tanks, which were all too frequently inadequately protected by their infantry. When the enemy tanks were depleted or dispersed, the panzers would roar forward and deal with the Allies' soft-skin vehicles and infantry. All the while the German tankers were covered by the antitank gunners and the infantry. Similar close support was expected (and usually received) from the artillery, anti-aircraft guns in an antitank role, and dive bombers.

Rommel also believed in the principle of mass attacks and leading from the front, where he could quickly influence the course of the battle. By striking against one point with the bulk of his motorized troops, the Desert Fox defeated superior enemy forces time and time again.

Rommel frequently compared desert warfare to war at sea. "No admiral ever won a naval battle from a shore base," he was fond of saying.[37] The Sahara even resembled the sea, with its huge areas of open space, its unpredictable storms, and its shifting waves. The waves and storms were made of sand instead of water, and the tank took the place of the destroyer, but many of the other naval principles remained constant. Speed and the quick decision remained trumps. Major General J. F. C. Fuller, one of the fathers of the theory of the Blitzkrieg, appears to agree with this assessment. He explained the Allied defeats this way: "In rapidity of decision and velocity of movement the Germans completely outclassed their enemy and mainly because Rommel . . . normally took personal command of his armor. . . . It was not that the British generals were less able than the German. It was that their education was out of date. It was built on the trench warfare of 1914-1918 and not on the armored warfare they were called upon to direct."[38]

Rommel himself once remarked, "Why should I bother about the superior number of British tanks when their commanders always use them in driblets? Against those driblets I am stronger with my army."

In recent years many people have incorrectly attributed Rommel's successes to the superiority of his tanks. This alleged technical superiority of the German Army was a myth, at least before 1944, when the Panzer Mark V (Panther) and Mark VI (Tiger) tanks made their appearance in significant numbers. Rommel fought his North African battles with the PzKw III and IV model tanks, which were equaled in performance by a number of Allied models, and were inferior to the Grants and Shermans manufactured by the United States and exported to Great Britain. Rommel's chief of intelligence put it this way: "Contrary to the generally accepted view, the German tanks did not have any advantage in quality over their opponents, and in numbers they were always inferior."[39] He attributed the success of the Afrika Korps to three major factors: the superior quality of the German antitank guns, the high level of cooperation achieved by various branches of the German military, and the magnificent tactical methods employed by the Afrika Korps and 90th Light Division.[40]

In July 1941 Hitler decided to reward Rommel for his victories and enlarge his sphere of command by reorganizing Axis forces in Africa.

Rommel was promoted to General of Panzer Troops, and given command of the newly created Panzer Group Afrika, of which the Afrika Korps was a part. He was also allowed to form the 90th Light Division from miscellaneous units already in Africa, although he received no new forces. The Panzer Group also included the XX Italian and XXI Italian Infantry Motorized Corps, to which the X Italian Infantry Corps was later added. However, since their defeat in February 1941 Italian morale sagged under the slightest pressure. Except for such units as the Ariete Armored Division, the Italian forces were of marginal value because they were almost all nonmotorized. Poorly equipped and poorly supplied, riddled by class-conscious, inefficient, and frequently anti-Fascist and anti-German officers, underpaid and badly fed, the Italian soldier had lost faith in his government. He only wanted to go home.

Morale levels were just the opposite in the German camp, where Rommel had the same effect on his men as he had had on the 7th Panzer in France. Major General von Esebeck, who commanded the 15th Panzer Division until being critically wounded near Tobruk, remembered how Rommel treated his soldiers, whom he called his "Africans": "He was always gay when he was speaking to young men. He had a smile and a joke for everyone who seemed to be doing his job. There was nothing he liked better than to talk with a man from his own part of the country in the Swabian dialect. He had a very warm heart. . . ."[41]

War changed his personal habits very little. Life only became a little harder and a little more primitive, but Rommel thrived on it, at least at first. He did not seem to care what he ate, and frequently forgot to eat at all. He usually carried a few sandwiches or a can of sardines and a piece of bread with him in the mornings. Quite often they returned with him at night, uneaten. For drink he carried only a small flask of cold tea, with lemon. Since Rommel realized that the more you drink in the desert the more you want, he usually brought the flast back untouched as well. One day Rommel invited an Italian general to lunch with him in the field. "It was rather awkward," Rommel said later. "I had only three slices of bread and they were all stale. Never mind, they eat too much [anyway]."[42]

Rommel's evening meal, the longest of the day, never lasted more than 20 minutes. He would have simple food, with an occasional glass of wine, but only with the meal. After dinner he would order the radio turned on, but only for the news, never for the music. After this he would write to his wife. If a major campaign was in progress, he sometimes had his batman,

Corporal Herbert Gunther, write a letter to her for him. He also continued his correspondence with his World War I comrades. Normally these letters were written in the general's own hand; very seldom were they dictated and typed, or written by an aide and simply signed by Rommel. No letter from these old veterans ever went unanswered. After answering any letters from these men, Rommel filled the rest of the evening with official correspondence. He might occasionally read a newspaper, but novels and radio programs (other than the news) had no place in his schedule.[43]

His relationship with other officers were strictly professional and formal most of the time. One of his aides, Lieutenant Heinz Schmidt, wrote: "He seldom mentioned his family or his private life, and, indeed, was almost reticent about intimate affairs of any sort. It was months before he called me anything but the formal Lieutenant, and only after he decided that I was more than a necessary additional limb did he address me by name, bother to find out my age, whether I was happy, or indeed, even think of me other than as something that filled a uniform and answered a command. It was, in fact, almost strange, after a long acquaintance, to find the impersonal General actually human."[44]

Rommel spent the period between July and November 1941 organizing Panzer Group Afrika and preparing for the next British attempt to relieve Tobruk. One of his main concerns was to pick talented men to command and staff the German elements of his Panzer Group. His first two successors as commander of the Afrika Korps fell sick almost as soon as they arrived. Lieutenant General Ludwig Cruewell, who had commanded the 2nd Motorized Division in France and the 11th Panzer Division in the Balkan campaign of early 1941, was finally chosen. He turned out to be one of the best subordinate commanders Rommel ever had. The unassuming Major General Alfred Gause was elevated from chief of staff of the Afrika Korps to chief of staff of the Panzer Group when Rommel moved up. Gause was replaced at the Korps by Colonel Fritz Bayerlein, who had been Heinz Guderian's chief of operations with the 2nd Panzer Group in Russia. A real bulldog of a man, Bayerlein had joined the Kaiser's army at age 16 and had risen through the ranks. Rommel had known him for years. Major Frederick Wilhelm von Mellenthin, who was distantly related to Frederick the Great, was appointed Group Ic (chief intelligence officer), while Colonel Siegfried Westphal became chief of operations.

Among Rommel's other staff officers, and one of the few who was not a professional soldier, was Captain Alfred Berndt, a fanatical Nazi who formerly worked in Goebbels' Ministry of Propaganda. Berndt wrote a war book and did much to advance Rommel's popularity with the German public. Berndt also served as an intermediary between the Desert Fox and the Nazis since he was politically acceptable to Hitler, had important contacts in both the government and the Army, and was liked by both Rommel and the Fuehrer.

While Rommel organized his new command and staffed it with competent people, events elsewhere presented him with problems he could not control. British air and naval forces based on Malta took control of the supply routes over and across the central Mediterranean. In September 1941 British aircraft, warships, and submarines destroyed 38 percent of the supplies en route to Libya. In October a whopping 63 percent of the tonnage bound for North Africa was sunk. Only 18,500 tons of supplies arrived, and Rommel could not meet his minimum daily requirements.[45] Unable to stockpile enough supplies, fuel, or ammunition, Rommel could only wait and fume in his tent while the British prepared for their winter offensive of 1941. Christened "Crusader," it began on November 23, and for over two weeks the armies were locked in a struggle of unprecedented fury. Advantages changed hands several times, but at last attrition took its toll. For the first time in his career, General Erwin Rommel was beaten. On the day the Japanese attacked Pearl Harbor he began to retreat with the remnants of his Panzer Group. By New Year's Day Cyrenaica had been lost. German garrisons continued to hold out at Bardia, Sollum, and the Halfaya Pass on the Egyptian-Libyan frontier, but these were doomed. The British were still confident when they halted their pursuit. Their leaders believed that, after they rested and built up supplies, there would be one more brief campaign in Africa, and that it would end with the Panzer Group's surrender at Tripoli. They thought that the Afrika Korps was a broken force, and that the German tide in the desert was permanently receding. They were dead wrong on both counts.

2

Rommel Strikes Back

"If Rommel had an outstanding quality," Brigadier Young wrote, "it was resilience. Like one of those weighted toy figures, no sooner was he knocked down than he was on his feet again."[1] The best corroboration of the truth of this assessment is seen in his surprise offensive of January 1942.

Rommel's fortunes often fluctuated in inverse proportion to those of Malta. Of this small island 50 miles south of Sicily, German Vice Admiral Assmann later said, "Had the Italians been Japanese they would have opened their war on the 10th of June, 1940, by doing a Pearl Harbor on Malta, which at that time was merely a defense base."[2]

Axis pressure on the strategic island varied from period to period, depending on Hitler's need for air power in the other theaters of war. In the early part of 1941 the British were forced to relax their hold on Rommel's Mediterranean sea routes. The Luftwaffe battered the island-fortress, and allowed the Italian Navy to dock convoy ships at Tripoli and Benghazi with minimum risk. The situation changed radically when the X Air Corps, which had virtually neutralized Malta, was reassigned from Sicily to the Balkans. Why Hitler made this move is unclear, for the X Air Corps remained virtually inactive for months, when it could have done immeasurable service by continuing to pound Malta. The Allies filled the power vacuum created by the departure of the X Air Corps, and reinforced Malta until it threatened the very existence of Panzer Group Africa. In November 1941, Allied ships, submarines, and aircraft sank 77 percent of the supplies sent to North Africa.[3] The island was a major factor in Rommel's defeat in the "Crusader" battles.

The High Command realized that if they allowed this situation to continue, the Afrika Korps was doomed. To neutralize Malta again, they recalled Field Marshal Albert Kesselring's veteran Second Air Fleet from Russia. However, they went one step farther and assumed the offensive themselves. The weapon they chose was perhaps the most feared in the world at that time: the famous German submarine.

The first six U-boats arrived in the Mediterranean in September and October 1941. In the next two months, 20 more of the deadly submarines successfully entered the Mediterranean by passing under the heavily guarded Strait of Gibraltar. Their presence also had an effect on the Italian submariners, who at once became more active and daring.[4]

The reports of the Axis naval successes must have read like a horror story to the War Office in London. A U-boat sank the *Ark Royal*, the only Allied aircraft carrier in the Mediterranean. The battleship *Barham* was struck by a German torpedo and disintegrated. Not to be outdone, Italian submariners penetrated the naval defenses of Alexandria and torpedoed the battleships *Queen Elizabeth* and *Valiant*. Although they did not sink, they would be out of commission for some time. An Italian sub also crippled the cruiser *Galatea*, which was subsequently finished off by a U-boat before it could drag itself to safety. Another group of Italian sailors proved equally resourceful. They laid a minefield north of Tripoli, into which the Royal Navy's Force "K" sailed. The cruiser *Neptune* and a destroyer went down, and the cruisers *Aurora* and *Penelope* were heavily damaged. This left the Allied naval commander, Admiral Cunningham, with no heavy units in the Mediterranean. Churchill was unable to reinforce him because every available vessel was in the Far East, trying to slow the latest Japanese advance.[5] Malta continued to be supplied by the RAF, now operating out of Cyrenaican bases, but it rapidly lost its offensive capacity, and Rommel began to receive regular supply shipments again. In early January 1942 a major convoy, carrying 55 new panzers, 20 armored cars, and a large quantity of fuel and other supplies, docked at Tripoli. "This was as good as a victory in battle," Colonel Bayerlein wrote.[6] Rommel now had the resources to launch a counteroffensive, to regain what he had lost in "Crusader," and to prevent another major British offensive that might jeopardize Tripoli itself. He knew that Field Marshal Sir Claude Auchinleck, the British commander-in-chief, Middle East, and Eighth Army Commander General Sir Neil Ritchie, were planning just such an attack.

By January 12, 1942, the German position in North Africa was not bad, despite the heavy casualties suffered in "Crusader." The British, on the other hand, were at the end of a very long supply line. The Axis frontier garrisons were still holding out, tying down major Allied formations. Other

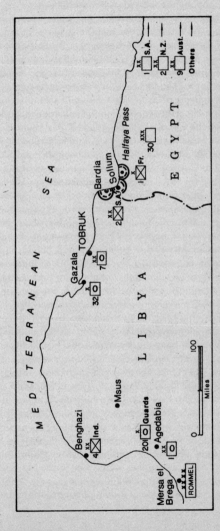

Map 2. British Eighth Army Dispositions, January 21, 1942. Although the Allies had an overall superiority of about three to one, their divisions were scattered all over the desert. This enabled Rommel to isolate and overrun their front-line units and disrupt their plans for an offensive against Tripoli.

top Allied formations, such as the 7th Armoured Division and the New Zealand Division, had suffered such heavy losses at "Crusader" that they had to be completely rebuilt. General Ritchie had only two major units in the forward area of western Cyrenaica: the inexperienced 1st Armoured Division, and the 201st Guards Brigade at Agedabia. The 4th Indian Division was held in reserve at Benghazi. These were all the forces the Allies would have if Rommel attacked. However, they considered the Desert Fox a spent force, and were not concerned about the possibility of a German resurgence.[7]

Panzer Group intelligence did not remain unaware of this attitude for long. They could tell what the British were thinking by analyzing their poor troop dispositions. In the briefing of January 12, 1942, the Panzer Group Ic, Lieutenant Colonel von Mellenthin, projected that the German forces on the front line would be superior to Ritchie's advanced units until January 25. After that date, reinforcements would probably make the Eighth Army the stronger antagonist.[8] Map 2 shows its dispositions.

Erwin Rommel stayed up all that night in the van that served as his headquarters. "It's in the small hours that my best new plans are hatched," he wrote Lucie a few days later.[9] No doubt he went over the intelligence estimates again. At 5:30 A.M. he went to sleep, but was up again by 6:30. That morning he called in a very select group of staff officers. To their astonishment, he announced that he was going to attack again on January 21. He told them what some of them already knew: that Auchinleck was preparing an offensive whose objective was to finish off the Axis empire in North Africa. "If we give the Tommies a break until February, they'll chase us out of here. Nothing could stop the 8th Army in that event. . . . So we must not wait. We must throw a monkey wrench into Tommy's plans."[10]

Rommel's battle plan was much like his first invasion of Cyrenaica the year before. The Afrika Korps would advance across the desert with its right flank on the Wadi el Faregh. Combat Group Marcks, comprised of elements of the 21st Panzer and 90th Light divisions, would advance along the Coastal Road. The XX Italian Motorized Corps would fill the gap between these two forces and form the center of the attack. Major General Veith and the nonmotorized elements of the 90th Light, along with the Italian infantry, would bring up the rear. Table 1 shows Rommel's order of battle.

The unique aspect of this offensive was that the Germans kept their plans secret, from friends as well as foes. The inability of the Italian

Table 1.

Panzer Group Afrika's Order of Battle, January 21, 1942

Afrika Korps	XXI Italian Infantry Corps
21st Panzer Division	Pavia Infantry Division
15th Panzer Division	Trento Infantry Division
	Sabratha Infantry Division
90th Light Division	
XX Italian Motorized Corps	X Italian Infantry Corps
Ariete Armored Division	Bologna Infantry Division
Trieste Motorized Division	Brescia Infantry Division

Command to keep secrets from the British was already notorious. To stop these security leaks, Rommel did not give the Italians their marching orders until the very eve of the attack. To keep them from learning of the offensive through his enemies at Fuehrer Headquarters, Rommel intentionally withheld the information from OKW* as well. Field Marshall Wilhelm Keitel, the Chief of OKW, Colonel General Alfred Jodl (Keitel's Operations Officer) and Colonel General Franz Halder, the Chief of the General Staff, all disliked Rommel and were jealous of his successes. Rommel knew that if he informed these men of his plans they would tell the Italians. These unusual precautions had some ugly repercussions later on, but they worked. When the panzers struck, they achieved complete surprise all along the line.

On January 21, Rommel issued the following order to his men:

From the Supreme Commander of Panzer Group Afrika:
ARMY ORDER OF THE DAY

German and Italian Soldiers!

Behind you lie heavy battles with a vastly superior enemy. Your morale remains unimpaired.

---

*Oberkommando der Wehrmacht, or the High Command of the Armed Forces

At this moment we are considerably stronger than the enemy facing us in the front line. Therefore we shall proceed today to attack and destroy the enemy.

I expect every man to give of his utmost in these decisive days.

Long live Italy! Long live the Great German Reich! Long live the Fuehrer!

> The Supreme Commander
> ROMMEL
> G.O.C., Panzer Troops[11]

This was possibly the last order ever issued by Panzer Group Afrika. The next day Hitler upgraded it to army status, and Rommel's forces received the designation Panzer Army Afrika. Rommel was given a personal reward: the Knight's Cross of the Iron Cross with Swords and Oak Leaves. However, he had no time to rest on his laurels, for the battle of Agedabia had already begun.

When Rommel's counteroffensive started, the Panzer Army was much stronger than it had been at the end of "Crusader." The Afrika Korps now boasted 111 tanks, with 28 in reserve. The Italians mustered another 89 tanks.[12]

On the other side, the last thing the British expected at this moment was a major German offensive. This explains why British forces were spread out all over eastern Libya. Even the front-line division was terribly scattered. The forward units of the Guards Brigade and the 1st Support Group were weakly deployed over 30 miles of front between Mersa el Brega and Wadi Faregh. Only one brigade of the 1st Armoured Division was even forward of Benghazi, and it was suffering from severe mechanical problems. Many of its tanks were simply worn out, and needed to be rebuilt or completely overhauled. However, the British logistical system was not equal to the task, and the 2nd Armoured Brigade would have to fight the upcoming battle in tanks that were no longer desert-worthy. The other brigade in the 1st Armoured Division, the 22nd Armoured, was far to the rear, being refitted and recovering from Sidi Rezegh. The division had a tank strength of 150,[13] and thus held some numerical superiority over the Germans. However, the quality of the panzers, coupled with the element of surprise and the experience of the veteran desert soldiers, more than made up for any quantitative deficiencies.

The British also had some problems they were not used to. The supply line was too long, and the available transportation inadequate. The Allies' forward troops received 250 tons too few supplies a day for even daily maintenance. Brigadier John Strawson, author of *The Battle for North Africa*, put it this way: "The drawbacks of the British might be summarized like this—intelligence was inaccurate, supplies uncertain, training inadequate and adaptability nonexistent."[14]

"Intelligence was inaccurate" is almost an understatement in this case. For once in its illustrious history, the British Secret Service was completely fooled. Rommel, not satisfied with withholding information from his superiors and allies, actually began telling them lies. First, he pretended that he was planning to abandon the Mersa el Brega positions. The Italian field commanders immediately reported this to Rome. Within hours the British Secret Service informed Auchinleck of this development.[15] This shows us how deeply the British Secret Service had infiltrated the top military councils in Rome, and yet Rommel was using their own spy network against them. His deception plan again shows us the genius of the Desert Fox.

Sir Claude Auchinleck was not easily fooled, and he refused to be taken in by the initial reports. However, reconnaissance reports soon poured in that seemed to corroborate the findings of the Secret Service. Even Sir Claude began to waiver and to believe. He was completely unaware that the panzers were on the move at night. Already most of Rommel's armored vehicles and tanks were hidden well forward under camouflaged nets. The well-disciplined Panzer Army Afrika soldiers remained hidden from Allied aircraft during the day, and only awaited Rommel's word of command to spring into the attack.

On January 19 a major sandstorm hit the area, and no further aerial reconnaissance flights were possible. Rommel might have ordered the storm. Unknown to anyone except the men involved, the German Afrika Korps brought up the last of its armor and camouflaged it near the British line under this perfect concealment.

The next day RAF scout flights resumed. They had some exciting reports. Mersa el Brega was on fire. The ships in its small harbor were being blown up. Rommel was undoubtedly destroying his excess supplies. The Panzer Army was about to retreat again. What they could not see from the air was that the houses were empty. The ships were old hulks. Rommel had simply created another of his deceptions. However, it succeeded in convincing the enemy that he would be retreating toward Tripoli in the near future.[16]

Shortly after dawn Rommel wrote to Lucie, as he habitually did before a battle. "I firmly believe that God is keeping a protective hand over me and will grant me victory," he said.[17] The German panzers struck the Allied line at 8:30 A.M. that day. The surprise was complete. Within a few minutes the Germans had penetrated the British front and were headed for Agedabia.

Rommel continued to play his game of duplicity with the Italians. This was Erwin Rommel at his most cunning. Just before the offensive started, he told General Gambarra, the Italian chief of staff in North Africa, that there would be no major offensive. "A small foray. A mere skirmish—you might call it a commando raid—is to be carried out."[18] Gambarra considered this so insignificant that he failed to pass the information on to Rome, just as Rommel had calculated.[19]

On the night of January 21 the commando party—an entire panzer corps and an elite infantry division—was clearing the area from the Wadi el Faregh to the Gulf of Sirte. That night the mobile elements of the 90th Light under Colonel Werner Marcks formed the vanguard for the night march on Agedabia, which fell the next day. Meanwhile, on the desert flank, the Afrika Korps engaged the confused Englishmen in a running tank battle that lasted three days. When it ended, the 1st Armoured Division had lost 100 of its 150 tanks,[20] 33 pieces of field artillery, several armored cars, and thousands of men.[21] The divisional staff was numbered among the prisoners. Thirty battleworthy Valentine tanks were also seized in a rear-area supply depot.[22] Soon these also would be in the battle line of the Afrika Korps.

Lieutenant Heinz Schmidt, now an infantry company commander, took part in this battle and wrote:

> We had our first skirmish with British tanks on the 2nd day of the march.... We sighted about 30 tanks stationary at the foot of a rise in hilly ground. When we received the order to attack, we were certain we had not yet been observed. We brought our 50mm anti-tank guns into position in a hollow. The enemy was totally surprised when we opened fire, and a dozen panzers raced down against the tanks. He [the Allied commander] decided his position was untenable and pulled out hurriedly with the loss of a few tanks.

> We had now developed a new method of attack. With 12 anti-tank guns we

leap-frogged from one vantage point to another, while our panzers, stationary and hull down, if possible, provided protective fire. Then we would establish ourselves to give them protective fire while they swept on again. The tactics worked well and despite the liveliness of the fire, the enemy's tanks were not able to hold up our advance. He steadily sustained losses and had to give ground constantly. . . .

We were not entirely happy about our petrol position. Yet one young officer, who said to Rommel, "Herr General, we need more fuel," received the brisk answer: "Well, go and get it from the British."[23]

General Ritchie could not bring himself to believe that this was a real Blitzkreig, and not just a reconnaissance in force. He overrode the pleas of desert veteran Godwin-Austen, the XIII Corps commander, who wanted to withdraw. As a result the 1st Armoured Division was slaughtered. As Strawson later commented: "Stubborn optimism might be all very well during a crisis of position warfare when nerve above all else was required; it was dangerous miscalculation when the initiative had been wholly surrendered."[24]

Ritchie tried to relieve the pressure on the trapped 1st Armoured by launching diversionary attacks with elements of the 4th Indian Division. Rommel refused to take the bait, and continued his systematic destruction of the British armor. The 4th Indian's diversions were totally ineffective.

On the other side, the Italians were at first shocked, and then indignant, when they learned of the magnitude of the battle in progress. General Cavallero, the Italian commander-in-chief, rushed to Rommel's headquarters and demanded he withdraw from the fight immediately. Surprisingly, Mussolini backed him in this demand, because he feared another major defeat. Cavallero denounced Rommel for his independent action and told him to "Make it no more than a sortie and come right back."[25] In what grew into a heated argument, Rommel refused to comply with the Italian's orders. "I intend to keep up the attack as long as I can," Rommel snapped. Cavallero left, growling.[26] Because of Rommel's failure to obey his orders, the Italian commander-in-chief held back his forces, and would not allow the Italian contingent of Panzer Army Afrika to participate any further in the campaign. Rommel went on without them. He had no intention of stopping. "Now the tables are turned with a vengeance," he wrote to his son, Manfred. "We've got the British by the short hairs, and I'm going to tear their hair out by the roots."[27]

Most of January 23-24 was spent in mopping-up operations, and in a vain attempt to surround the remnants of the 1st Armoured. The survivors of this division were in full flight across the desert, and for the most part could not be headed off.

Rommel had another of his periodic brushes with death during these actions. He and Colonel Westphal flew over the battle area to check on the Afrika Korps' progress. A flight of 12 Hurricane fighters flew directly over them, but remarkably did not see them. Twice British anti-aircraft fire riddled the airplane, but failed to knock it out of the sky. When they landed, it looked like "Swiss cheese." Amazingly, none of the Germans was so much as nicked.²⁸

By January 25, the forward elements of the Eighth Army were in total panic. Rommel gave up his encircling effort and ordered an immediate pursuit in the direction of Msus. Colonel von Mellenthin wrote that "the pursuit attained a speed of 15 miles per hour, and the British fled madly over the desert in one of the most extra-ordinary routs of the war."²⁹ The 15th Panzer Division advanced an incredible 50 miles in only four hours. At 11:00 A.M. this unit burst into Msus, and took the critical supply depot almost completely intact. Although they found little gasoline in the place, it was still a fantastic victory. That day alone the British lost 96 tanks and armored cars, 38 guns, and 190 trucks to the 15th Panzer.³⁰ After the first five days of the counteroffensive, the British had lost 299 tanks and armored vehicles, 147 guns, and 935 prisoners. Rommel reported his own losses at three officers, 11 enlisted men, and three tanks.³¹

January 26 was spent in preparing the finishing touch to the campaign: the capture of Benghazi. The next day Rommel started out with a feint toward Mechili. Ritchie took the bait and rushed the larger part of his greatly reduced command to that town. Meanwhile, Rommel had doubled back on Benghazi. It was spring in the desert, and in that very brief season everything was green. Plants that bloom only once for a very short period were alive now. It might have been Europe, judging from the landscape. For once, the soldiers traveled through a beautiful countryside, and their morale was sky high. This beautiful weather did not last long, for the next day a sandstorm, accompanied by a heavy downpour, struck the Afrika Korps. Nature halted the day's advance short of where Rommel would have liked. Cold, hungry, and wet men slept in the open until dawn. Then the advance began again.³²

Rommel closed in on Benghazi on January 29. Near the city he captured the British depots that were scheduled to supply the Allied advance on Tripoli in February. He also retook an Axis depot lost in the retreat from Sidi Rezegh. The supplies inside had not even been touched. At noon the following day, as he re-entered the Cyrenaican capital, he received a message from Mussolini. It suggested that Rommel "on this favorable occasion should take Benghazi." Rommel sent back a curt three-word reply: "Benghazi already taken." The Arab population cheered the Germans and greeted them like liberators, just as they had done for the British less than two months before.[33] A thousand men from the 4th Indian Division were trapped inside the city; they surrendered when it fell.[34]

For this absolutely brilliant campaign, climaxed by the capture of Benghazi, Hitler promoted Rommel to Colonel General, the second-highest rank in the German Army. Ritchie continued his retreat to the Gazala line, and did not seek another battle. Rommel's pursuit forces reached the line on February 6, but were too weak to assault it, so the campaign ended here.

This operation was one of Rommel's masterpieces. From the beginning to the end he was in complete control. He boldly seized the initiative and held it throughout. With superb self-confidence and self-reliance he surprised his enemies, then chased them in confusion out of Benghazi. For the second time he had conquered Cyrenaica. The Allies, who had been planning an operation that might have terminated the German stay in North Africa, were now busy constructing a defense line several hundred miles farther back. They also had two more shattered divisions to rebuild. Despite an overall enemy superiority of between 2.5 and 3 to 1 in Libya, Rommel again proved the value of a brilliant leader of men against those who are merely regimented. He had seized his moment, and made the best of it. In the final analysis, this is what made him great.

Although this campaign settled no decisive strategic questions, it did settle one issue: The Allies were not about to hurl Erwin Rommel's men off the African continent in the foreseeable future. In fact, the Desert Fox was already planning his next campaign, the one that would carry him to the pinnacle of his military career. He had gained the initiative in mid-January. He would not give it up again for months.

3

The Gazala Line

In February 1942, Erwin Rommel, as ever, wanted to assume the offensive. For once he had some supply reserves, taken from the British in the Cyrenaican rout of the month before. On February 16 he conferred with Hitler at the Wolf's Lair, the Fuehrer Headquarters in East Prussia. During the next two days, Colonel Westphal had two conversations with Colonel General Jodl. Neither Rommel nor Westphal had any luck. Hitler and the High Command were preoccupied with the Eastern Front, where the Nazi armies had just barely escaped annihilation in the Soviet's first winter offensive. They were noncommittal when the desert soldiers tried to get permission to attack the Eighth Army, now solidly entrenched behind the Gazala line. Rommel and his operations officer left Germany in a very depressed state of mind.[1]

Rommel's emotional outlook undoubtedly improved in the next two months as supplies poured into Tripoli and Benghazi. In the months of March and April, between 93 and 99 percent of all supplies sent to North Africa got through undamaged. Kesselring's air raids on Malta continued with unabated fury. The British submarines left for safer parts, while the Messerschmitt fighters strafed and sunk the British cargo vessels. In March, the Second Air Fleet dropped 2,000 tons of bombs on the island, and increased the total to 7,000 tons in April.[2] All RAF forces on the island were forced to evacuate or were destroyed. Now it was Malta's turn to starve. Of the 26,000 tons of supplies dispatched from Alexandria to the island-fortress in March, only 5,000 reached port.

Grand Admiral Raeder, who had always appreciated the island's strategic value, saw an opportunity to deal the British a decisive defeat, and at the same time raise the stock of the German Navy with the Fuehrer. Raeder persuaded a lukewarm Hitler to cooperate with the Italians for an invasion of Malta. The landings, christened Operation "Hercules," were timed for the full-moon phase of June.

Six Italian divisions were assigned to the "Hercules" project. The plans called for an initial landing by 30,000 German and Italian paratroopers under the command of the Prince of Piedmont. The elite Nazi airborne specialist, Major General Hermann Ramcke, was named chief instructor of the Italian Folgore Parachute Division. Ten Luftwaffe air transport groups under Major General Conrad assembled in Sicily for the drops, landings, and supply efforts. The total forces involved amounted to 100,000 men and 500 transport aircraft, quite apart from Kesselring's fighters and bombers. The British had only 30,000 men to oppose this massive force, and little hope for substantial reinforcemtns as long as Kesselring maintained the pressure.[3]

In the desert, Rommel and Cruewell were building up supplies for the offensive, which still lacked approval from the High Command. Ludwig Cruewell had just received another promotion. He was now deputy commander of the Panzer Army. General Walter Nehring was sent to Libya to take command of the Afrika Korps. He arrived with a message from Hitler. "Tell Rommel that I admire him," the Fuehrer had said. After all the months of backbiting from his enemies at Fuehrer Headquarters, this comment must have heartened Rommel.[4]

Rommel also got two new divisional commanders as permanent replacements for Neumann-Silkow and von Ravenstein. Major General Georg von Bismarck assumed command of the 21st Panzer, and Major General Gustav von Vaerst took over the 15th Panzer. They were both experienced and talented leaders.

Lieutenant Wilfried Armbruster joined Rommel's personal staff during this buildup period, and was to stay with him until the end in Africa. Armbruster was also talented; not only could he speak Italian, but he could also imitate Rommel. When Rommel shouted in fury at the Italian generals, Armbruster roared the translation in exactly the same tone of voice.[5]

On March 20, Cruewell's 50th birthday, he visited his former headquarters at Umm er Rzem. Some enlisted bakers managed to cook up some cream and chocolate tarts for the popular general. Real French champagne was brought out of hiding, and officers and men had a regular little party.[6] It was well that they could not see into the future, particularly that of the guest of honor; it would have spoiled the celebration.

Other, less happy thoughts occupied the mind of Erwin Rommel. He continued to press Hitler and the High Command for authority to launch another offensive. By April, the German position in Russia had stabilized enough to give Hitler time to consider offensive actions elsewhere. Toward the end of the month he met with Mussolini, Kesselring, and Cavallero at Obersalzberg. Since the Italians were not yet ready to attack Malta, Hitler overrode the objections of Admiral Raeder and decided to let Rommel attack the Gazala line before the Italians tried to overwhelm the island. Hitler instructed Rommel to capture Tobruk, and then go on the defensive, while the other Axis forces took Malta.[7] At least this was the way Hitler envisioned future Axis operations in North Africa in April 1942.

On the desert, a second race for supplies began. This one resembled the one that took place prior to the British "Crusader" offensive the year before, with one important difference: This time, Malta was neutralized. Auchinleck originally planned to strike in mid-May, but he became alarmed over Rommel's growing armored strength. In view of this, the War Cabinet in London allowed him to postpone the attack until the middle of June. There was really no excuse for this, because the British had an overall ground force superiority of more than two to one, and the desert was not a secondary front to the Allies. Churchill and his subordinates were rushing supplies to Egypt and Libya on a priority basis. The Prime Minister spared no effort to support the Eighth Army.

Rommel, convinced that his staff was doing all it could to prepare for the offensive, went on a short leave in mid-February. On February 18 he had dinner with Hitler at his East Prussian headquarters. The Fuehrer flew into a denunciation of Winston Churchill as "the very archetype of a corrupt journalist. He himself has written that it's incredible how far you can get in war with the help of the common lie. He's an utterly amoral, repulsive creature. I'm convinced he has a refuge prepared for himself across the Atlantic. . . . He'll go to his friends, the Yanks." To this outburst, Rommel apparently made no reply.[8]

Erwin Rommel spent the next three weeks at home in Austria. It amazed him to see how his son had grown. If the war continued, he too might be drafted, as millions before had been. This thought brought no pleasure to his father. Indeed, little during the three weeks did, for Rommel was once more preoccupied by the coming campaign. "I just could not settle down at home," he wrote. Finally he gave up and flew back to Cyrenaica.[9]

The British in Libya were trying to draw him into a static battle of

position, for which they were specially trained. For this reason they constructed the Gazala line, one of the technical marvels of the war. The
Italians had built some fortifications in the area prior to the outbreak of
hostilities, but these were pitiful indeed compared to the British effort. It
was a huge series of thick minefields that extended 40 miles from the
Mediterranean Sea to Bir Hacheim. In fact, as Colonel von Mellenthin
stated, it was mined "... on a scale never yet seen in war."[10] Over a million
mines were laid. The line also included several isolated strongpoints, called
"boxes," which were designed to cover the minefields and prevent the Axis
from penetrating them. The boxes were usually about two miles in diame-
ter, and garrisoned by a reinforced brigade. The Allied command referred
to these forces as brigade groups, but in this book they will be called
brigades so that the terminology can remain standard.

Each box had almost every modern defensive device at its disposal:
minefields, barbed-wire entanglements, bunkers, listening posts, machine-
gun nests, artillery and antitank concentrations, and even tanks. The
artillery was assigned the task of covering the gaps between the boxes.
Inside each box was an abundance of supplies, food, water, and ammunition. Each position had the potential to hedgehog for several days.

To the rear of the boxes lay the operational reserves: armored and
motorized infantry formations that were prepared to launch counterattacks
as required. They were also assigned the mission of holding critical positions in case of a major Axis breakthrough. For this reason they camped in
strongly fortified positions of their own: Tobruk, Knightsbridge, El Adem,
and others.

As fine as this defensive network was, it had one major deficiency: It
could be outflanked. Once again, the British militantly refused to recognize
the fact that their left (desert) flank was vulnerable. Once again, Erwin
Rommel prepared to apply the principles of mobile warfare against an
opponent who could not accept the fact that it was no longer 1918.

Even without the Gazala line, the Allies had an overall two to one
superiority over the Germans.[11] In first-line tank strength, von Mellenthin
put the Panzer Army's total at 333 German and 228 Italian tanks, against
900 British tanks.[12] Major General Playfair's figures are similar. In the
British *Official History*, he placed the Allied tank superiority at 849 to
560.[13] His exact figures are shown in Table 2.

General Playfair's figures are somewhat deceiving if taken strictly at face
value, because they do not take into account the quality of the vehicles

Table 2

Opposing Tank Strength, May 1942

	Allies		**Axis**	
Medium tanks	Grants	167	PzKw III's	223
	Crusaders	257	PzKw III (Specials)	19
			PzKw IV's	40
Total with armored divisions		424		282
Light tanks	"I" tanks	276	PzKw II's	50
	Stuarts	149	Italian mediums	228
Grand Totals		849		560

Source: Playfair, *History of the Second World War, The Mediterranean and Middle East*, Vol. III, Her Majesty's Stationery Office, London, 1960; p. 220.

involved. In fact, the Nazi war machine had lost whatever technical superiority it ever had in the Western Desert with the arrival of the Grant tank. This American-made vehicle weighed 30 tons, or more than any existing panzer up to this time. It had a six-man crew, and two main battle guns: a 75-millimeter and a 37-millimeter cannon. The 75-millimeter guns outclassed Rommel's PzKw III's smaller gun. The only tank the colonel general had to compete with the Grant was the PzKw III (Special) with its high-velocity 50-millimeter gun, but there were only 19 of these in the entire Panzer Army. Rommel did have four PzKw IV Specials, but no ammunition for them arrived before the battle started.[14]

The Allies also maintained numerical supremacy in other critical areas besides tank strength and quality. They had a 10 to 1 domination in armored cars,[15] 8 to 5 in artillery,[16] and 6 to 5.5 in aircraft. The RAF outnumbered the combined German-Italian Air Forces in airplanes by a net total of 604 to 542.[17] The poor quality of Italian equipment makes this figure even more significant.

The Allies should have had a superiority in antitank weaponry, but they did not. The British six-pounder antitank gun was more effective than Rommel's 50-millimeter, but not as good as the Russian 76-millimeter gun,

a captured weapon that the Panzer Army was now receiving from the
Eastern Front in significant numbers. However, the real reason for the
German lead in antitank gunnery lay in better tactical employment. Rommel's men used the 88-millimeter anti-aircraft gun in an antitank role,
while the British were very reluctant to use their 3.7-inch AA gun in a
similar role against the panzers. As a result the rear areas of the Eighth
Army were somewhat safer from Luftwaffe attack than the rear of their
opposite number against the RAF, but their front line units were frequently overrun when they might have been saved.

Besides equipment shortages and deficiencies, Rommel was also ham-
pered by a severe shortage of men in key units. For instance, the average
company strength in the 90th Light Division stood at 50 men in mid-May,
or about 35 percent of the normal requirement. Some of the Italian
divisions were now of only regimental size.[18] However, including Italians,
Rommel was outnumbered only 90,000 to 100,000.[19] Of course, this figure
is also deceptive if taken at face value. Many of the Italians had already lost
faith in their government and had little taste for the type of engagement
that produced long casualty lists.

British aerial parity, excellent camouflage techniques, commendable
radio security, and armored car superiority prevented Rommel's intelligence network from gathering a true picture of the situation facing them.
When they attacked, the Germans did not know of the existence of the
Grant tank or of the extent or depth of the minefields. They thought the
belts ended near Trigh el Abd (near the center of the Allied line) when in
fact they extended many miles south of this.[20] They did not know that the
22nd Armoured and 32nd Army Tank brigades were close behind the
Gazala line. They also failed to note the existence of the Knightsbridge box,
held by the 201st Guards Brigade, or the location of the 29th Indian Brigade
at Bir el Gubi. They also did not learn that the 3rd Indian Motor Brigade
was in position southeast of Bir Hacheim. In all, they missed or failed to
correctly identify two armored and three infantry brigades, plus the extent
of the minefields and the changes in the technological sphere. As Rommel's intelligence chief later admitted: "Perhaps fortunately, we underestimated British strength, for had we known the full facts even Rommel
might have balked at an attack on such a greatly superior enemy."[21] Tables
3 and 4 show the orders of battle.

The British Gazala line was manned by an impressive infantry-heavy
force. It included the 1st South African Infantry Division, supported by the

Table 3.

Allied Order of Battle, Gazala Line
May 26, 1942

Front Line

1st South African Division
    3rd South African Brigade
    2nd South African Brigade
    7th South African Brigade

50th Infantry Division
    151st Infantry Brigade
    69th Infantry Brigade
    150th Infantry Brigade

1st Free French Brigade*

Reserves

2nd South African Division
    6th South African Brigade
    4th South African Brigade

9th Indian Brigade

32nd Army Tank Brigade

1st Army Tank Brigade

1st Armoured Division
    2nd Armoured Brigade
    22nd Armoured Brigade
    201st Guards Brigade (Armoured)

7th Armoured Division
    4th Armoured Brigade
    7th Indian Motor Brigade
    3rd Indian Motor Brigade

29th Indian Motor Brigade

*This included the attached Jewish Battalion.

32nd Army Tank Brigade, holding the northern sector; the 50th (Northumbrian) Infantry Division in the center, with its three brigades, the 151st, 69th, and 150th, running north to south, and the 1st Army Tank Brigade in close support; and the 1st Free French Brigade (plus the Jewish Battalion) holding the southern flank at Bir Hacheim. In reserve, the Eighth Army held its armored muscle. The 1st Armoured Division, with the 2nd and 22nd Armoured brigades and the 201st Guards Motor Brigade, lay astride the Trigh Capuzzo, behind the center of the Gazala line. Covering the all-important southern flank the 3rd Indian Motor Brigade, as previously mentioned, lay southeast of Bir Hacheim. Also in the immediate vicinity was the 1st Armoured Division, with its 7th Motor, 1st Armoured, and 4th Armoured brigades. Even farther to the left-rear, the 29th Indian Brigade assembled at Bir el Gubi, to guard against the unlikely possibility that Rommel would surface 30 miles behind the Allied front. More realistically, the 29th Indian served as an infantry reserve. The 2nd South African

Table 4.

Axis Order of Battle, Gazala Line
May 26, 1942

Pinning Force: General Cruewell

15th German Rifle Brigade*

XXI Italian Infantry Corps
  Sabratha Infantry Division
  Trento Infantry Division

X Italian Infantry Corps
  Brescia Infantry Division
  Pavia Infantry Division

Strike Force: Colonel General Rommel

XX Italian Motorized Corps
  Trieste Motorized Division
  Ariete Armored Division

Afrika Korps
  21st Panzer Division

5th Panzer Regiment
104th Panzer Grenadier Regiment
155th Panzer Artillery Regiment
3rd Reconnaissance Battalion†
200th Panzer Engineer Battalion

15th Panzer Division
  8th Panzer Regiment
  115th Panzer Grenadier Regiment
  33rd Panzer Artillery Regiment
  33rd Reconnaissance Battalion†
  33rd Panzer Engineer Battalion

90th Light Division
  155th Panzer Grenadier Regiment
  200th Panzer Grenadier Regiment
  361st Panzer Grenadier Regiment
  190th Motorized Artillery Regiment
  580th Reconnaissance Battalion
  900th Motorized Engineer Battalion

*This consisted of detached elements of the 90th Light Division.
†Temporarily attached to 90th Light Division.

and 5th Indian Infantry divisions, camped in the Tobruk area, completed the British dispositions. Map 3 shows the Allied defenses.

Rommel's plan was much simpler than Ritchie's arrangements, mainly because Rommel had less to work with. Essentially he divided his force into two parts: the Cruewell Group to the north and center, and the strike force to the south. Group Cruewell consisted of the XXI and X Italian Infantry corps, and two regimental combat groups of the 90th Light Division, operating under the Headquarters, 15th Rifle Brigade. Their major mission was to launch diversionary attacks against the Gazala line in an effort to pin down the Allied reserves. The XXI Italian Corps was to demonstrate in the northern sector against the South Africans, while the X Italian

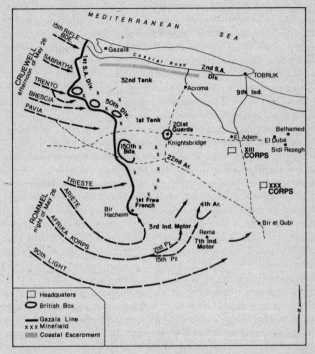

Map 3. The Initial Attack on the Gazala Line, May 26-27, 1942

Infantry Corps tied up the British 50th Infantry Division and whatever else it could engage. While Cruewell did this, Erwin Rommel would lead the strike force in a sweep to the south. With the bulk of the Panzer Army's tank force he would overrun any Allied forces south of Bir Hacheim and come up behind the Gazala line. The main attack force consisted of the Afrika Korps, most of the 90th Light Division, and the XX Italian Motorized Corps (Ariete Armored and Trieste Motorized divisions) under the brave General Baldassare.

Rommel's plan represented a bit of a gamble, because the attack force would be in a critical position if Bir Hacheim held out longer than expected.

Both Gause and Bayerlein pointed this out. Rommel agreed with their estimates, but responded with the remark, "That chance has to be taken."[22]

There were two basic flaws in Rommel's plan: First, the British should have expected it. Oddly enough, both Auchinleck and Ritchie believed the main attack would come in the center, although neither discounted a sweep around Bir Hacheim.[23] Rommel set the pattern for the Gazala offensive in both the first and second Cyrenaican campaigns, when he swept around the British southern flank and defeated the Eighth Army. They really should have expected him to do the same thing here.

The second flaw in Rommel's plan was that it was overly ambitious. Rommel led the Afrika Korps far into the enemy rear, while he left the Italians to deal with Bir Hacheim. When this position proved to be too strong, Rommel would be in deep, deep trouble.

Rommel's men spent most of April rehearsing the plan. Morale was high, despite the heat. There was some relief from another quarter. Rommel finally got to see the last of General Gambarra, whom he detested. The Italian chief of staff for North Africa was relieved by Mussolini and replaced by General Curio Barbasetti. "Apparently Gambarra was sent packing because in the presence of some officers he said he only hoped to see the day when he might lead an Italian army against us Germans," Rommel wrote. "The Idiot!"[24]

While training continued at an intense pace, Rommel went out on reconnaissance missions to see if he could learn anything important. On one such foray he almost lost his life. An enemy shell splinter came through the windshield and struck him in the stomach. Fortunately for him it was spent, or the career of the Desert Fox would have ended then and there. However it only caused a large bruise and some minor discomfort. His luck had held again.[25]

In late March an incident took place that amused the Swabian. He decided to headquarter temporarily in a stone house at Umm er Rzem, near Derna, because it would provide good protection against sandstorms. He found a message, obviously chalked on the door by a retreating British soldier. It read, "Please keep tidy. Back soon."[26] The enemy, it seemed, had his share of wit.

The strain of offensive preparations was also relieved, to a degree, by fan mail. This stream of letters from Germany both amused and annoyed the Desert Fox. "One secretary is not enough," he complained. "Lovelorn letters from all shapes and sizes of females are on the increase. . . . The newsreels have brought the younger females particularly out of their composure."[27]

Despite this remark, General Rommel seems to have enjoyed playing the hero, at least a little, for the letters were a diversion from grim reality. Now, however, more serious problems faced him. The Afrika Korps was ready. The time had come to attack.

At 2:00 P.M. on May 26 the Axis offensive began. Group Cruewell launched the initial (diversionary) assault at this unusual hour. The main combat unit employed in this work was the 361st Panzer Grenadier Regiment of the 90th Light Division. Rommel had spent a day in "Crusader" pinned down with these former French Legionnaires. They were an ill-disciplined lot, but excellent warriors. When Rommel approached their camp, he always gave his driver the same order: "Padlock the spare tires. We're coming to the 361st."[28]

On this day the 361st's job was to convince the British that the main assault had come. This would draw their attention away from Rommel, who was heading south. The mock offensive was well supported. Heavy artillery and Stukas pounded the British and South African positions, while dust units—trucks with aircraft engines mounted on their rear beds— threw up huge clouds of sand in an attempt to create the illusion of deploying panzer and motorized infantry columns.[29] The main force of the Afrika Korps also took part in the exercise by moving as if it intended to strike along the Trigh Capuzzo. By nightfall the British command was fooled into thinking the attack would come in the center of their line.

The feint had worked well enough to give Rommel at least a degree of surprise when he did surface. As night fell, all appearances indicated that the Axis forces would attack along the Trigh Capuzzo at dawn the next day. It was 10:30 P.M. before Rommel gave the code word "Venezia," and the Panzer Army began the long swing to the south. The night march excited Rommel as much as his men, who were also confident of victory. Rommel later wrote: "My staff and I, in our places in the Afrika Korps column, drove through the moonlight towards the great armored battle. . . . I was tense and keyed-up, impatiently waiting the coming of day."[30]

During the night, 7th Armoured Division and XXX Corps Headquarters received fragmentary reports from the South African and other armored-car scouts. These brave and independent men operated well forward of friendly lines, much like the cavalry scouts of previous centuries.

They correctly reported that major Axis columns had turned south, in the general direction of Bir Hacheim. The 7th Motorized Brigade's advanced outposts radioed in similar reports. However, Generals Messervy and Norrie, the 7th Armoured and XXX Corps commanders, did not grasp the significance of these dispatches. Precious hours slipped by, and no important decisions were made on the British side. The Allied generals apparently wanted to wait until dawn, when the armored-car reconnaissance reports could be confirmed by the Royal Air Force.[51] Unfortunately for them, dawn would be too late.

By daybreak of May 27, the great Axis flanking movement had succeeded. Rommel wheeled north with his four divisions, toward Bir Hacheim and points east. One of the original five divisions of the strike force, Trieste, had turned east too soon, and was bogged down in the minefields north of Bir Hacheim. Ariete, on Rommel's left flank, pivoted to attack the French at the southernmost point of the Gazala line. Rommel led the Afrika Korps, in the center of the attacking line, toward the rear of the Eighth Army. On the right flank the 90th Light Division, minus some units but augmented by the three German reconnaissance battalions, fanned out to the east. Before the sun had risen very high, the desert soldiers claimed their first victims. The Ariete, reinforced by elements of the 21st Panzer Division, smashed the 3rd Indian Motor Brigade south of Bir Hacheim. On the other flank the tough 90th Light overran the Retma Box, which was only partly manned by the 7th Motor Brigade. The men of the 90th did not halt but struck out to the northeast for El Adem, pursuing the survivors of the motor brigade and disrupting the rear of the 7th Armoured Division as they went. Meanwhile, in the center of the thrust, the 15th Panzer Division and most of the 21st Panzer Division caught the 4th Armoured Brigade before it could completely deploy into combat formation. The major battle was fought here, between the 8th Panzer Regiment and the 4th Armoured Brigade. During this battle, Rommel had his first nasty surprise of the campaign. For the first time he met the Grant tank, and found its 75-millimeter gun was much superior to the 50-millimeter gun of the PzKw III. To complicate matters even further for Lieutenant Colonel Willy Teege, the German spearhead commander, the 21st Panzer's divisional artillery, the 33rd Panzer Artillery Regiment, had not been able to keep up with the advance. However, aid was quick in coming, for Colonel Mueller led his 5th Panzer Regiment directly into the fray. Fighting became desperate all along the line. Erwin Rommel rushed forward with Generals Nehring and von Vaerst, and assumed personal command of the battle. The Grant tanks took heavy tolls on the panzers. Entire German crews were wiped out by direct hits from their powerful main battle gun. However, German leadership was the decisive factor. By employing superior tank tactics, adapted to the terrain, the men of the Afrika Korps finally broke up the 4th Armoured Brigade. Of its two regiments, the 8th Hussars was almost wiped out. The 3rd Royal Tank Regiment also suffered heavy losses, including 16 Grant tanks.[32]

As the remnants of the 4th Armoured fell back, the Afrika Korps surged forward and shot up the communications and supply echelons of the 7th Armoured Division. The Afrika Korps' advance was so rapid that they even managed to capture the divisional headquarters. General Messervy just had time to hide his badges of rank before he was taken prisoner. Later he escaped in the confusion of the battle. Nevertheless his division, a mainstay of the Eighth Army, had been temporarily eliminated as a cohesive fighting unit.

Meanwhile, 10 miles farther north, the 2nd Armoured Brigade lay idle in its camp near the Trigh Capuzzo. A concentrated effort by this brigade and the 4th Armoured just a couple of hours earlier might easily have repulsed Rommel's main attack. This piecemeal British effort was to be repeated throughout this battle. It would soon cost the Eighth Army the lives of many of its best men.

As the remains of the British armored units fell back toward Bir el Gubi, Rommel decided to pursue in the direction of the Trigh Capuzzo. He wanted to reach Acroma by nightfall. The occupation of this place would isolate the bulk of Gott's XIII Corps in the main Gazala line, and probably force him to abandon that strong position. However, Rommel made a serious mistake in ordering this move, for he had badly underestimated the strength of Allied armor. By sending the Afrika Korps forward at pursuit speed, he strung their columns out all over the desert. By advancing to the north, Rommel hoped to force Ritchie to defend the area south of the Coastal Road with his remaining mobile forces. The British general refused to fall into this trap, and altogether avoided another frontal confrontation with the Afrika Korps. Instead, he let the spearheads of the Korps pass west of Knightsbridge, and then struck Rommel's supporting columns in both flanks with the 2nd Armoured and 1st Tank brigades. The 2nd Armoured attacked Rommel's right flank, and the 1st Tank ambushed his left, attacking from the direction of the Gazala line. Of these attacks, von

Mellenthin later wrote, "The Grants and Matildas charged home reck-lessly—our tanks took a severe hammering, one rifle battalion suffered such losses that it had to be disbanded, and supply columns were cut off from the panzer divisions. It is true that our antitank gunners exacted a heavy toll, but in some cases the British tanks forced their way up to the very muzzles of the guns and wiped out our crews. . . . "[33]

The unexpected British counterattacks completely isolated Rommel and the Afrika Korps from Cruewell and the rest of the army. The Korps was cut off from its transport and supply columns. Now Rommel, not the Eighth Army, was in a trap. To the northeast, the 90th Light was also cut off and almost out of water. The crisis of the battle occurred at 4:00 P.M., when British tanks attacked the left flank of the 15th Panzer Division. The panzer infantry battalion covering von Vaerst's flank was wiped out, and his whole division was in danger of annihilation.[34]

General Walter Nehring, the Afrika Korps leader, responded imme-diately. "A flak front!" he roared at Colonel Alwin Wolz, the commander of the 135th Flak Regiment. "Wolz, you've got to build up a flak front to act as a flank defense with all available guns." The 88-millimeter anti-aircraft guns were quickly pushed into position. The regiment formed a line two miles long, with overlapping fields of fire. The British, having dealt with the infantrymen, attacked this new line with their Grants just as Wolz completed it. However, they soon discovered that not even the Grants could withstand the jolt of the 88-millimeter gun. They soon withdrew, with losses.[35]

The Allies were not through with Wolz's line. They bombarded it with heavy artillery and destroyed several guns, along with their crews. Fortu-nately for the Germans, nature intervened before they could launch another attack. A *ghibli* (sandstorm) sprang up and covered everything with dust. The battle was over for the day.[36]

Among those seriously wounded in this fight was Gustav von Vaerst, the promising Hessian commander of the 15th Panzer Division. He would be out of action for some time.

The British attacks of May 27, uncoordinated as they were, had caused heavy losses on both sides. They had forced Rommel to turn back to meet them. They also disrupted the German commander's control of the battle. The affair west of Knightsbridge deteriorated into a series of small unit actions. This effectively halted the advance of the Afrika Korps,[36] just when it looked as if Rommel would succeed in cutting the XIII Corps off from the rest of the Eighth Army. The leading elements of the Afrika Korps had actually penetrated to within sight of the Coastal Road before the signal to return reached them.[37]

During the night of May 27 the 90th Light Division hedgehogged south of El Adem. Many miles away the Afrika Korps leaguered north of Bir el Harmat, near a feature called Rigel Ridge. They had come close to achieving their very ambitious objective, but having failed were in a bind themselves. They had lost over a third of their tank strength, and the excessively heavy fighting had cost them dearly in fuel and ammunition. Certainly their supply allotment would not last as long as predicted. Now they were behind enemy lines, with very little gasoline. The 15th Panzer was in especially bad shape. To make matters even more dangerous, the Italians had failed to take Bir Hacheim. The Trieste Motorized Division was still lost, and the Ariete's attack had been thrown back by the Free French. Allied raiding parties from the Gazala line boxes now struck freely at Rommel's exposed rear area, and his supply line was completely severed. By midnight the seriousness of the German intelligence failures that had resulted in Rommel's underestimations of enemy strength and dispositions became apparent.

Perhaps the worst of these omissions was the German failure to locate the 150th Brigade Box a few miles west-southwest of Rommel's night camp. The 150th prevented the Trieste and Pavia divisions from breaching the Gazala minefields and sending supplies to the trapped Germans. The panzer soldiers had stumbled into a deadly trap. They were virtually surrounded, behind enemy lines, and nearly out of gasoline. The fact that the trap was largely an accident on the Allies' part made it no less dangerous.

May 28, 1942, should have seen the annihilation of the Afrika Korps. That it did not is less attributable to the brilliance of Rommel than to the ham-fisted way the British generals fought the battle. Instead of launching a coordinated assault on the surrounded Germans, the Allied armor engaged in a few minor skirmishes. The 22nd Armoured Brigade spent the day observing Rigel Ridge, where the 15th Panzer was camped. The 15th, now under Colonel Eduard Crasemann, did nothing at all, but not due to a lack of will; it was immobilized due to a lack of fuel. Had the British attacked in strength, this elite force would almost certainly have been wiped out.

South of Knightsbridge, the Ariete advanced. Rommel wanted to fill the gap between the 90th Light and the Afrika Korps. The Italians skirmished with the 1st Army Tank and 2nd Armoured Brigades. The 90th Light Division faced the most serious thrust of the day. Over 100 tanks from the 4th Armoured Brigade pinned it down six miles east of Bir el Harmat, Rommel's battle headquarters. The salvation of this division lay in its antitank guns, which held the enemy at bay. The 90th Light was in no immediate danger as night fell.

The 21st Panzer Division provided all the offensive punch that was left in the Afrika Korps. It advanced northward, took the position known as the Commonwealth Keep, occupied the coastal escarpment, and brought the Via Balbia under artillery and tank fire.

All this time, the completely fresh 32nd Army Tank Brigade lay idle behind the front of the 1st South African Division. Under a bold commander, it could easily have won the battle and mauled, if not destroyed, Rommel's strike force. As things were, it did nothing all day long.

Rommel spent the day trying desperately to get a vital supply column to the endangered Korps. Early in the morning he was under British artillery fire, and his command vehicle was struck by shell fragments from enemy guns. A little later he made his way through the minefield, although he was fired on by both the British and the Italians. The colonel general rushed back to the Panzer Army's headquarters, but found it had been dispersed by British tanks in his absence. He finally managed to get a small supply column through the minefields to the Rigel Ridge area.[38] The situation was somewhat eased, but not dispelled.

The Italian Trieste and Pavia divisions scored the most significant success on May 28. They cut a series of small gaps in the minefields in the vicinity of the 150th Brigade Box. The gaps were still hard to use and very dangerous, due to the enemy's artillery, but they held the promise of some relief for the trapped "Africans."

Rommel decided to relieve the pressure on his main force by getting the Italians to open another major battle to the northwest. He ordered Cruewell to ". . . break through the minefield from the west to disengage the rear." Cruewell went to the Panzer Army Artillery Headquarters to plan a bombardment with Major General Krausse, the artillery commander. Next Cruewell flew back to the front lines, but the flares that were supposed to be shot off to mark friendly lines were never fired. Cruewell found himself over British lines at an altitude of only 500 feet. Enemy machine-gun fire riddled the light plane. The engine was destroyed, and the pilot slumped

over dead. Cruewell, in the back seat, was helpless. Miraculously, he survived. As if guided by the hand of Fate, the airplane landed itself. General
Cruewell was removed, unhurt, by members of the 150th Brigade. He
would live to see Germany again, but for him the war was over. The Panzer
Army lost its second in command, and one of its best leaders.[39] To him, it
must have seemed the end of the world. His wife, at only 34 years of age,
had died suddenly, just a few weeks before. Cruewell might live to return to
Germany, but he would have little to come home to. Without him, the
attack by the Italian Sabratha Division came to nothing.[40]

When Colonel Westphal learned that General Cruewell was missing,
Westphal became concerned that certain nervous Italian generals would
take charge, since Rommel was pinned down behind enemy lines. Westphal was afraid they might order a retreat and leave the armor in the lurch.
Fortunately, Field Marshal Kesselring happened to be visiting Panzer
Army Headquarters when the news arrived. The operations officer asked
the Luftwaffe commander-in-chief to assume command in the Italian
sector. The field marshal was at first reluctant to take this unusual step, but
Westphal finally convinced him to do it. The field marshal subordinated
himself to a colonel general. Kesselring's unselfish act is almost unprecedented in German military annals.

Having a field marshal working for him did not improve Rommel's
position in the pocket, for the British became aggressive again. The 2nd
Armoured Brigade moved west from Knightsbridge, in an obvious attempt
to cut off Ariete from the Afrika Korps. Rommel prevented this by
attacking it with the partially refueled 15th Panzer Division. In doing so, he
touched off another major battle, and further depleted his previous supplies. the 22nd Armoured Brigade soon joined the fight, as did the 21st
Panzer Division, Ariete, and many of the antitank gunners from the nearby
90th Light.[41] The battle of May 29 was indecisive except that it convinced
Rommel he would have to turn around and break the Gazala line from the
east to secure his supply line.

The British had again missed an opportunity to score a decisive victory. It
had been all the hard-pressed Axis strike force could do to repulse two
British armored brigades. Yet within a few miles of the scene of combat the
entire 4th Armoured Brigade lay uncommitted. All they did this day was
watch a few combat groups from the 90th Light. Several miles farther
north the men of the 1st and 32nd Army Tank brigades spent the day

playing cards and drinking tea. On the other hand, Rommel had concentrated all three of his armored divisions at the decisive point. By doing so he kept them alive for another day.

As night fell on May 29, the Afrika Korps was still in effect "in the pocket." A few supplies did trickle through, though only at great risk. The X Italian Infantry Corps had opened a few small gaps in the minefield in the vicinity of the Trigh Capuzzo, because the 50th British Infantry Division had simply been assigned too much frontage to cover it all completely. As a result, there was a 15-mile gap between the 150th Brigade Box at Sidi Muftah and the 1st Free French Brigade Box at Bar Hacheim. Several sectors of this gap could not be covered by direct Allied fire. Eventualy the Italian sappers discovered the locations of these exposed sectors and infiltrated them. However, the supplies they managed to get through to the strike force did not allow for extended operations. Their position was steadily deteriorating. Erwin Rommel knew that he must re-establish uncontested supply contact with the rest of the Panzer Army, or the Afrika Korps, Ariete, and the 90th Light would be forced to surrender within a very few days.

During the night of May 29-30, Rommel established defensive positions in an area that soon became famous as "the Cauldron." The 21st Panzer held Sidra Ridge on the northern face of the Cauldron, while the Ariete faced east on Aslagh Ridge. The 90th Light faced west opposite the 150th Infantry Brigade Box at Got el Ualeb, which the Germans had finally pinpointed. The 15th Panzer camped just southwest of the infantry division.[42]

The Eighth Army's generals were elated over Rommel's short retreat. They thought the battle was won. "Rommel is on the run," Ritchie signaled Auchinleck.

"Bravo, Eighth Army!" came the reply. "Give him the coup de grâce."

They would have been interested in Rommel's own, curt order: "Got el Ualeb must fall. The 150th Brigade must be evicted." It was a do-or-die situation. If the 150th held, it meant the end of Rommel's army.[43]

Ritchie's attempt at administering the coup de grâce went astray on May 30. Again the Allies launched unconcentrated attacks while the bulk of their armor remained unengaged. General Lumsden's 1st Armoured Division (the 2nd and 22nd Armoured brigades) railed against Ariete's front, but was defeated by the Italians, who were well supported by German antitank

and anti-aircraft (88-millimeter flak) units. Fifty-seven British tanks were
knocked out.[44]

While holding off the Allied armor, Rommel invested the 150th Brigade
Box and launched his first attack on Got el Ualeb. Here he received yet
another nasty surprise. The desert soldiers discovered a new British antitank weapon. It was the 57-millimeter antitank gun, or the six-pounder. It
weighed 1.22 tons, was served by a five-man crew, and could fire 15 rounds
of armor-piercing ammunition per minute. The British had gained technical (but not tactical) parity with the Nazis in the field of antitank gunnery.
The American Army later adopted this weapon.

Despite their technological advances, the 150th Brigade found itself in
serious trouble as May 30 wore on. They had over 3,000 men, 124 guns, 80
heavy Matilda tanks,[45] and plenty of supplies and ammunition. They could
hold out for a while, but against the large Axis concentration massing on
their rear, they could hardly be expected to hang on for long.

During the afternoon Rommel again made his way through the minefield, and returned to Army Headquarters to confer with Kesselring and
Hitler's personal adjutant, Major von Below. Later Rommel returned to the
pocket, determined to lead the decisive attack himself.[46]

He would have rested easier if he had known what transpired in British
Headquarters that night. Major General Lumsden, the commander of the
1st Armoured Division, at last came to the conclusion that only a combined
tank-infantry attack could force the collapse of the Cauldron. Generals
Norrie and Ritchie were preoccupied with the planning of "Limerick," a
thrust into the Italian lines. They never seemed to be ready to launch the
actual blow, and kept postponing it from day to day. As a result, Rommel
was left free to deal with the 150th Brigade with the bulk of his original
strike force.[47]

On May 31 the brave men of the 150th stood against the fury of
Rommel's attacks for the second consecutive day. The Trieste Motorized
Division had at last freed itself from the minefield, and joined up with the
Swabian colonel general. The entire XX Motorized Corps, the 90th Light
Division, and much of the Afrika Korps bogged down against the deter-
mined Britons. Colonel Siegfried Westphal, operations officer of the
Panzer Army and one of Rommel's most trusted subordinates, was among
the casualties. He went forward with Rommel, and was seriously wounded
by British mortar fire.

Despite their exhaustion, the greatly superior numbers of Rommel's forces began to tell on the embattled Britons. Erwin Rommel finally forced the British commander to commit his last reserves, and then personally led an attack that broke through the outer perimeter.[48] Unless Ritchie did something within the next few hours to relieve the pressure, the 150th was doomed. This was the situation as the night of May 31-June 1 fell on the battlefield.

On the other side of the line, the Afrika Korps was also on its last legs. It had enough strength for one more day of battle. If supplies could not reach it by then, it would be finished. Only the superb discipline of the individual soldier had kept it going for this long.

Major Archer-Shee of the 10th Hussars was with the Afrika Korps that night, as a reluctant guest. He had been captured early in the battle, when the 3rd Motor Brigade was overrun. Like the Germans, he was parched with thirst. He found himself among the Indian Brigade's prisoners near Rommel's headquarters, on the edge of the minefields. The camp itself was ringed by 88-millimeter guns. The Allied POWs had received no water for quite some time. The major worked up his courage and demanded to speak to Rommel. To his surprise, he was taken to him. In broken German Archer-Shee informed the colonel general that if the prisoners could not be given food or water, the Axis had no right to hold them. They should be returned to Allied lines immediately, he said.

Rommel listened sympathetically. Then, to the major's surprise, he said, "You are getting exactly the same ration of water as the Afrika Korps and myself: half a cup. But I quite agree that we cannot go on like this. If we don't get a convoy through tonight I shall have to ask General Ritchie for terms. You can take a letter to him for me. . . ."[49]

On the first day of June, Rommel threw the last of his strength against the battered 150th Brigade, which still received no help from the Eighth Army. The first attack by the 5th Panzer Regiment was beaten back, and a dozen more panzers were destroyed. The Kiehl Combat Group was also repulsed. After a Stuka attack, General von Bismarck sent in the 104th Panzer Grenadier Regiment. They made surprisingly rapid progress. The fighting soon became hand-to-hand. Rommel was right up front with his men. "The enemy's weakening!" he yelled in the Swabian accent he always lapsed into when he was excited. "Wave a white flag and he'll surrender," he ordered. Captain Reissmann, the assault commander, did not believe this, but naturally he obeyed the order. To his astonishment, the British began to walk out of their positions, their hands raised.[50]

The Afrika Korps was saved. The 150th Brigade and its tank support unit, the 44th Royal Tank Regiment, were both destroyed. They lost a total of 3,000 men, 101 tanks and armored cars, and 124 guns.[51] It had been a close-run thing. General Bayerlein later told Desmond Young: "If we had not captured it [the 150th Brigade Box] on June 1st, you would have captured the whole Afrika Korps. By the evening of the third day we were surrounded and almost out of petrol. As it was, it was a miracle that we managed to get supplies through the minefield in time."[52] Indeed, some of the Allies had already claimed their victory. On June 2, Moscow radio declared that Colonel General Rommel had been captured. They had confused him with the unhappy Cruewell. For his part, Cruewell conducted himself with typical Afrika Korps spirit after his capture. He arrived in Cairo, and was shown the famous Shepheard's Hotel. He looked about the luxurious accommodations and said, "It will make a grand headquarters for Rommel!" Adolf Hitler was so pleased with this remark that he had Cruewell's words broadcast around the world.[53]

The victory over the 150th Brigade was not without its costs, for Rommel lost another vital member of his staff that day. Major General Alfred Gause had gotten too close to the front, and was nearly hit by a British tank shell. The force of the blast hurled him backward through the air. He landed against the side of a panzer and suffered a brain concussion. Rommel had lost his two senior staff officers within 48 hours of each other. This came right on top of the losses of Generals Cruewell and von Vaerst earlier in the week. Yet, in keeping with Rommel's philosophy that no one was indispensable, both were replaced, and Rommel continued to take his staff officers forward with him. Bayerlein became chief of staff of the Panzer Army, and Colonel von Mellenthin succeeded Westphal as operations officer.

Despite his thin margin of victory and the serious personnel losses in the higher echelons, Rommel had broken the encirclement. A near-fatal trap had been broken, and, with the fall of Got el Ualeb, instantly became a major asset. A serious salient suddenly existed in the Eighth Army's Gazala line. With the enemy's front pierced, Rommel now prepared to deal with its southern anchor at Bir Hacheim. Unbelievably enough, the spirit of optimism still reigned at Eighth Army Headquarters. Ritchie signaled Auchinleck: "I am distressed over the loss of 150th Brigade after so gallant a fight, but still consider the situation favourable to us and getting better daily."[54]

* * *

Field Marshal Albert Kesselring was totally unprepared for what he found as acting deputy commander of Panzer Army Afrika. While Kesselring was beyond doubt a brilliant military thinker, as he later proved in the Italian campaigns of 1943-45, nothing in his education or background prepared him for Erwin Rommel's method of leadership. At first Kesselring was appalled. Then he grew angry. This was the emotion he felt when he visited Major General Gause and Colonel Westphal in their hospital room at Derna on the Mediterranean Sea. "My dear Gause," Kesselring began, "I don't want to upset you but things can't go on like this. Rommel must not cruise about at the front line. He's no longer a divisional or corps commander. As an army commander it must be possible to reach him. You must make him see this." Kesselring went on in this vein for some time.

Perhaps the Luftwaffe marshal expected some degree of sympathy from these two men. After all, they were General Staff trained, and Rommel's theories of leadership had led them to hospital beds. If Kesselring did expect accord, he was disappointed. "Herr Feldmarschall," Gause replied at last, "the colonel general can't be restrained. He simply drives off and then the wireless truck can't keep up with him or gets shot up.... But how could he lead here in Africa from the rear? This is the type of warfare where everything has to be decided from the front." As Kesselring considered this statement, Westphal interjected: "Herr Feldmarschall, it's impossible to pin Rommel down. In order to make grave decisions he has to have a picture of the terrain."

Kesselring remained unconvinced. "One day it might have disastrous consequences, gentlemen," he said, gravely.[55]

It is well that the conservative and orthodox Kesselring could not see and hear through space. He would have been even more unhappy, because Erwin Rommel was off and running again.

"Get into the car, Bayerlein," Rommel called. "I'm driving to Bir Hacheim." Thus was Colonel Fritz Bayerlein introduced to his new job as chief of staff of the Panzer Army.[56] Both the move and the statement were typical of Bayerlein's new boss. No warmth or welcome can be found in this order. His former friend at the Infantry School at Dresden was just another subordinate now. The move was also vintage Rommel. He had just narrowly avoided annihilation the day before. A lesser man might have been content to escape, withdraw, and rebuild. Rommel ignored his losses and immediately pressed on toward the next objective.

Since May 26, the day the offensive began, the Italians had been attacking Bir Hacheim without success. Rommel shook his head. "A whole division! Well, we'll soon take that."[57] This proved to be easier said than done, because the French garrison, supplemented by a battalion of Jews, was in the process of putting up the most stubborn resistance experienced by the Germans in the entire North African war, with the possible exception of the Australian defense of Tobruk in the spring of 1941.

The Bir Hacheim Box was the southern anchor of the Allied front. If the Bir Hacheim Box fell, the entire Gazala line would be untenable. It was defended by over 4,000 determined and desperate Frenchmen and Jews. Their defensive network included a thousand well-camouflaged machine-gun nests, artillery emplacements, bunkers, and trenches, all well hidden and protected behind extensive minefields.

Rommel's first attacks were launched by ad hoc German-Italian combat groups, and were turned back by General Pierre Koenig and his men. The colonel general then called for Stukas to soften up the fortress. However, this time the Eighth Army recognized the value of the position, so the Royal Air Force was waiting for the slow dive bombers with its fighter aircraft. So many German planes were lost that Kesselring screamed at Rommel in rage. "We can't go on like this, Rommel!" he yelled. "Attack the bloody nest with all available ground troops. Abandon these economical combat tactics."[58]

Rommel responded by ordering another ground attack. He chose as its leader Colonel Wolz, the commander of the 135th Flak Regiment. The capable Wolz had done well a few days before, when his 88s saved the Afrika Korps from destruction. However, Combat Group Wolz could not come any closer to a penetration than its predecessors had done.[59]

The Swabian colonel general decided that the position would have to be taken by siege after this repulse. On June 2 he sent the 90th Light and Trieste divisions to invest the French box. With the other mobile elements of his army, Rommel turned to meet the anticipated British counterattack, "which to us seemed to be very long in coming," Colonel von Mellenthin later commented.[60]

With the British inexcusably quiet, the Afrika Korps used the lull to recover and repair some of its damaged tanks. On June 2 they had only 130 serviceable first-line battle tanks left, compared to the 320 with which they started the battle. The British, with about 400 tanks left (a clear three to one superiority!), failed to attack.[61]

Meanwhile, the two Axis motorized divisions tightened the noose on Bir Hacheim. They received priority support from the Luftwaffe, which gained local air control over the fortress. During the siege the pilots flew 1,300 sorties against the French and Jews, despite Bir Hacheim's excellent anti-aircraft defenses and frequent interdiction flights by the RAF. Many of these raids were carried out by Stukas, which suffered heavy casualties. Up to 40 a day were shot down.[62] Still they kept coming, and materially weakened the Allies' ability to resist.

On June 4 the lull entered its third day. Rommel decided to regain his former tank strength further by carrying out a panzer salvaging operation in the Bir el Harmat area the next day. Accordingly, elements of the 15th Panzer opened up several gaps in the minefields to the southwest of Bir el Harmat. As events transpired, this turned out to be a great piece of good luck for the German commander, because the British chose the next day finally to get around to delivering their long-delayed counterattack.

4

The Cauldron and Knightsbridge

On June 5, the great battle entered its eleventh day, with no decision in sight. On this morning, the Eighth Army tried to flush the remains of Rommel's original Gazala line strike force out of its positions in "the Cauldron." The basic idea was good; actually, it was long overdue. However, the British execution of this maneuver turned out to be extremely poor. In fact, one participant likened it to sticking your arm into a wasps' nest.

Had Rommel known that the Allies would take so long to attack his positions, he undoubtedly would have attempted another major assault on the Bir Hacheim Box, surrounded but still holding out to the south. However, he could not have imagined the confusion that existed at Eighth Army Headquarters. Here, no strong leader directed his forces with the ruthlessness required to win a modern battle. Perhaps Brigadier W. G. F. Jackson put it best when he wrote: "There has to be a unifying force to steer all the many strong-willed men in an agreed direction. That force is the commander's will, but it cannot make any impact without a policy and plan which all can understand."[1] This sense of direction was almost totally lacking in the higher echelons of the Allied desert army.

After inexcusably long discussions with corps and divisional commanders, General Ritchie decided to restore the Gazala line and destroy the Afrika Korps by a series of frontal assaults. There were two major faults in his plan. First, it was another piecemeal, unconcentrated effort. Second, Ritchie used only about half of his available strength. Once again a British commander violated the cardinal military principles of mass and concentration.

Ritchie's plan called for an initial attack by the 32nd Army Tank Brigade on the northern flank of the Axis salient. The main effort would be on the eastern face of the Cauldron, the center of Rommel's line. Here the 10th

Indian Brigade would penetrate the Ariete's front on Aslag Ridge in a night
assault. The 22nd Armoured and 9th Indian brigades would follow them,
and at dawn attack through the Indian lines and thrust into Rommel's rear.
The 201st Guards Brigade formed the Allied reserve at the Knightsbridge

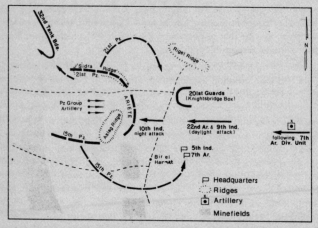

Map 4. The Battle of the Cauldron, June 5-6, 1942. In this
battle, the Eighth Army tried to crush the Afrika Korps and
Ariete, which it had virtually surrounded; however, in the end it
suffered a serious defeat itself.

Box. Map 4 shows the battle, and illustrates a major Allied reconnaissance
failure: the fact that no one discovered that elements of the 15th Panzer
Division had breached the minefield near Bir el Harmat, which, in the
absence of countermeasures, left the entire British southern flank and rear
in a badly exposed position.

The Allies also violated every principle of control in this battle. Their
command arrangements can best be described as weird. The XIII Corps was
to command the attack on Sidra Ridge, while the Aslag Ridge battle was a
XXX Corps responsibility. The 5th Indian Division was to command
during the actual breakthrough against Ariete, and the 7th Armoured

Division would take over the advance of the 22nd Armoured and 9th Indian brigades after the penetration. The 5th Indian Division would maintain control of the 9th Indian Brigade when it moved up, but not during the pursuit. They would, however, continue to control the 10th Indian.[2] Much of this was to be done at night, which just added to the confusion.

The 5th Indian and 7th Armoured divisions established a joint headquarters at Bir el Harmat, but no one was in actual overall command of the main assault. General Norrie, the XXX Corps commander, should have been placed in charge of the entire operation, but he was not. He apparently did not try to assume that responsibility himself, either, which makes him at least partially responsible for the ensuing disaster.

The battle opened badly for the British, but they did not know it. Four Allied artillery regiments opened up on the Ariete positions at 2:50 A.M. on June 5. Their bombardment was totally useless, because it fell well short of the Italian line. Hundreds of high-explosive shells landed on empty sands.[3]

When the 10th Indian Brigade started its night advance, it captured all its initial objectives with deceptive ease. This was because the Italian main defensive line lay a considerable distance farther west than Allied planners imagined. At dawn the attack ran into considerable trouble. The Ariete, always the best of the Italian divisions, had been well alerted, and resisted fiercely. Despite the terrible inferiority of their tanks, they inflicted heavy casualties on their adversaries. Besides this, the Eighth Army's new tactics were causing them some tremendous difficulties. The British were using combined arms tactics on a large scale for the first time in the desert war. They had at last adopted the right concept, but their experience in using it in battle was nil. After suffering some unnecessary losses, they finally managed to clear Aslag Ridge of Italians. The Ariete fell back on the Panzer Army artillery positions, in good order and firing all the way. When they were on line with the Panzer Army artillery, Rommel committed most of the 8th Panzer Regiment (15th Panzer Division) to the fight. The major Allied thrust ground to a quick halt.

Meanwhile, the 201st Guards, the 4th Armoured, the 2nd Armoured, the 9th Infantry, and the 69th Infantry brigades lay nearby, listening to the sounds of the battle, totally unengaged.

On the northern flank, the 32nd Army Tank Brigade attacked the 21st Panzer Division on Sidra Ridge. The Panzer Army operations officer, Colonel von Mellenthin, later denounced it as ". . . one of the most ridiculous attacks of the campaign."[4] The British tankers were supported by only twelve field guns and very little infantry. They advanced in broad daylight across open terrain: a perfect target for the Germans. Naturally the British tankers were stopped cold by the panzers, the antitank gunners, and the grenadiers. The veterans of the Siege of Tobruk were cut to ribbons. Finally, they retreated into a minefield! The 32nd Army Tank Brigade lost 50 of its 70 tanks and practically ceased to exist. Their survivors were pulled out of the battle, only to reappear again at Tobruk, after which they disappeared forever from the desert war.

By noon, the British counteroffensive had shot its bolt on both sectors. At this late moment, the British finally brought up the bulk of the 2nd and 4th Armoured brigades, but it was far too late. Rommel was ready to launch some attacks of his own. Unlike the pitiful efforts of the morning, they were controlled by the will of a determined leader, and as such were devastating.

General von Bismarck, the commander of the 21st Panzer Division, started the renewed offensive by moving southeast toward Bir el Tamar. Already he had destroyed the 32nd Army Tank Brigade. By striking through the gap created by this victory, he hoped to double the British right (northern) flank back on its center. Almost simultaneously, elements of the 15th Panzer Division, led by Colonel Crasemann and accompanied by Rommel himself, emerged from the minefields to the south. The failure of the British reconnaissance units to find the gaps in the Bir el Harmat minefield now became apparent with disastrous clarity. Nothing was available to prevent the Germans from forcing the Allied left flank back on its center. It was the classic double envelopment. If it was not on the same scale as Stalingrad, it was at least of the same effectiveness. The desert warriors immediately overran the headquarters of the 5th Indian and 7th Armoured divisions. Whatever command control the Allies ever had in this battle was lost now. Soon the encirclement was complete. The 9th and 10th Indian brigades, much of the 22nd Armoured Brigade, and four artillery regiments were trapped in the Cauldron.

General Briggs, the commander of the 5th Indian Division, fled to El Adem, where he began to reorganize the remnants of his command. General Messervy re-established the headquarters of the 7th Armoured Division in the Knightsbridge Box. He now had command of the 4th and 22nd Armoured brigades, but it was too late. The confusion of the sudden defeat had paralyzed the British command. This state of immobility was intensified and prolonged by the Luftwaffe. They chose this moment to bomb the Knightsbridge Box. The 201st Guards Brigade suffered badly; the British reserves were temporarily neutralized.

Even at this late moment, a determined and coordinated counterattack by the remaining British tank units might at least have rescued their encircled strike force from the Cauldron, but no attempt was made. The next day, June 6, the Afrika Korps crushed the pocket and forced the surrender of those units still able to offer organized resistance. Rommel took 3,100 prisoners, and captured 96 guns and 37 antitank weapons.[5] Among the prisoners was Brigadier Desmond Young, the commander of the 10th Indian Brigade. Rommel had captured the man who would later become his foremost biographer. Large numbers of Allied tanks were destroyed in this pocket, blown up to prevent capture, or incorporated into the Afrika Korps. Colonel von Mellenthin put the total Allied tank losses in the two-day Battle of the Cauldron at 100.[6] This is the minimum figure. Carell put their losses at 170 tanks,[7] while Brigadier Jackson stated that only 132 of the original 424 Allied medium tanks were still serviceable on June 7.[8] Most of these were lost in the Cauldron. Although the exact losses may never be known, one thing is certain: The Eighth Army had been defeated piecemeal. Rommel was now free to deal with Bir Hacheim, which still held out in his rear.

Rommel realized that he would not be completely out of danger until Bir Hacheim fell. The collapse of this position would also give him complete freedom of maneuver. However, despite several attacks, Bir Hacheim still showed no inclination of collapsing. "That accursed Bir Hacheim!" Rommel swore again and again.[9] From the beginning of the offensive it had defied all his efforts to take it.

On the night of June 6-7, the 90th Light Division cleared several lanes in the minefield. The next morning it launched an all-out attack in conjunction with Combat Group Wolz. This charge was also turned back by the French and Jewish defenders.

On June 8 Rommel regrouped and tried a new tactic. He assembled the engineer battalions from the various German divisions (the 33rd, the 200th, and the 900th) and placed them under the personal command of Colonel Hecker, the Panzer Army engineer officer. He then ordered Hecker to penetrate the minefield so the 90th Light could reach and destroy the French and the Jews. Two combat groups and several Luftwaffe units supported Hecker's night attack, which was stopped within 500 yards of the fortress. A large part of the Jewish Battalion was either killed or taken prisoner.[10]

The next day OKW sent an order to Erwin Rommel. It spoke of the "numerous German political refugees" (that is, Jews) who were fighting on the side of the Free French. The order read: "The Fuehrer has ordered that they are to be terminated with extreme prejudice. They are to be liquidated mercilessly in combat. Where they are not, they are to be shot afterwards, immediately and forthwith, on the orders of the nearest German officer, insofar as they are not temporarily reprieved for the extraction of intelligence. The communication of this order in writing is forbidden. Commanders are to be given oral briefing."[11]

No one in Rommel's command remembers hearing this order. No copy was found in Rommel's files after the war.[12] Like other orders that displeased him, it disappeared. Apparently he decided to ignore Hitler's command, burned his copy of the order, and never mentioned it to his subordinates. It was a dead issue.

The survivors of the Jewish Battalion were treated humanely by their captors, and were turned over to the Italians. Although these brave men had done little to affect the overall outcome of the war, they had done much to explode the myth that the Jew cannot fight. Five years later some of these men reappeared on the stage of history, as the forerunners of the Israeli Army.

Colonel Hecker was less concerned about where the Jews would reappear than with the fact that they had disappeared from his front. On June 9 he renewed the attack, but it bogged down again. Hecker himself was wounded when his command vehicle ran over a mine.[13]

When Hecker reported his defeat, Rommel grew angry again. "This accursed Bir Hacheim has taken a sufficient toll!" he roared. "I'm going to leave it. We'll attack Tobruk."

Colonel Hecker did not like this idea. He told Rommel, "Herr Colonel General, give me a battalion of German infantry to continue the attack. Now that we have already taken several strongpoints, I am convinced that we can bring the battle to a victorious conclusion."

Rommel regained control of his temper. After a brief conference with Colonel Bayerlein, Rommel said to the wounded Hecker: "You're right. I'll give you Lieutenant Colonel Baade with at least one battalion." Ernst Baade commanded the 115th Panzer Grenadier Regiment of the 15th Panzer Division. Rommel committed most of the regiment to the battle.[14]

The German engineer's determination paid off. Koenig and his men resisted fanatically, but the fortress began to crack on June 9. Elements of the 90th Light advanced to within 220 yards of the perimeter. Ritchie succeeded in relieving some of the pressure by sending the 7th Motor and 29th Indian brigades toward the box. The 90th Light was forced to turn and face them.[15]

This diversion bought only one more day for the 1st Free French Brigade. The next day, June 10, the 90th Light returned to the siege and gained ground with significantly fewer casualties. That evening Pierre Koenig radioed Ritchie: "Am at the end of my tether. The enemy is outside my HQ." Ritchie knew the end had come. He ordered Koenig to break out that night.[16]

The French had fought very well, and their breakout also did them credit. Although the brigade was mauled, most of the men succeeded in escaping after some bitter hand-to-hand fighting. Among those to get away was Koenig. Later, he became military governor of the French Occupation Zone in Germany.[17] The next morning Bir Hacheim finally fell to the 90th Light. They took only 500 prisoners, most of them wounded. It had been a bitter though unequal fight. The road to Tobruk was now clear of all obstacles except one: the British armored forces in the vicinity of the Knightsbridge Box.

Even as late as June 11, more than two weeks after Rommel unleashed his offensive, the British still had not lost the battle. Ritchie had about 330 tanks (250 cruisers and 80 infantry tanks) left to oppose Rommel's 230 tanks (of which approximatey 160 were of German manufacture). Some of Ritchie's tanks had been damaged early in the offensive, but were now repaired. The Allies also had a definite numerical superiority in men, particularly against the German contingent. The 90th Light Division, for instance, was down to 1,000 men. In short, the British still had both armored and infantry superiority. However, they had lost their positional domination. The Gazala line was a useless hulk. Its entire southern flank had been ripped wide open.

On the morning of June 11 Rommel ordered the 21st Panzer Division to demonstrate against the British forces holding the northern rim of the Cauldron. Meanwhile, he sent the 15th Panzer, Trieste, and 90th Light divisions toward El Adem.

That night General Norrie, the XXX Corps commander, gave his orders for the next day. The 7th Armoured Division (now composed of the 2nd and 4th Armoured brigades) would deal with the 15th Panzer, while the 1st Armoured Division (22nd Armoured and 1st Army Tank brigades) took on the 21st Panzer. The British made one fatal mistake in issuing this order: they violated radio security. The German Wireless Intercept Service promptly informed Rommel of the enemy's plans.[18]

Rommel was delighted by this news. Since he knew his opponent's moves in advance, it would be easy to construct a trap for him. Rommel ordered the 15th Panzer to hedgehog. The 21st Panzer was ordered to maneuver south of the Knightsbridge Box, elude the 1st Armoured Division, and strike the 7th Armoured Division in the rear. Caught between these two veteran divisions, the 7th Armoured could easily be destroyed. The plan worked out almost exactly as Rommel envisioned it.

On June 12 the British lost their command of the battlefield right from the start. A reconnaissance unit from the 90th Light surprised the unlucky General Messervy and forced him to hide in a dried-up water hole to avoid capture. As a result, the 7th Armoured Division was leaderless most of the day.[19]

Unwittingly, the reconnaissance force from the 90th Light delayed Rommel's timetable, but did not materially alter his plan. The climax was simply delayed a few hours, and General Nehring was forced to launch a pinning attack with the 15th Panzer and parts of the 90th Light. It was an excellent day for the German antitank gunners. The weather conditions were very hazy. Under this perfect cover the gunners could easily get within killing distance of the British armoured vehicles without being seen. Tank after tank was knocked out.[20]

As soon as the 2nd and 4th Armoured brigades were decisively engaged against Nehring's forces, Rommel ordered the 21st Panzer Division to attack from the north. Its timing was perfect. The panzers plowed straight into the British rear and had the disordered Allied division in a crossfire within moments. The 4th Armoured Brigade took the blunt of the blow and was completely routed. The 2nd Armoured Brigade was also mauled. Too late General Lumsden, the commander of the 1st Armoured Division, realized what had happened. He rushed his forces south to the scene of the battle, trying to catch the 21st Panzer in the rear. By the time he arrived, however, the Afrika Korps was pursuing what was left of the 2nd Armoured Brigade in a northwesterly direction, toward the Knightsbridge Box. The arrival of Lumsden's 22nd Armoured Brigade delayed Rommel's pursuit, but also cost that unit many of its tanks. Darkness put an end to the slaughter.

That night the exhausted survivors of the two British armored divisions reached the Knightsbridge Box, seriously depleted in number. They had lost 100 to 120 tanks. The 4th Armoured Brigade was scattered. It left the battle area and did not halt its retreat until it reached the coastal escarpment. The armored brigades that remained in the area could hardly be considered battleworthy. The balance of tank forces had swung decisively in favor of the Axis. Rommel had achieved armored superiority. By doing so, he had won the campaign. The question remained: Could he cash in on his victories? He had won impressively before, but Tobruk, a key to final victory in the desert, had always eluded him. Now, once again, he advanced toward the objective with which he was obsessed. Only one overriding question was left unanswered: Could the Eighth Army deny it to him again?

5

The Second Battle
of Tobruk

The battles of the Gazala line merged imperceptibly with the second drive on Tobruk in June 1942. At the time the average soldier was generally unaware of the difference. Even some of the top commanders failed to appreciate the distinction. This was especially true of the Eighth Army's top leadership. Although the Gazala line was a doomed position following the defeat of the British armor near Knightsbridge, the Allied leadership was characteristically slow in recognizing it. Both Auchinleck and Ritchie wanted to hold onto the line (or what was left of it), with a possible view of striking toward the west, against Rommel's lines of communication, sometime in the vague future. Even Prime Minister Churchill agreed with this unrealistic assessment of the situation. He signaled Auchinleck in Cairo: "Your decision to fight it out to the end is most cordially endorsed. We shall sustain you whatever the result. Retreat would be fatal. This is a business not only of armour but of will-power."[1]

In this case Churchill's estimation was pure wishful thinking, for retreat was already inevitable. Fortunately for the Allies, the XIII Corps commander did not share the blindness of his superiors. General Gott, the old warhorse of the desert army, was now directing all the British forces in the Gazala-Knightsbridge area. This unification of command would have been commendable three weeks earlier; even three days earlier it might have averted defeat. Now it was too late, because the Afrika Korps rapidly closed in on the Knightsbridge Box. The 21st Panzer came in from the west and overpowered the 2nd Scots Guard Battalion, while the 15th Panzer and 90th Light divisions closed in on the eastern flank. Although the box itself had not yet been attacked, Gott recognized the signs of a double envelopment when he saw them. Rather than risk the sacrifice of what few tanks the Eighth Army had left, he abandoned Knightsbridge and retreated northward, toward the coast.[2]

Erwin Rommel wasted no time in ordering a pursuit. During the night his men prepared for their attack of the next day. The colonel general knew Gott would have to make a stand, or abandon the infantrymen still in the Gazala line to their fate. This would be highly unlikely, since there was not a single brigade at stake here, as at Got el Ualeb or Bir Hacheim, but two full infantry divisions.

At dawn on June 14 Rommel resumed his attacks with customary vigor. He was at the head of his men, urging them on toward the Coastal Road. Ritchie finally issued the order to abandon the Gazala line. However, this was done far too late, because Gott would still have to make the stand. He would have to lose more valuable tanks so that the foot soldiers could escape. He chose to defend positions in the vicinity of the Acroma Box, only a few miles due south of the Via Balbia. Rommel immediately concentrated against him. The Battle of Acroma was fought under circumstances distinctly unfavorable to the British.

On June 13, the Allies had 95 tanks;[3] following the Battle of Acroma, they had 70 remaining.[4] Although their casualties were not as high as they might have been, they were significant. This battle proved that even the combined elements of all British armor could no longer make a successful stand against the Afrika Korps. The 1st Armoured Division was finished as a battleworthy unit. Its survivors were withdrawn from the battle area and sent to Egypt. The remnants of the 7th Armoured Division also retreated toward the frontier. Meanwhile, the men in the Gazala line burned or blew up what ammunition and supplies they could. The 1st South African Infantry Division retreated full speed down the Coastal Road, harassed by Stukas along the way. Late in the day elements of the 15th Panzer reached the Coastal Road and cut off their retreat. However, an immediate attack by the relatively fresh South Africans threw them back. Most of the division's men made good their escape to Tobruk, and later to Egypt.[5]

The 50th (Northumbrian) Infantry Division, minus the previously destroyed 150th Brigade, avoided capture in a unique way. Its commander realized that it was too late to try to escape via the Coastal Road. Rather than fleeing eastward across the desert and running a good chance of having to oppose the entire Afrika Korps with rifles on open terrain, General Ramsden attacked to the west. He quickly broke through the surprised Italians of the Brescia and Pavia divisions, turned south, bypassed Bir Hacheim, led his division on a long sweep across the desert, and finally joined up with friendly forces near Maddalena several days later. In the process the Northumbrians had to abandon all the equipment that would slow them up, including all their heavy weapons. Now they would have to be re-equipped, and would not be able to participate in the defense of Tobruk.[6] On the other hand, their escape was one of the great adventures of the Desert War. They had lived to fight another day, and would be ready to defend Egypt, if things came to that.

During the night of June 14-15, Rommel urgently tried to force his men onward, to cut the Coastal Road. Small elements of the 15th Panzer Division had already tried, but they were too weak to finish the job. However, if Rommel could get the bulk of the Afrika Korps to the Coastal Road in time, they might yet bag the 1st South African Division. Unfortunately for him, the men of the Afrika Korps did not respond. They had been in almost continuous action for 19 days. They had been surrounded, shot up, and nearly starved into submission. Two thirds of their armor had been knocked out. They simply could not keep going. Exhausted, filthy men sprawled out on the ground and slept like the dead. Nothing their officers said or did could raise them. Rommel was finally forced to admit that there were limits to physical endurance that not even the Afrika Korps could exceed. Resigning himself to this fact, he let them sleep.

It was 8:00 A.M. on the morning of June 15 before Rommel could again get the Afrika Korps moving. He found it was too late to cut off the retreat of the South Africans, but the 15th Panzer Division did capture their rear guard on the Via Balbia. The other two German divisions received orders to sweep eastward, toward El Adem, where the 29th Indian Brigade held a fortified box. Rommel wanted to strike immediately. As he proved in France two years before, Rommel was a great believer in running a defeated enemy into the ground. He would allow the Allies no rest. Ritchie must be prevented from establishing a new front south of Tobruk. For these reasons the 21st Panzer and 90th Light divisions again found themselves deployed for battle on the morning of June 15. They attacked the strong-points of El Hatian and Batruna, southwest of Tobruk. El Hatian held out, but Batruna collapsed. Another 800 prisoners fell into German hands.[7]

On the British side uncertainty reigned, as usual. Both Ritchie and Auchinleck were reluctant to accept the fact that the Eighth Army was beaten. True, they had lost most of their armor, but the infantry was more or less intact. The 10th Armoured Division was on its way to the front, and could restore the balance of power if they could hold out a little longer. Besides this new force, 150 other tanks were in the repair shops. Many of these would be serviceable in a few days, and the RAF still had limited air superiority.[8] The top British leaders still had hopes of stopping the Desert Fox.

Field Marshal Auchinleck wanted Ritchie to halt Rommel south of Tobruk (that is, at El Adem). Failing this, Auchinleck believed the fortress should be abandoned. His instructions to Ritchie read, in part: ". . . but on NO account will any part of the 8th Army be allowed to be surrounded in Tobruk and invested there . . ."[9]

Ritchie disagreed with this policy. At this point, Churchill intervened personally. Despite a categorical statement from the Royal Navy that it was not prepared to supply a second siege of Tobruk, he ordered Ritchie to hold it at all costs.

Ritchie, Auchinleck, and Churchill all were too far away to properly appreciate the true situation, although Auchinleck did come closer to reality than the other two. Rommel, on the other hand, was well forward with his men, and knew exactly what was going on and what he should do. He headed straight for El Adem, the gateway to Tobruk.

By 6:15 P.M. the 90th Light was skirmishing with the 29th Indian Brigade at El Adem. The three German regiments penetrated south and southeast of the box, and threw back British reconnaissance forces. The 21st Panzer was also nearing Tobruk from the east, while the XX Italian Motorized Corps reassembled in the Knightsbridge area in preparation for their movement to Tobruk. The X and XXI Italian Infantry corps were engaged in mopping-up operations in the Gazala line.[10]

All these moves indicated that Rommel planned to continue operations with little or no rest. However, British planners seemed to have failed to grasp this fact. They still entertained hopes of successfully defending Tobruk, even though their army, for the moment at least, was a broken reed.

That night von Mellenthin reported to Rommel that the 1st South African, 50th Infantry, 1st Armoured, and 7th Armoured divisions were no longer fit for battle. This meant that only the 2nd South African Division and the 11th and 29th Indian brigades could be within the Tobruk perimeter.[11] This was a good intelligence estimate. It missed only the 201st Guards and 32nd Army Tank brigades. These omissions are excusable, considering the small amount of time available for reconnaissance and the depleted state of some of these forces. Mellenthin probably left the 32nd out of his calculations because of the casualties it suffered during the Battle of the

Cauldron, where the 21st Panzer had reduced it to the size of a reinforced company. The Prussian officer did not know that the Allies were feverishly trying to rebuild this crippled brigade with all available resources.

Rommel listened to the colonel's briefing and announced: "It is my intention to take Tobruk by a coup de main. For this purpose the outlying area of Tobruk, south and east of the fortress, must be gained without delay, and the British 8th Army pressed away further to the east."[12] His specific orders were as follows:

21st Panzer Division: Take El Duda and Belhamed, southwest of the fortress;

15th Panzer Division: Advance to the El Adem area, act as the Army reserve, and await further orders;

Trieste Motorized Division: Replace the 15th Panzer west of Tobruk;

Ariete Armored Division: Cover the rear of the 15th Panzer and the desert flank of the Panzer Army by occupying defensive positions deep in the desert, south and southwest of the El Adem Box;

90th Light Division: Attack and capture the El Adem Box;

Xth Italian Infantry Corps: Invest Tobruk on the southwest;

XXIst Italian Infantry Corps: Invest Tobruk on the west.[13]

At 7:30 P.M. Rommel broke his tradition of eating alone and invited two of his most helpful subordinates, Colonel Bayerlein and von Mellenthin, to join him for dinner. At first, the table talk centered around skiing and garrison life at Wiener Neustadt, but it soon reverted back to Tobruk, which was on everyone's mind. Rommel pondered the problem for a moment and then fell asleep in his chair. He had been in action since 5:00 A.M.[14]

The next day, June 16, the Italian infantry completed the mopping-up of the Gazala line. They captured another 6,000 prisoners in the process, plus thousands of tons of supplies and whole convoys of undamaged vehicles.[15] These were immediately incorporated into the Panzer Army.

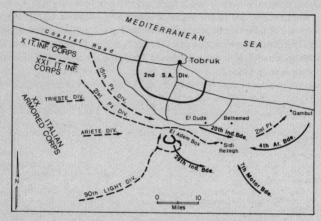

Map 5. The Investment of Tobruk, June 16-18, 1942. Because
the Allied High Command refused to allow a timely retreat,
over 30,000 men were trapped inside the fortress. The attempt
by the 4th Armored and 7th Motor brigades to prevent the
encirclement of Tobruk failed.

Farther east the investment of Tobruk began. Map 5 shows this
maneuver. The 90th Light's attack was the most important, at least
according to Rommel's plan, so the colonel general personally accompanied this division, and the Panzer Army Artillery gave it priority of fires.
However, the main battle did not take place here, but farther east, in the
sector of von Bismarck's 21st Panzer Division. General Ritchie had
received some reinforcements, and succeeded in building up the 4th
Armoured Brigade to a strength of 100 tanks, without Rommel's finding
out about it. He sent this rejuvenated force into battle immediately, in
hopes of preventing the isolation of Tobruk by keeping the Coastal Road
open. Along with elements of the 20th Indian Brigade, it clashed with the
21st Panzer Division in the Third Battle of Sidi Rezegh. Despite heavy
RAF attacks, Georg von Bismarck defeated the British tank forces. His men
took Sidi Rezegh at 6:15 P.M. On his southern flank the Ariete Division,

along with the 3rd and 580th Reconnaissance battalions, turned back the 7th Motor Brigade.[16] The Eighth Army's only effort to relieve the fortress had failed.

Meanwhile, the greatly reduced 90th Light failed to take El Adem because of a courageous and stubborn Indian defense. Rommel and the divisional commander, Colonel Marcks, had a stormy scene before the colonel general agreed to call off the attack. That night the 29th Indian Brigade broke out of the box. This left Tobruk invested on the western and southern sides.[17] Only the eastern flank of the fortress still maintained a tenuous contact with the Eighth Army. If Rommel could but take Gambut, Tobruk would be completely cut off from the rest of the Eighth Army. Only one unit stood in the way: the battered but defiant 4th Armoured Brigade, which had been practically rebuilt.

That afternoon Field Marshal Kesselring visited Rommel's new headquarters. Kesselring promised to support the attack on Tobruk with all available aircraft.

The next day, June 17, witnessed the isolation of Tobruk. Rommel predictably moved on Gambut, the former major RAF base, now nearly abandoned. He engaged the 4th Armoured Brigade with the entire Afrika Korps and Ariete. The battle raged for some time, but ended in another British defeat. The 4th Armoured lost half of its tanks and melted away toward the Egyptian frontier. Because of this defeat General Ritchie relieved the unlucky General Messervy of his command. It was the first of a series of sackings that would shake the Eighth Army over the next few weeks. Meanwhile, Gambut fell at 10:00 P.M. that night. Fifteen serviceable aircraft and a huge amount of petroleum fell into German hands. Later that night Rommel cut the Via Balbia. Tobruk was again surrounded.

The 20th Indian Brigade was not as lucky as the 4th Armoured. The fall of Gambut left it isolated near Belhamed. Ritchie ordered it to break out under the cover of darkness. Unfortunately, it ran directly into the Afrika Korps near Gambut. The entire brigade was destroyed.[18]

On June 18 the Second Siege of Tobruk began. Rommel's men mopped up the area between Gambut and Tobruk, and cleared the last pockets of resistance. The Swabian general ran into some trouble himself. As he was driving up the road south of Tobruk with part of his battle staff, he came upon several empty German trucks. They had run into a hastily set minefield, and their drivers and passengers had obviously been taken prisoner. Rommel calmly got out of his vehicle and with his bare hands began clearing the road of mines. His escort joined him, and within five minutes they were off and running again.[19] Meanwhile, the men of the 90th Light pursued the rear guard of the Eighth Army toward the Egyptian frontier. They made good speed, and took the supply dumps between Bardia and Tobruk intact. This move further confused the British as to Rommel's intentions. Did he plan to assault Tobruk, or invade Egypt? Actually, he planned to do both, in that order.[20]

While the Allies retreated, Italian infantrymen continued to approach Tobruk by a series of forced marches. Unlike the 90th Light and Trieste, which were motorized, most of the Italian infantry units had to travel on foot, and it took them much longer to get into position. The Pavia Division and elements of the newly arrived Littorio Armored Division screened the fortress to the west and south.[21]

The Eighth Army was in a bad way as the Italians dug in before the fortress. Of its five infantry divisions, three had been badly shot up. Their two armored divisions and various independent brigades were nearly wiped out, and they had lost much of their artillery. Despite these heavy losses, Ritchie had promises of early help. The Americans were arriving in the United Kingdom in strength, which allowed Churchill to release British forces for the North African Front. The Eighth Armoured Division would reach Suez by late June, and the 44th Infantry Division would arrive in early July. The eleven artillery regiments also en route would more than replace those lost since May 26. In addition, the 2nd New Zealand Division, so badly slaughtered in "Crusader," had been completely rebuilt in Syria. It was already on its way to the frontier, and would be in action within a week. On the other side of the hill, Adolf Hitler had ordered the Second Air Fleet to prepare to return to Russia, where his armies were advancing on Stalingrad.[22] If Tobruk could hold out only a few weeks, the events of 1941, which culminated in the German loss of Cyrenaica, might easily be repeated in 1942.

Inside the fortress General Klopper, the garrison commander, had an impressive force. His infantry included the 2nd South African Division (consisting of the 6th and 4th South African Infantry brigades) and the 11th Indian Brigade. They manned the outer perimeter. In reserve were the armored forces: the 201st Guards and the 32nd Army Tank brigades. The latter force, all but wiped out in the Cauldron, had made a remarkable recovery. It now included 52 Matilda and Valentine tanks. Klopper stationed the 201st Guards in the Fort Pilastrino area, and the 32nd formed the mobile reserve for the eastern half of the fortress, in the King's Cross sector. The Allies also had the 4th Anti-Aircraft Brigade, five regiments of artillery, and 70 antitank guns at various points within the garrison.

Rommel's plan to capture the fortress involved a clever ruse. He bypassed the city initially and made for the Egyptian frontier. This gave the British command the impression that Rommel was not going to launch a frontal attack on the fortress, but was going to resort to another siege. This was exactly the impression that Rommel wanted them to have.

On June 18 Rommel issued his final plan for the attack on Tobruk. The 90th Light would advance along the Coastal Road toward Egypt. On the night of June 19 it would retrace its steps and strike the perimeter from a road march shortly after dawn on June 20. The Afrika Korps would join it from the east, after beginning its approach march along the Trigh Capuzzo. The main blow would fall in the southeastern sector, against the positions held by the 11th Indian Brigade. It was to be preceded by a massive aerial and artillery bombardment. Infantry and engineer units would pave the way for the tanks by bridging the antitank ditch.

In accordance with the overall plan, Major General Krausse positioned the bulk of the Panzer Army Artillery east of El Adem. The artillerymen were astonished to find a stockpile of shells that they had abandoned during the retreat of November 1941. The British had not even bothered to destroy them. Krausse would have an abundance of ammunition for his all-important bombardment.[23]

Everything went as Rommel planned. He accompanied the 90th Light's advance to Bardia on June 19. They met no resistance. This in itself indicated that the British would not interfere with the attack on Tobruk. As planned, the motorized division returned at full speed that night. Before dawn they joined the Afrika Korps and the XX Italian Motorized Corps in front of Tobruk.

Inside the fortress, all was not well. The garrison did not resemble the Australian force that originally denied the port-city to the Axis army. The garrison had just suffered a defeat that badly damaged its morale. Besides, the fortress was in poor repair. Most of its land mines had been dug up and transported to the Gazala line. No one had taken care of the barbed-wire entanglements, the antitank ditch, or the trenches. Klopper had only a week to make good months of neglect. There simply was not time to do everything that needed to be done.

Rommel, on the other hand, was ready. Before 4:30 A.M. he was up, and wrote his customary prebattle letter to Lucie. "Today's the big day," he said. "Let's hope Lady Luck stays faithful to me. I'm dog-tired, otherwise okay."[24]

At 5:20 A.M. on June 20 the Air Fleet struck. "Kesselring had been as good as his word and sent hundreds of bombers in dense formations," Colonel von Mellenthin later wrote. "They dived on the perimeter in one of the most spectacular attacks I have ever seen."[25] The Indians were pulverized.

The XXI Italian Infantry Corps, supported by tanks, started the ground battle by launching a feint attack on the southwestern sector. The engineers and the Afrika Korps infantry (now temporarily under Headquarters, 15th Rifle Brigade, which Rommel activated again for this occasion) rushed toward the perimeter, along with the XX Italian Motorized Corps. The Indians, who were demoralized by the Gazala defeat anyway, were stunned by the intensity of the bombardment. Although fierce fighting developed in some quarters, most of the shattered brigade gave way quickly. By 8:00 A.M. the antitank ditch was bridged. Within half an hour the 15th Panzer Division was rushing across this improvised structure, toward the city. Rommel was up front, cheering his men on. "Speed it up, boys!" he shouted. "We've got our finger on the trigger."[26]

If the British armor had struck back immediately, before a significant number of panzers crossed the bridge, they might have managed to hold out. Even this is doubtful. However, the 32nd Army Tank Brigade did not begin its counterattack until 10:00 A.M. By that time the panzers from both the Afrika Korps' divisions had been crossing for an hour and a half, and the Ariete had also established a foothold a little farther west. Once the Afrika Korps breached the perimeter in strength, the fortress was doomed. It was all over but the killing.

The 32nd Army Tank Brigade, so recently butchered in the Cauldron, had to face the entire Afrika Korps alone. General Nehring, the Afrika Korps commander, took personal charge of the 15th Panzer Division. General von Bismarck directed the 21st Panzer from the sidecar of a motorcycle. Together they descended on the hapless British armored brigade, which lasted about an hour before it was wiped out. Only the tanks in the repair shops escaped destruction. By 11:00 A.M. 50 Matildas and Valentines lay burning. Nothing but a few artillery battalions were now left to stop Rommel from taking King's Cross, the vital crossroads about six miles from the port and five miles from the point of breakthrough. It fell at

2:00 P.M. Rommel then divided his forces. The 15th Panzer Division moved off in the direction of Fort Pilastrino, where the last of the British armor lay. Bismarck received the honor of attacking the city itself.

Following the destruction of the 32nd Tank Brigade, the fortress crumbled with incredible speed. Nehring and the 15th Panzer overwhelmed the 201st Guards Brigade on Pilastrino Ridge. The last major tank unit in the fortress was done for. To the north, von Bismarck burst into the city with such speed that several ships from the Royal Navy did not have time to escape. In an engagement reminiscent of Rommel at St. Valery in 1940, several ships were sunk by the divisional artillery and the panzers. Map 6 shows the fall of the town and fortress.

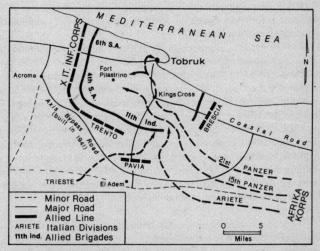

Map 6. The Fall of Tobruk, June 20-21, 1942. After a tremendous initial bombardment, Rommel struck the fortress with all his mobile forces at its weakest point. The garrison crumbled, and Tobruk fell with incredible speed.

By nightfall, two thirds of the fortress was in Axis hands. Klopper considered launching a breakout, but realized it would lead only to a further loss of life. Most of his transport was already in the hands of the Afrika Korps anyway.

After dinner that night, Rommel visited with Colonel Bayerlein. Rommel was too excited to sleep. He said, "You know, it's not just leadership that produces a triumph like this. You've got to have troops who will accept every imposition you put on them—deprivation, hardship, combat and even death. I owe everything to my soldiers."[27]

Finally Rommel managed to doze off in a corner of his car, his head propped up against the window. Outside his staff lay on the ground, wrapped in blankets.[28] They were up again well before dawn.

At 5:00 A.M. on June 21, Colonel General Erwin Rommel entered Tobruk, the prize that had eluded him for so long. He found it was "little more than a heap of rubble."[29] A few minutes later he received the surrender of the survivors of the 32nd Army Tank Brigade Headquarters. That was about all that was left of the gallant little brigade because all its tanks were destroyed, except for 30 in the repair facilities. It was a headquarters without a command.[30]

Rommel set up headquarters in the Albergo Tobruk, where he tended to the details of the surrender. A meeting between Rommel and Klopper was arranged. At 9:40 A.M. the South African officially capitulated. Rommel captured the entire 32,000-man garrison: 19,000 British, 10,500 South Africans, and 2,500 Indians, along with a huge quantity of supplies. The fortress had fallen so rapidly that its end was almost anticlimactic.

A group of South African officers demanded that they be housed in separate POW compounds from the black South Africans. Rommel rejected this request out of hand. He pointed out that the blacks were South African soldiers too. They wore the same uniforms, and fought side by side with the whites. They would be housed in the same POW cages and enjoy all the rights of any other prisoners of war.[31]

Numerous explanations for this tremendous Allied military disaster have been offered. Without belaboring the point, the evidence shows that seven major factors contributed most significantly to the rapid collapse of the fortress. First, the German strength was much greater in 1942 than it had been in 1941. Second, Axis morale was much higher, while Allied morale was much, much lower. Third, the Allies had allowed the legendary fortress to deteriorate physically since November 1941. The mines had been removed, and the antitank ditch and trenches were partially silted up. Fourth, the Germans had a much greater knowledge of the terrain and the lay of the city's defenses than had been the case the year before. Rommel knew the southeastern quadrant was the weakest section, and this is where he struck. He had attacked blind in the strong southwestern sector the year before. Fifth, the British lacked the antitank equipment necessary to defend successfully. They had only 70 antitank guns to protect 33 miles of perimeter. This was totally inadequate. Sixth, the Allied artillery control was unbelievably poor. Even the 25th Royal Army Field Artillery Regiment did not fire a shot until 7:45 A.M. on June 20, despite the fact that its mission was to provide direct support for the 11th Indian Brigade. By 7:45, the Indians had been facing the combined might of Kesselring's aerial bombardment, the Panzer Army's artillery barrage, and the attacks of a reinforced panzer corps for 2½ hours. A final, possibly overriding factor must be cited, and this is leadership. The attack that overwhelmed the fortress was a model of what ruthless determination by a great commander can accomplish. On the other side of the coin, the Allies failed to provide the kind of leadership that General Morshead furnished for the Australians in the previous siege of Tobruk. However, this cannot detract from Rommel's own success. His attack of June 20 was perhaps the most brilliant he ever directed, with the exception of his victory at Monte Matajur in 1918. Both were masterpieces.

On June 22, 1942, Erwin Rommel reached the pinnacle of his military career. A grateful Fuehrer promoted him to field marshal. At 50, he was the youngest man in the Nazi Army to attain this, Germany's highest military rank. Later he wrote: "To have become a field marshal is like a dream to me. All these mighty events of the past weeks trail behind me like a dream."[32]

Rommel celebrated in a typically restrained fashion. He ate a canful of pineapples and had a small glass of well-watered whiskey from a bottle recently liberated from the British.[33] After dinner, he became more somber. "Hitler has made me a Field Marshal," he wrote to his wife. "I would much rather he had given me one more division."[34]

6

The Drive on Alexandria

In his victories of the Gazala line and Tobruk, Rommel captured more than 2,000 vehicles and 2,000 tons of fuel. With this, he believed that he could lead his victorious but nearly exhausted soldiers all the way to the Suez Canal. Carried away by his undeniably brilliant series of triumphs, he lost sight of his own earlier warning: "Without Malta the Axis will end by losing control of North Africa."

After the fall of Tobruk, Rommel cabled Lieutenant General Enno von Rintelen, the German Military Attaché in Rome: "The first objective of the Panzerarmee—to defeat the enemy's army in the field and capture Tobruk—has been attained. Request you ask the Duce to lift the present restriction on freedom of movement, and put all the troops now under my command at my disposal, so I can continue the battle."[1] In other words, Rommel was requesting permission to invade Egypt.

Not because of this message, but certainly because he feared Rommel would do something like this, Field Marshal Kesselring flew to North Africa. On June 21 he met with the Desert Fox in his command vehicle. The two held diametrically opposing views, and both had some valid points. Kesselring maintained that Malta must be captured before an invasion of Egypt, or the Luftwaffe would not be able to support ground operations, since some pressure on Malta would have to be maintained. Even so, the island might recover its offensive potential, and then Rommel's supplies would be cut off. Better, the aviator said, to eliminate Malta first. Then Rommel could advance into Egypt with all available air support, without having to worry about his exposed supply lines.

Rommel argued that now was the time to strike the decisive blow. The Eighth Army had only two infantry divisions left more or less intact. If given time, they would recover and receive substantial reinforcements, some of which were already on the way. The Panzer Army might never have a chance like this again. Besides, Rommel asked, when would the Italian Army be ready to take Malta? This operation had already been postponed several times, and there was nothing to indicate that it would not be delayed again and again in the future.

They were both strong-willed men, and neither would give in. Finally, according to Colonel von Mellenthin, the discussions became "exceedingly lively." Rommel had to admit that the Panzer Army had sustained heavy losses, but he countered by saying that the British had suffered more, and that the Reich now had a unique opportunity to take the Suez Canal. If this opportunity were not seized, it might never come again.[2]

No agreement was reached when the conference ended. As Kesselring left, he made no secret of his intention to withdraw all air units to Sicily. However, not even this could sway Rommel from the course he had determined to pursue.

With Rommel and Kesselring at loggerheads, the final decision was left to Adolf Hitler. The Italian General Staff, the German Naval Staff, Kesselring, Mussolini, and General von Rintelen all lined up against the invasion of Egypt. Nevertheless, Hitler decided in favor of his former bodyguard. On June 22 he answered a letter from Mussolini, in which the Italian dictator had urged him to consolidate the successes of May and June. Hitler replied without mentioning Malta. He wrote of "a historic turning point," which had now been reached. It could be of "decisive importance" in the outcome of the war. The Eighth Army had been "practically destroyed." It was unlikely that such a unique opportunity would ever again present itself in this theater of operations. "The swiftest and most complete exploitation" was therefore essential. He called for "uninterrupted pursuit." He concluded: "The goddess of good fortune in battle approaches the leaders of men but once, and whoever fails to seize her in his arms will not often be able to reach her again thereafter."[3]

Mussolini accepted Hitler's decision of June 22 without further argument. Mussolini was lured by the possibility of a triumphal march into Egypt and the further expansion of the Fascist Empire. In any event he trusted Rommel's judgment more than that of his own advisers.[4]

As for Rommel's arguments, General Warlimont of the High Command later wrote that he "... could in any case hardly have acted differently ..." in ordering the pursuit.[5]

General Warlimont and Rommel were not exactly the best of friends, either personally or professionally. If this man, a member of OKW in Berlin, endorsed Rommel's decision after the fact, then the logic behind the decision must have been compelling. In fact, this was the case. With American industrial production beginning to make itself felt, while Germany bled herself white on the Russian Front, any chance of scoring a decisive victory had to be taken. This is exactly what Rommel wanted to do. He realized the risks and, if he failed, he would do so striving for victory and not stalemate. Had Kesselring's conservative approach been adopted, the end in North Africa might have been delayed, but it still would have come. At least Rommel's approach gave the Axis a chance to win and perhaps change the disastrous course the war was now taking.

Rommel rested only one day after the fall of Tobruk. His order for the continuation of the offensive was distributed during this short lull. It ended with the words: "Now for the complete destruction of the enemy. We will not rest until we have shattered the last remnants of the British Eighth Army. During the days to come, I shall call on you for one more great effort to bring us to this final goal."[6]

On the other side of the wire, the Allied Army was stunned by the sudden collapse of the Tobruk garrison. They made rapid plans to defend Egypt against the coming invasion. Gott's XIII Corps (now consisting of the 1st South African, 7th Armoured, 10th Indian, and 50th Infantry divisions) would delay in the frontier areas as long as possible. Then it would fall back 120 miles to Mersa Matruh. Here it would join General Holmes' newly formed X Corps, which consisted primarily of veteran formations. All along his route of advance to Mersa Matruh, Rommel's columns would be subjected to the most intense RAF attacks. In case the Mersa Matruh line did not hold, Auchinleck planned one last stand before the Nile, at a place called El Alamein. On this line Norrie's XXX Corps dug in. Once he left the frontier Gott would give up the 1st South African Division, which would proceed to Alamein with all possible speed.[7]

On June 23 Rommel reached the frontier. Gott forced him to deploy, but retreated without engaging in a major battle. Then events proceeded as Auchinleck hoped they would. The Panzer Army outdistanced what little fighter cover it had, and suffered heavy losses at the hands of the Royal Air Force. The RAF opposed the German offensive with well over 500 planes; Luftwaffe support for Panzer Army Afrika was minimal.

The lack of air cover did not slow up the forward surge of the Afrika

Korps. The vanguard covered over 100 miles in 24 hours. Sidi Barrani changed hands. The spectacular advance reached a point 30 miles east of Mersa Matruh by June 25.

The morale of Rommel's "Africans" was very high. Their panzer strength was very low. Rommel entered Egypt with only 44 German tanks. Ariete and Trieste were in even worse shape. Together they had only 14 tanks, 30 guns, and 2,000 men.[8] The constant fighting and lack of mainte-nance was taking its toll. Rommel was plagued by constant breakdowns.

Fortunately for the Italians, the Littorio Armored Division arrived from the homeland to boost the thinned ranks of the XX Motorized Corps. Unfortunately for them, they lost one of their best commanders. General Baldassare, the leader of the XX Corps, was killed in a skirmish on June 25. Baldassare was one of the few Italian generals whom Rommel truly respected. He called him a "brave and efficient commander," and genuinely mourned his death.[9]

On the morning of June 26 Rommel's spearhead reached a point ten miles southwest of Mersa Matruh. It was low on fuel. The RAF had so badly mauled Rommel's transport and supply columns that all his captured stockpiles did him little good, because he could not get them to his front-line soldiers. In fact, the British Air Force operated so successfully that it must be given the major credit for saving Egypt from the Panzer Army. A German plane flying over the Western Desert was now a rare sight. It would become even rarer from here on in.

Rommel wasted little time pondering what he did not have. Instead, he planned to use all available resources in the Battle of Mersa Matruh, which he hoped would be the decisive battle of the Desert War.

Matruh itself was a partially fortified coastal town. The perimeter originally had been built by Wavell in 1940, when he opposed the Italian invasion. Later Auchinleck had worked on it while Rommel besieged Tobruk in 1941. It consisted of a dense minefield to its west and south, but none on its eastern flank. South of the town the coastal escarpment forked into two escarpments, called the Northern Escarpment (lying seven miles south of Mersa Matruh) and the Southern Escarpment (situated 15 miles south of the fortress). Two thin minefields covered the approach between the two escarpments.[10] In all, 200,000 mines protected the area from Axis encroachment.[11]

Rommel recognized that his Egyptian invasion depended on one overriding factor: speed. If the Eighth Army were allowed time to catch its breath they might recover and check his advance. Then the Panzer Army would be in serious trouble. Rommel decided to attack Matruh immediately. There was no time for an effective reconnaissance. "We entered the battle with only the vaguest idea of British dispositions," his operations officer later admitted.[12]

Going into the battle, Rommel assumed that the Eighth Army had four infantry divisions (the 50th British, the 2nd New Zealand, the 5th Indian, and the 10th Indian) holding a line from Matruh to the southern edge of the escarpments. He also assumed that their left flank (the area south of the escarpments) was covered by the 1st Armoured Division.[13]

Rommel's plan called for the encircling of the Allied infantry divisions around Matruh. The first prerequisite for such a move would be the defeat of the 1st Armoured. Rommel ordered the 21st Panzer to attack between the escarpments, while the 15th Panzer Division struck south of them. Meanwhile, the 90th Light would advance on the left flank of the 21st Panzer, swing north, and cut the Coastal Road east of Matruh. The X and XXI Italian Infantry corps would cover the western front of Matruh while the XX Italian Motorized Corps supported the southern attack.[14]

The actual British dispositions were quite different from what Rommel guessed. The British Army was divided into two wings: The newly arrived X Corps under General Holmes defended the area north of the escarpments, while General Gott's XIII Corps was responsible for the battle south of the escarpments. The X Corps included the fresh 10th Indian and battered 50th British Infantry divisions. Gott led the 1st Armoured, 5th Indian, and 2nd New Zealand divisions, all positioned south of the escarpments. Between the two forks of the escarpment, Ritchie had only two thin minefields and two battalion-sized motorized infantry columns from the 29th Indian Brigade. They were very weak and, following their rout of the week before, were also very demoralized. This was all that held the center of the British line. In short, the Eighth Army had two strong wings with a very weak center. By sheer coincidence, Rommel planned to attack them in their weakest sector. Map 7 shows detailed British dispositions and Rommel's attack.

Rommel's whole plan for a decisive victory hinged on the Eighth Army remaining immobile. Ritchie planned his battle exactly as Rommel hoped. However, Auchinleck objected to risking the bulk of the army in a last-ditch-type effort. Besides, the X and XIII corps were largely static and

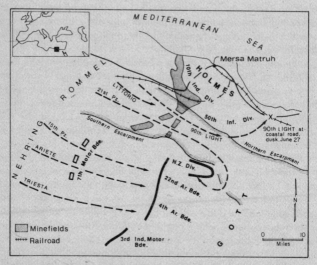

Map 7. The Battle of Mersa Matrush, June 26–27, 1942. Attacking without reconnaissance, Rommel just happened to strike the Eighth Army at its weakest point, and defeated the Allies due to sheer luck.

dispersed, operating in semi-independent modes that violated every rule of unified command. This type of arrangement had already resulted in more than one Allied defeat. On June 25 Auchinleck arrived at Matruh, dismissed Ritchie, and assumed personal command of the Eighth Army. His first orders countermanded the stand-fast approach of his former staff officer. Just as in "Crusader," Auchinleck's personal intervention saved the Eighth Army.

On the afternoon of June 26, Rommel struck. He had only 60 serviceable panzers left in the Afrika Korps. This slight increase in strength was a result of the skill of his fast-working mechanics, and not to any reinforcements from the Fatherland. He faced an armored division refitted and reinforced to 160 tanks, 60 of which were of the superb Grant model. Purely by accident the main German strike force advanced against the weakest part of Auchinleck's line. They quickly smashed the two Indian columns and penetrated the Allied center. South of the escarpments General Nehring (with the 15th Panzer Division and XX Italian Motorized Corps) shot up 18 American-made medium tanks in the opening skirmish.[15] However, the Royal Air Force and a shortage of fuel prevented either force from exploiting its success.

At dawn Rommel resumed his advance between the two Allied jaws. The 90th Light, a command reduced to 1,600 combat effectives, destroyed the famous Durham Light Infantry Regiment (of the 50th Division) 17 miles south of Matruh and took 300 prisoners.[16] This unit was completely isolated from and unsupported by the rest of the Allied army, a typical example of the waste caused by British tactical doctrine at this stage of its development.

Rommel himself accompanied the 21st Panzer Division between the escarpments. Deep in the Allied right rear he clashed with Major General Freyberg's 2nd New Zealand, a completely rested and refitted division. The 21st Panzer, on the other hand, was nearly exhausted. It had only 23 tanks and 600 infantrymen left. Freyberg had little trouble containing its attack at Minqa Qaim. To the north, the 90th Light was also in trouble. It was pinned down by elements of the 50th British Infantry Division.[17] South of the escarpment, the 15th Panzer (with approximately 37 tanks) and the remnants of Ariete and Trieste (14 tanks, 30 guns, and 2,000 men)[18] clashed indecisively with the 1st Armoured Division.

Between the two Allied wings, Rommel could have easily been surrounded. However, neither he nor Auchinleck had any idea of the true situation. Rommel left the 21st Panzer in the afternoon and joined the 90th Light. Under his direction this unit outflanked the British and shortly after dark cut the Coastal Road 20 miles east of Matruh. Colonel von Mellenthin remembered: "All this was undoubtedly very disturbing to the British commanders, but if they had kept their heads they should have realized that it was the Panzer Army which was in greater danger of destruction. 90th Light with only 1,600 men was on the coast road about fifteen miles away from the nearest troops of the Afrika Korps, and was hardly capable of tackling the British 10th Corps, which it had 'cut off' so impudently."[19]

Meanwhile, Bismarck's 21st Panzer scored two successes against the New Zealanders, now aided by strong elements of the 22nd Armoured Brigade. First, one of their shell splinters struck the brilliant General Freyberg in the neck and nearly killed him.[20] Second, they managed to get south of the division and scattered its main transport park.[21] General Gott witnessed the flight of the transport and erroneously concluded that the panzers had come over, and not around, the New Zealanders. He decided that this fine division was finished, when in fact it was easily holding its own. The Allied Army was not defeated, but General Gott was, which was just as good for Rommel's purposes. The XIII Corps commander ordered his men to withdraw during the night. Due to poor Eighth Army communications, General Holmes was not informed of the withdrawal. He continued to hold fast at Matruh, confident of early relief, and completely unaware that he was being left in the lurch.

During the night of June 27-28, the 1st Armoured and 2nd New Zealand broke contact. The tankers fell back south of the escarpments and avoided further shooting. The New Zealanders, on the other hand, plowed straight through the 21st Panzer. By this time, Rommel was back with this division. He became involved in this "wild melee," and was soon surrounded by burning vehicles. The confusion was total and indescribable. Germans fired on Germans, while the RAF bombed and strafed New Zealanders in the darkness. However, most of the tough Allied division, now led by Brigadier Inglis, made good its escape.[22]

Early on the morning of June 28, General Holmes found himself surrounded by the enemy. It was too late now to do anything but hold on until nightfall, and break out in the darkness. He would have a good chance to do this because Rommel was off and running again. With the Afrika Korps he headed toward Fuka and Alamein, in pursuit of the XIII Corps. He was sticking to the cardinal rule: The Eighth Army must not be allowed a respite, even if it meant bypassing the opportunity of destroying an entire corps. Rommel would not allow himself to be diverted from his goal by a few thousand infantrymen. In continuing his pursuit to the east, Rommel made the move that was strategically correct.

At 5:00 P.M. on June 28 the 90th Light Division and elements of the X and XXI Italian Infantry corps stormed the fortress of Mersa Matruh. The fighting lasted all night. In the darkness another confused breakout occurred. Approximately 60 percent of the British X Corps escaped.[23] The Axis simply did not have enough manpower to stop them all. The next morning resistance in the town collapsed. A rear guard of 6,000 men was captured, and 40 Allied tanks destroyed. The 50th British and 10th Indian Infantry divisions were temporarily *hors de combat*, and the 2nd New Zealand was badly shaken. On June 29 numerous columns of Axis and X Corps vehicles streamed across the desert, trying to avoid each other, all heading eastward. The last fortress port in the Western Desert had fallen. Rommel's leading elements were only 125 miles from Alexandria. He called on his nearly exhausted but happy veterans for one more effort. They headed toward the XXX Corps positions at El Alamein, the place both sides now recognized as the Allies' last ditch in North Africa.

By now over half of the Axis forces traveled in captured British vehicles, powered by British gasoline. Their leading vehicles ran over land mines and were strafed by the RAF. They were replaced. The advance continued.

That morning the 21st Panzer intercepted some British columns near Fuka and took another 1,600 prisoners.[24] Rommel joined Captain Briel, the vanguard commander, at 11:00 A.M. "Well, Briel," he said, "you will advance with your men to Alexandria and stop when you come to the suburbs. The Tommies have gone." Briel was stunned. So they had won the war. Rommel smiled and continued. "When I arrive tomorrow we'll drive into Cairo together for a coffee."[25]

This proved to be a premature order. Briel was halted near the railroad station of El Alamein, 60 miles short of Alexandria.

The Desert Fox in field uniform, 1942.

Rommel's panzer troops in action in France, 1940.

The Desert Generals. Left to right: unknown officer, Rommel (commander, Panzer Army Afrika), Veith (commander, 15th Panzer Division), Nehring (commander, Afrika Korps), and Cruewell (deputy commander, Panzer Army Afrika), unknown officer.

Italian troops camping at an oasis.

Italian soldiers of Panzer Army Afrika digging in. Rommel soon concluded that most Italian troops were unreliable in combat.

The 5th Panzer Regiment prepares to move out.

A heavy howitzer battery prepares to change position. A light Panzer Mark II can be seen in the left background.

A reconnaissance battalion "goes to ground" as a ghibli begins.

Rommel's communications vehicle (foreground) and command vehicle (background).

Field Marshal Erwin Romm[el], an official photograph take[n] in December 1942.

Field Marshal Albert Kesselring, Luftwaffe commander and Rommel's nominal superior.

The High Command. Nearest to table, left to right: Field Marshal Wilhelm Keitel, Field Marshal von Brauchtisch (then commander-in-chief of the Army), Hitler, and Colonel General Halder. All three soldiers disliked Rommel.

Rommel at Fuehrer Headquarters. Hitler flew into a rage when the field marshal asked to be allowed to retreat.

Afrika Korps improvisation: a 150-millimeter heavy infantry gun is mounted on the carriage of a damaged panzer to create a self-propelled assault gun. Such ingenuity characterized the Afrika Korps.

Tanks of both armies burning during the "Crusader" battles.

The Afrika Korps in action, late 1941.

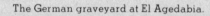 A desert in flames, December 1941.

The German graveyard at El Agedabia.

7

The First Battle of El Alamein

Rommel's advance on the Nile continued at full throttle on the morning of June 30. The 15th Panzer Division overran a battery of British 150-millimeter guns near El Alamein[1] and thus added to their varied collection of equipment. They had all makes of field and antitank guns: American, British, Russian—and even some weapons of German manufacture. Over half their transport vehicles were products of Allied factories.

About noon on that day the pursuit was halted by heavy artillery fire from Tel el Eisa, a prominent hill located just south of the Coastal Road, about five miles west of the El Alamein railroad station. The preliminaries of the First Battle of El Alamein had begun.[2]

The Alamein "line," as Allied propaganda broadcasts called it, hardly existed. It had been fitfully worked on each time Egypt was threatened with invasion, and forgotten about as soon as the danger was over. Despite this neglect, it was still a highly strategic position. It extended 40 miles, from the Mediterranean Sea to the Qattara Depression. Both of these physical features were impassable obstacles. This made the Alamein line the only position in the entire Western Desert that could not be outflanked. Rommel would have to go through this "line" to take Cairo and the Suez, for he could not go around it.

Norrie's XXX Corps began work on the Alamein line on June 26. He assumed responsibility for the northern half of the front. The veteran 1st South African Division under General Pienaar held the sector from the El Alamein Box (on the sea) to Ruweisat Ridge. The fresh 18th Indian Brigade, recently brought up from Syria, defended the vital ridge itself, reinforced by the 2nd South African Brigade of Pienaar's division. A few days later, after the Battle of Mersa Matruh, the 1st Armoured Division, consisting of the 4th and 22nd Armoured brigades, reinforced the South Africans and Indians in the northern sector.[3]

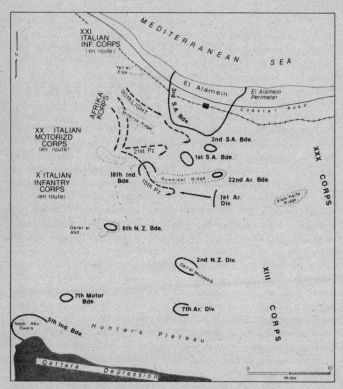

Map 8. The Alamein Line, July 1, 1942

Gott's XIII Corps manned the area south of Ruweisat Ridge. Unlike the northern sector, the terrain here was not generally flat, but broken and rough. The 2nd New Zealand Division formed Gott's right (northern) flank, with the 6th New Zealand Brigade occupying the forward positions at Bab el Qattara (or Kaponga). The left flank was held by the sole surviving brigade of the 5th Indian Division. It defended the Naqb Abu Dweis Box, overlooking the Qattara Depression. The 7th Armoured Division, which had only the 7th Motor Brigade under its supervision, formed the corps reserve.[4]

The X Corps, so recently mauled at Matruh, did not stop at the El Alamein line but continued on to the Nile Delta, to reform, re-equip, and prepare to evacuate Egypt, if that became necessary. Only the 50th Infantry Division of Holmes' corps stayed in the Alamein area. Auchinleck ordered it to halt near his headquarters on the eastern edge of the Alam Halfa Ridge, 15 miles behind the front line. Here it formed the reserve for the Eighth Army.[5] Map 8 shows the initial engagement and the critical terrain features.

General Norrie told his men that this was the last ditch. With grim determination the British, South Africans, and Indians dug in to face Rommel's attack, which they assumed would come within 24 hours. Thousands of miles away, in London, Rommel's advance almost toppled the Churchill government. On July 1 Member of Parliament (MP) Aneurin Bevan rose and pointed out that the Prime Minister had won debate after debate, and lost battle after battle. Members of Churchill's own Conservative Party joined the movement against him. The motion of censure was seconded by Conservative MP Admiral Keyes, whose son had died trying to kill Rommel in the Bera Littoria raid the year before. One of the House of Commons members denounced the class-ridden mentality of the army. "In this country," he said, "there is a taunt on everybody's lips that if Rommel had been in the British army he would still have been a sergeant." Churchill managed to stay in power only by the skill of his oratory. He attributed the disasters that had recently befallen the Eighth Army to Rommel's skill as a leader and to the ineptness of his own military commanders. The next day the German newspapers headlined the Prime Minister's speech. Rommel's name was spoken everywhere. In East Prussia, Hitler was amused and reflective. "The mere name [of Rommel] suddenly begins to acquire a value," he commented. "Imagine what would happen if we kept on plugging the Soviet Marshal Timoshenko. In the end our own soldiers would come to regard him as some kind of superman."[6]

If the reaction to Rommel's drive was remarkable a continent away, it was even more so in Africa. In Alexandria, 60 miles from the front lines, panic set in. Military men, diplomats, and civilians alike lost faith in the Eighth Army's ability to deny Rommel his prize. The British Fleet left the port of Alexandria as Rommel's vanguard approached. Demolition squads prepared to blow up the harbor installations. Most of the soldiers left the city. Many civilians fled to Cairo, which suffered massive traffic jams due to the emigration. Telltale smoke was seen coming from the British Embassy: The diplomatic staff was burning its secret papers. Similar sights could be seen at the various military headquarters in the city. Long columns of trucks, loaded with the office equipment of the General Headquarters and the British General Staff, sped off in the direction of Palestine. The American Liaison Staff also disappeared, while the dependents of British soldiers were told to pack for a rapid departure. Those units of the X Corps that were still operational dug in on the Nile Delta. Rommel was so near that Auchinleck actually considered giving up Egypt and sending the Eighth Army to the Sudan, Palestine, and Iraq.[7] The Rommel legend had grown to such an extent that his very name was enough to cause panic in the enemy's capital. Unfortunately for him, his name was about all he had left. His entire German contingent was not enough to equal an under-strength peacetime division. He arrived at Alamein with 55 worn-out panzers, 15 armored scout cars, 77 field guns of various calibers, 65 antitank guns (including a few 88-millimeter anti-aircraft guns), and about 2,000 weary infantrymen.

Rommel knew he was badly outnumbered in all categories, particularly that of air power. The RAF more than doubled the number of daily sorties they flew against the Panzer Army since the battles of the Gazala line. The Luftwaffe, on the other hand, was barely able to furnish even token support for the Panzer Army.

To make matters even worse, the Axis supply lines collapsed completely. Of the 60,000 tons of supplies Rommel's forces needed each month, Axis authorities could deliver only 3,000.[8] As a result, Rommel had to depend entirely on his captured stocks, which were already beginning to run low.

In his *Papers*, Rommel cited several reasons for the supply failure. They all revolved around one theme: "Peace reigned in Rome." The Italian officials were either too corrupt or too incompetent to do their jobs properly.[9] In fact, some were undoubtedly selling secrets to the British. German sea convoys had a much better chance of reaching North Africa than Italian convoys, which were frequently sold out to the British Secret Service, and often met a Royal Navy submarine pack somewhere in the central Mediterranean.

Rommel's men had been in almost daily combat for five consecutive weeks. They were hamstrung by a lack of fuel, transport, and ammunition. While they struggled across the desert, Churchill and Roosevelt lavished all the resources of the Western democracies on the North African Front. They sent the Eighth Army huge consignments of guns, trucks, tanks, airplanes, land mines, armored cars, and men. Giant convoys of up to 100,000 tons, loaded with every conceivable war material, left America for the Suez Canal. However, due to German naval and air forces in the Mediterranean, the convoys would have to take the long route around the Cape of Good Hope, on the southern tip of Africa. This delay would give Rommel time for one last stroke. It would be decisive, one way or the other.

Erwin Rommel knew the odds were changing. They had always been against him, but now they were shifting even more in favor of the Allies. With their American-made tanks and new-model antitank guns, the Eighth Army was rapidly gaining qualitative superiority in the desert. Quantitatively they had always been superior, but now the difference threatened to become overwhelming. When the Grant and Sherman tanks arrived in strength from the United States, the Allies would have definite qualitative dominance. "If this were achieved," Rommel later wrote, "it would clearly mean the end for us."[10]

The German field marshal planned his attack on the Alamein positions using the same formula as at Gazala and Mersa Matruh. The Afrika Korps would advance south, as if heading for the southern end of the line. That night they were to turn northeast and circle behind the Alamein and Deir el Abyad strongpoints. As at Mersa Matruh, the 90th Light was to cut the Coastal Road from the rear. "When Alamein is encircled and our panzer divisions are to the rear of the main enemy forces in the south, the enemy will collapse as he did at Mersa Matruh," Rommel predicted.[11] However, as Rommel briefed his officers on this plan, something ominous happened: The meeting was broken up by a British air raid. The marshal took cover in a hole, but others were not so quick. Corporal Herbert Gunther, who had been Rommel's orderly for some time, was seriously wounded. The unexpected attack was a foretaste of things to come.

As at Mersa Matruh, Rommel began the First Battle of El Alamein with only the vaguest notion of the Allies' dispositions. Unlike at Matruh, he was not lucky. His reconnaissance forces failed to locate and identify the 4th Armoured Brigade and other key enemy formations. Under the circumstances these failures were understandable, and even predictable, but they were nevertheless fatal to Rommel's plan of July 1.

Things went wrong almost from the beginning. The attack was scheduled to start at 3:20 A.M. It actually began at 6:30 A.M. By then it was daylight, and the Afrika Korps was again subjected to artillery and air bombardments. The 90th Light lost its way and ran into the Alamein Box instead of bypassing it. Since the light division was so low in manpower, it could no longer defeat an enemy force of more than regimental size. The 3rd South African Brigade kept it well pinned down until a sandstorm provided it with enough cover to withdraw. The storm lasted from about noon until 4:00 P.M. Under this natural screen the 90th Light moved south, but when the dust finally settled the German division found itself in open terrain among the three South African brigades and in the range of the 1st Armoured Division artillery. The howitzers and field guns of these units tore the exposed infantry unit to ribbons. Support columns and even some combat elements panicked, and the tough 90th Light was almost routed. Rommel rushed up with the Kampfstaffel and rallied the division, but not even he could get it moving forward again.[12] Rommel himself went forward, but was pinned down by Allied artillery fire for two hours before some Stukas silenced these particular gun positions and restored the field marshal's freedom of movement.[13]

Meanwhile, to the south, General Nehring led the Afrika Korps to the Deir el Shein area, where he ran into the 18th Indian Brigade. He had only 1,000 infantrymen left, but decided he would have to eliminate the Indians before continuing the advance. Nehring committed the bulk of the Afrika Korps to battle at Deir el Shein. During the sandstorm his engineers breached the British minefield, and when the wind died down the main attack started. After fierce resistance, the Afrika Korps stormed the position. The courageous 18th Indian was annihilated, and 2,000 more prisoners were taken. However, the Korps lost 18 of its 55 remaining tanks. ". . . the fighting edge of the Afrika Korps was finally blunted," Colonel von Mellenthin later recalled.[14]

On July 2 Rommel regrouped and set forth on another effort to break through to the sea. By 10:00 A.M. his advance had stalled again. The South Africans again checked the 90th Light, while the Afrika Korps unsuccessfully attacked the 1st Armoured Division on Ruweisat Ridge. Thirty-seven tanks were simply not enough to do the job.

The next day Rommel launched what proved to be his final thrust. By now he had abandoned his plan to get into the rear of the XIII Corps. Instead of two attacks, as in the previous days, he decided to make one concentrated movement around the Alamein Box, using all his German forces and the Littorio Armored Division. However, Auchinleck also grew aggressive, and beat Rommel to the punch. Auchinleck sent the 2nd New Zealand Division into a bayonet charge against Ariete, which promptly broke down. The best Italian unit in the army was routed, and Rommel's southern flank was in grave danger. The Italian armored division lost 28 of its 30 field guns and several tanks. Rommel was at first surprised and then angered by the sudden change of events. "The Italians were no longer equal to the very great demands being made on them," he concluded.[15] Due to the threat on his desert flank, the field marshal was forced to pull the 15th Panzer Division out of the main attack and send it south. As a result, the attack failed.[16] The Desert Fox now had no choice but to temporarily admit defeat, and go over to the defensive. He would await the arrival of the X and XXI Italian Infantry corps, which were still marching to the front, perfect targets for the Desert Air Force.

Grimly, the weary and filthy men of the Afrika Korps and the 90th Light Division dug in. Mercifully they did not know what lay in store for them, but they did know one thing: The glorious advance on Cairo was at an end.

Now, when it was too late, Rommel began to receive some reinforcements from Europe. Kesselring flew some miscellaneous combat units from Crete to Tobruk, where they joined with units already in Africa to form the 164th Light Afrika Infantry Division. Naturally, it would take some time to make the division fully operational, but at least it was coming. A few weeks later the Luftwaffe began ferrying the men of the Ramcke Parachute Brigade across the Mediterranean. The Italians also contributed to the buildup by dispatching three divisions released by the cancellation of the Malta invasion. These forces were the Folgore Parachute Division, and the Pistoia and Friouli Infantry divisions.[17]

On the other side of the line, Auchinleck rebuilt the 5th Indian Division from one brigade to three, and brought Morshead's 9th Australian Division—the famous Desert Rats of Tobruk—from Syria to El Alamein. Strong elements of the 8th Armoured Division also landed at Suez; the entire division would be landed in Egypt and operational by the middle of July.[18] Clearly, the Eighth Army was winning the race for reinforcements, just as they had won the battle for supplies. By August they had 400 tanks, 500 guns, 7,000 vehicles, and 75,000 tons of other supplies in Alexandria alone. Between January and August 1942, the Eighth Army received almost 1 million tons of supplies.[19]

Meanwhile, the Afrika Korps was in bad straits. On July 4 they had only three dozen panzers in running order, and a few hundred infantrymen to back them up. German artillery units had only two rounds per gun, on the average, and most of these units were now using captured British field pieces. Fortunately, some 1,500 rounds of 25-pounder ammunition had been taken at Deir el Shein. The Italians also had some artillery shells stockpiled.[20] The cannon was therefore the strongest weapon left in the arsenal of the Panzer Army Afrika.

On this day, Rommel took the 21st Panzer Division out of the front line in order to form a mobile reserve. It proved to be a premature measure, for the Allies thought the Panzer Army was retreating, and attacked through the division's former positions with 40 tanks. The 21st Panzer beat them back, but only with great difficulty.

In early July Auchinleck came up with a plan designed to destroy Rommel's army once and for all. Unlike in previous battles, the main targets in this campaign were to be Italian units. Auchinleck realized they were used up, so he deliberately concentrated against them, knowing that Rommel would be forced to use his German forces to save them. By adopting this dangerous policy, he pushed Erwin Rommel to the very edge of defeat.

Because of the almost superhuman efforts of his maintenance personal, Nehring could summon about 50 operational panzers to his battle line on the morning of July 8. Almost all of them were worn out, in serious need of overhaul, major repairs, or complete rebuilding. Yet there was never time for this. Tanks were simply not designed to endure the kind of punishment that the Desert War inflicted on them, and the unceasing operations were beginning to tell on the equipment of the Afrika Korps. The infantry units were also seriously depleted. The two panzer grenadier regiments of the Afrika Korps were now down to 300 men apiece. Each of them had only 10 supporting antitank guns remaining. Both the 15th and 21st Panzer had a small regiment of artillery left (seven batteries per regiment), but, as we have seen, their ammunition supply was extremely low. The 90th Light

Division was in equally poor condition. It averaged less than 400 men in each of its four regiments, and only 30 antitank guns and two batteries of artillery had survived the fighting since Gazala. The three reconnaissance battalions had a total strength of only 15 armored cars, 20 armored troop carriers, and three batteries of artillery, all of which had been captured. Headquarters, Panzer Army Artillery controlled the greatest firepower: 11 heavy batteries, 26 88-millimeter anti-aircraft guns, and 25 20-millimeter anti-aircraft guns.[21]

Conditions were not better and were frequently worse in the Italian contingent. The XX Motorized Corps (two armored divisions and one motorized division) had a total of 54 tanks. Its eight motorized battalions had a net total of only 1,600 men. The Corps antitank guns numbered only 40. Six light artillery batteries rounded out a dismal picture.[22]

On July 8, the elements of the X and XXI Italian Infantry corps facing the El Alamein line totaled 11 battalions of about 200 men each. They had 30 light and 11 heavy batteries. The Italian Army artillery provided another four heavy batteries.[23]

At full strength, the establishment of the Panzer Army would have been as follows: Afrika Korps, 371 tanks, 246 antitank guns; 90th Light Di-

Table 5

Panzer Army Afrika Tank Strength, July 8, 1942

Unit	Number of Tanks Authorized	Number of Tanks on Hand	Percent of Authorized Strength Available
Afrika Korps	371	50	13.5
90th Light	—	—	—
XX Italian Motorized Corps	430	54	12.6
Panzer Army Totals*	801	104	13.0

Source: Rommel, p. 251.

*Excluding the totals for the X and XXI Italian Infantry Corps, which are unavailable. However, they were also very weak in this category.

Table 6

Panzer Army Afrika Antitank Gun Strength, July 8, 1942

Unit	Number of AT Guns Authorized	Number of AT Guns on Hand	Percent of Authorized Strength Available
Afrika Korps	246	20	8.1
90th Light	220	30	13.6
XX Italian Motorized Corps	120	40	33.3
Panzer Army Totals*	586	90	15.4

Source: Rommel, p. 251.

*Excluding the totals for the X and XXI Italian Infantry Corps, which are unavailable. However, they were also very weak in this category.

vision, 220 antitank guns; XX Italian Motorized Corps, 430 tanks, 120 antitank guns. Tables 5 and 6 show the relative weakness of the Panzer Army. Small wonder Rommel commented, ". . . my formations no longer merited the title of divisions."[24]

To boost his badly undermanned defenses, Rommel employed what was for him a new device: the land mine. He requested thousands from Berlin, and dug up others from captured minefields around Gazala, Tobruk, and Mersa Matruh. His natural grasp of this defensive technique was fantastic. He learned rapidly, and the minefield soon became the bulkhead of the Axis defensive line.

From July 5 to 7, Auchinleck sent the XIII Corps against Rommel's southern flank. The 2nd New Zealand Division provided most of the muscle for this push. This division had already pretty well exhausted itself in halting Rommel's drive on Alexandria. It proved to be too weak to break the German-Italian line, but it did force Rommel to commit some of his armor to the south,[25] and further depleted his dwindling reserve of captured petroleum.

The British opened their offensive on Rommel's northern flank at dawn on July 8 with a massive artillery bombardment. Ten thousand shells fell in the three-mile sector held by the remnants of the 15th Panzer Division. This demonstration only served to underline the tremendous extent of

Allied resources. Allied forces actually succeeded in establishing a foothold in the panzer division's front line on July 8, but were thrown back when the divisional reserve counterattacked.[26]

By July 9, Erwin Rommel had defeated two major British attacks. That morning his reconnaissance forces discovered that the Allies had abandoned the important Qaret el Abd Box on the southern flank. Rommel could not understand this move, but he nevertheless decided to seize the opportunity it presented. He immediately sent the 21st Panzer and Littorio Armored divisions south to occupy Qaret el Abd. That evening he and von Bismarck planned an attack on the British XIII Corps. If successful, Rommel might regain the initiative for the Panzer Army. Unknown to Rommel, he was doing exactly what Auchinleck hoped he would do. The British commander-in-chief planned to draw the Axis armor to the south while he struck Rommel's northern flank a devastating blow on the morning of July 10. For once Rommel had been outwitted.

Rommel spent the night of July 9-10 on the southern flank, making the final preparations for the next day's attack. He originally planned to sleep in a captured hospital, but was chased out by an active flea colony.[27] He woke up at 5:00 A.M. on the morning of July 10, startled by the sound of hundreds of cannon, which were bombarding his positions to the north. He had been asleep for only two hours, but was alert almost instantly. He suspended his own attack, which was scheduled for 6:00 A.M., and headed for the endangered sector with his Kampfstaffel.

On and near the Coastal Road, the British artillery blew the forward positions of the Italian Sabratha Division into oblivion. Then the fresh 9th Australian Division, supported by British tanks, unleashed a violent attack that sent the Italians running. The entire Sabratha Division melted away in minutes. Colonel von Mellenthin described the battle this way:

> Our tactical headquarters lay only a few miles behind the front. As I drove up to the front hundreds of Italians streamed towards me in panic-stricken rout. They were the men of the Sabratha Division, and it was not difficult to see that the whole division had been overrun. Something had to be done to stop this huge gap. I immediately got in touch with Headquarters and scraped together everything I could in the way of staff personnel, flak, infantry, supply units, field kitchen companies ... and with these heterogenous troops faced the Australian attack. In bitter hand-to-hand fighting, in which staff officers manned machine guns, we managed to halt the first enemy rush.[28]

At this most opportune moment, a new German unit appeared on the battlefield. It was the 382nd Grenadier Regiment of the 164th Light Afrika Division, the vanguard of that unit. It had no vehicles, but marched directly into the battle and repulsed the Australians.[29] When Rommel arrived with his combat group, the attack was broken. The Allies had penetrated to within 3,000 yards of Panzer Army Headquarters.[30] Rommel's comments about all this are barely printable. "The Tommies have nettled two battalions of the Sabratha shits," he said. "Seebohm is missing. It makes you puke."[31] Lieutenant Seebohm was the brilliant and highly successful head of the Wireless Intercept Service, which had played such a decisive role at the Battle of Knightsbridge. He had led a combat group into the battle after Sabratha broke, and was later found among the dead. Most of his irreplaceable unit was also destroyed.[32] Besides crippling Rommel's intelligence network, this battle proved that the Indians were no longer capable of repulsing the attacks being launched against them.

Auchinleck's fourth major assault came the next day, July 11. Again he singled out an Italian unit, this time the Trieste Motorized Division, stationed south of the Coastal Road. After a terrific aerial and artillery bombardment, he sent the Australians forward. They overran Trieste and broke through Axis lines. Rommel threw the few remaining German reserves into this battle, which was finally decided by the Panzer Army Artillery, which fired into the Allied infantry at close range and broke up the Allied attack. However, the Panzer Army Artillery expended almost all their shells, and no reserves of this precious commodity existed. Now they would have to fight almost entirely with captured guns and British-made shells: a truly desperate measure! Rommel's position had become very critical.

Rommel now drew the inevitable conclusion that the strain on the Italian units was too great for them, and they could no longer be counted on to hold their lines against even a weak British attack. He therefore closed all German rest camps and ordered every available German soldier to the front. The event he feared most of all had taken place: The initiative had passed, and the front was static.[33]

Auchinleck's Eighth Army was now in its element. These men had been specifically trained in World War I-type tactics which envisioned nothing but this kind of static, positional warfare. This training had cost them thousands of men and almost lost the war for the British Empire, but now it paid off at last. They had been lucky, but the British currently held almost the only position in North Africa that Rommel could not outflank. Auchinleck could build up and keep Rommel pinned down at the same time.

Erwin Rommel recognized the danger, of course, but there was very little he could do about it. He decided to take one desperate gamble, and deliver a frontal assault against the Alamein Box. To do so he ordered the 21st Panzer Division to leave the Qaret el Abd sector and return to the north. On July 12 the Afrika Korps regrouped for the attack. The Allies unwittingly accommodated this maneuver by remaining inactive. They were busy consolidating their gains of the past three days. The next day, July 13, the panzers struck.

Rommel's plan called for the bypassing of the 26th Australian Brigade in the forward position of Tel el Eisa, which Sabratha had lost on July 10. The German tanks would then push east approximately five miles and overrun the Alamein Box. The assault, Rommel wrote, was supported by "every gun and airplane we could muster."[34] Unfortunately, the infantry of the 21st Panzer Division deployed too far to the rear, and the immediate effect of the aerial bombardment was lost. By the time the Germans charged, the South Africans (who covered the southern approaches to the box) had recovered. The attack failed.[35] Rommel tried to advance again the next day, with similar results. He had lost the element of surprise, and the Australians and South Africans had been reinforced during the night.[36]

This abortive attack ended Rommel's aggressive efforts for some time. During the night of July 14-15, Auchinleck resumed his piecemeal, anti-Italian offensive, which was proving so successful. He struck the Pavia and Brescia divisions on Ruweisat Ridge with the 5th Indian and 2nd New Zealand divisions. They were supported by the 1st Armoured Division, which was to exploit any successes scored by the infantry.[37]

The veteran Allied infantrymen broke right through Italian lines with great speed and little difficulty. Resistance collapsed almost immediately and the Italians poured to the rear or surrendered in droves. "It's enough to make one weep," Rommel moaned.[38]

The New Zealanders committed two serious errors in the darkness: They failed to locate the 8th Panzer Regiment on their left flank, and they failed to finish off some small German infantry units whose positions they had overrun. Unlike the Italians, these warriors did not lay down their arms and march obediently toward the prisoner-of-war camps. They found their way, individually and in small groups, to rally points. There they reorganized, hedgehogged, and continued to wage war. At dawn one of these groups ambushed the New Zealand antitank gunners as they came up, and left the forward Allied division without enough antitank protection. The situation for the Allied spearhead became critical when the 1st Armoured Division failed to support the New Zealanders as ordered, and Rommel counterattacked with the 3rd and 33rd Reconnaissance battalions.[39] Naturally the 8th Panzer Regiment joined in the battle with its 20 remaining tanks. General Nehring personally led the main attack and overran the 4th New Zealand Brigade. The German thrust was finally halted by the British 2nd Armoured Brigade,[40] but not before Rommel's troops captured part of the vital ridge and 1,200 of the tough New Zealanders.[41]

Defeat after defeat piled up on the Panzer Army's Italian contingent. The German units became a sort of fire brigade, because they rushed from point to point, all along the front, stemming the crisis of the moment. After each fire they were weaker than before, in men, ammunition, and fuel. All thought of resuming the offensive was forgotten.

Auchinleck launched his sixth major attack on July 16, in the sector of the Coastal Road. The Australians finished off the remnants of the Sabratha Division, but were again turned back by the 382nd Grenadier Regiment,[42] which was rapidly gaining experience in desert warfare.

The next day the battle of attrition continued. The Australians, with strong tank support, attacked in the direction of Miteiriya Ridge. They smashed the Trieste and Trento divisions, but were forced back to their original positions by a strong German counterattack. However, Rommel had to use his last reserves, and they were almost out of ammunition. That night Rommel told Kesselring and Cavallero: "If something is not done about supplies soon, we shall collapse."[43] Kesselring might have replied "I told you so," but he did not.

During the next three days the Eighth Army confined itself to harassing operations while it regrouped for its eighth major thrust. Rommel took greater advantage of the lull by building up his positions and withdrawing some German units from the line. Once again he created a small tactical reserve. Some more elements of the 164th Light Afrika Division arrived at the front, as did the Italian Folgore Parachute Division. As welcome as these men were, they lacked experience in North Africa and were not yet "desertworthy." Nevertheless they went directly to the front line.[44]

On the night of July 21-22 the British struck again. This time Auchinleck chose a German target: the surviving men of the 15th Panzer Division, who were still clinging to their positions south of Ruweisat Ridge. Auchinleck hoped they had worn themselves out and were at the end of their will to resist. They were not. After an initial Allied breakthrough, the desert veterans closed their lines and cut off the Australian spearhead. Five hundred more prisoners were taken.[45]

At 8:00 A.M. Auchinleck unleashed his main attack. The Allied units involved included the 5th Indian Division, the 6th New Zealand Brigade, and the 23rd Armoured Brigade of the newly arrived 8th Armoured Division. They were told to wipe out the German foothold on Ruweisat Ridge. The Second Battle of Ruweisat Ridge had begun in earnest.

The Eighth Army failed miserably in this battle. They did not properly clear the minefields, locate German units, discover panzer concentrations, or coordinate infantry/armor attacks. A mixed German-Italian combat team held on and proved that not all the Italians had lost the will to fight. Many of these men resisted to the last bullet. Their heroic stand gave Rommel time to concentrate the Afrika Korps against the 23rd Armoured Brigade. He was still outnumbered, but the inexperienced British tankers played right into his hands. They came under furious antitank fire, turned to avoid it, and drove right into a minefield. Before they could extricate themselves the 21st Panzer barred their way and wiped out what was left of the brigade.[46] At least 87 tanks were lost,[47] and the figure was probably higher. One of the few British survivors summed up the battle this way: "Two years' training, a voyage half-way round the world, and in a half an hour it was all over."[48] One source put the total Allied losses at 140 tanks and 1,400 men captured or destroyed.[49] On the other side the equivalent of three Axis infantry battalions had been wiped out, but the panzer casualties were negligible.[50] This Axis line was still holding, if only barely.

Despite the growing discontent in the higher echelons of the Eighth Army, caused by the high casualty rates for very little substantive gains,[51] Auchinleck convinced his generals to attack again on the night of July 26-27. On the northern face of the attack the Australians overran a battalion of the 164th Light, but were beaten back by Combat Group Briehl, the 3rd Reconnaissance Battalion, and the Kampfstaffel. The main assault came from the 50th British Infantry Division, which struck Rommel's center and routed an Italian battalion, but then ran up against much of the Afrika Korps and the newly arrived 200th Infantry Regiment of the 164th Light Afrika Division. The 1st Armoured Division was supposed to support this thrust, but failed to do so. Its commander, Brigadier Fisher (General Lumsden had been wounded), refused to follow the infantry claiming that the gaps in the minefield were not properly cleared. As a result the 69th Infantry Brigade was left in the lurch, and crushed.[52] In this repulse the British lost 32 tanks and 1,000 men.[53]

The balance of losses of July 15, 22, and 27 was highly in favor of Rommel's Panzer Army. Since the attacks began, the Allies had lost 13,000 men, as opposed to 7,000 for Rommel. However, only just over 1,000 of these were Germans. The Eighth Army, shaken by the failure of ten successive attacks, went over to the defensive. A lull descended on the North African Front.

It is ironic that the British stopped attacking just when Rommel was on the very verge of defeat. Lieutenant General Fritz Bayerlein later told Brigadier Young: "We were very much impressed and very much disturbed by the way you attacked us all through July. You very nearly succeeded in breaking through our positions several times between the 10th and 26th. If you could have continued to attack for only a couple of days more you would have done so. July 26th was the decisive day. We then had no ammunition at all for our heavy artillery and Rommel had determined to withdraw to the frontier if the attack was resumed."[54]

8

High Tide in the Desert

After the defeat of Auchinleck's July offensives, there was a lull on the Western Desert. Behind the lines, however, there was feverish activity. Rommel desperately tried to build up sufficient supply and petroleum reserves to assume the offensive once more. He realized that time was running out on Panzer Army Afrika. His spectacular series of victories in June had given the Allied political leaders in Washington and London their greatest shock since the fall of France. The British and American Allies spared no effort in assembling men, supplies, tanks, and other weapons for the North African Front. All this took time, of course, and as we have observed, the giant convoys could not use the Mediterranean route to deliver the supplies due to the presence of the U-boats and the Luftwaffe. The convoys would have to journey from New York to Suez or Alexandria via the Cape of Good Hope in South Africa. Shipping time would take eight to twelve weeks. This then was all the time Erwin Rommel had left. He would have to win the Desert War in that period, or face ultimate defeat in North Africa.

The British did not wait for the American convoys to add muscle to the Eighth Army. Fresh soldiers streamed in from India, Syria, Palestine, Iraq, and other points. German intelligence estimated that by August 20 Auchinleck would have 70 infantry battalions, 900 tanks and armored vehicles, 550 guns, and 850 antitank guns ready for action.[1]

From May 26 to July 30, Rommel's men had captured 60,000 Allied soldiers and knocked out 2,000 Allied tanks and armored cars. The Panzer Army now existed on the spoils of these victories. For example, 85 percent of its motorized transport was of Anglo-American manufacture. These battles, however, had not been won without loss. A total of 2,300 Germans had been killed, 7,500 wounded, and 2,700 captured or missing. Only 34,000 Germans remained fit for combat.[2]

The Italians had also suffered heavy casualties. A thousand of them were dead, 10,000 wounded, and 5,000 captured or missing. However, unlike the Germans, they were demoralized, and could no longer be counted on against the British.[3]

The tide of the war was turning, and Rommel knew it. Hitler, still obsessed with the Eastern Front, sent him a bare minimum of reinforcements. Mussolini did somewhat better, but not much, as all he could send were nonmotorized infantry divisions. In his tent, Rommel fumed. "What I need here," he wrote Gause, "are not still more Italian divisions—let alone the Pistoia, with no combat experience at all—but the German soldiers and German equipment with which alone I am ultimately going to have to carry through my offensive."[4]

More important than any other single event of the past two months was the inescapable fact that the Royal Air Force had achieved complete domination of the North African skies. Supply columns were being shot up as far west as Tobruk, 370 miles behind German lines. This Rommel could afford least of all.

Behind the minefields on either side, the refitting of battered units went on at full speed. Soon the British had six divisions on the front line and six in reserve, including three armored divisions. All were at or near full strength. On the other side, Axis repair shops were far from idle. Rommel's mechanics worked miracles, and soon the number of available panzers rose to about 200, while almost 300 Italian tanks were pronounced serviceable. Unfortunately, many of these German-Italian tanks were almost completely worn out by a year and a half of almost constant operation. They needed thorough overhauls, and not a few needed to be completely rebuilt, but there was not time for this. They went back to their units, ready to break down again under the slightest strain. Rommel knew this, but was powerless to do anything about it.

In August 1942, the failures of the Italian Navy to provide the proper support for their supply convoys became more and more critical. They were (with some justification) thoroughly intimidated by the Royal Navy, and could seldom be induced to leave port. Rommel had 2,000 vehicles, 120 tanks, and 100 field guns in Europe awaiting transport to North Africa. However, the Italian Navy proved incapable of shipping them overseas.[5]

The lack of Italian success in the central Mediterranean greatly devaluated the strategic importance of Tobruk. The Italian Navy usually chose the shorter, less dangerous routes to Tripoli and Benghazi, 1,400 and 750 highway miles, respectively, from El Alamein. As a result, the angry Rommel had to haul his supplies the remaining distance by truck. This further exposed his limited transport to RAF attacks and greatly increased the chance of a breakdown. It must be remembered that 85 percent of Rommel's transportation vehicles were captured Allied trucks, and naturally very few spare parts for them were available. Breakdowns on a 750-mile haul are not unusual. Frequently the failure of a single small part rendered a truck as useless as if it had been hit by a British bomber.

Favoritism in supply allocation was another major problem that Rommel could never solve. In theory, the proportion of German and Italian cargoes was supposed to be based on a one-to-one ratio. In practice, it was far from that. Supply responsibility lay with the Commando Supremo, whose officers generally hated Rommel and despised Mussolini. They funneled resources to their favorites and ignored all others. In August the Italian contingent received 27,500 tons of supplies, as opposed to 8,200 tons for the Germans. This tonnage amounted to only 32 percent of the minimum monthly requirements for the four German divisions.[6] In September the Commando Supremo sent the Pistoia Infantry Division to Libya as a garrison force not under Rommel's control. Soon it had received 300 to 400 of its vehicles. The 164th Light Afrika Division, already heavily engaged, received only 60 of its vehicles. While several Italian units were completely rebuilt or refitted, the Germans did not receive a single replacement vehicle of any type in the critical month of July.[7] At one point the Afrika Korps dwindled to a strength of less than 50 operational tanks, while the 120 panzers previously mentioned lay on the docks in Italy, awaiting shipment.

Perhaps all this would not have been so terrible, except for the fact that the Italian High Command neglected their own most valuable units. The elite Folgore Parachute Division, for instance, got almost no vehicles, and had to march to the front on foot. By August the XX Italian Motorized Corps was short half of its transport vehicles and tanks. Conditions grew so bad that only four of its 10 motorized battalions could remain mobile. Of its 220 surviving tanks, over half were worn out and incapable of prolonged operation.[8] The Commando Supremo should have sent replacements for these, or at least provided this corps with the best available maintenance support units and facilities, but it did not.

To alleviate the situation, Rommel proposed to the High Command that Kesselring be charged with total responsibility (and authority) for supply.

Of course, this idea was quickly rejected by Rome. As a result, German forces in the Panzer Army were consuming twice as many supplies as they received by the first three weeks in August. They subsisted almost entirely on the enemy supply dumps captured at Gazala, Tobruk, and Mersa Matruh. These were rapidly depleting, with no hope of renewal. German manpower and equipment levels were also at a low ebb. On August 20 the German forces were below assigned strength by 16,000 men, 600 tanks, 175 armored vehicles, and 1,500 other vehicles. This figure includes the captured Allied equipment that had been incorporated into the Panzer Army.[9]

The complete domination of the air by Allied fighters and fighter-bombers further slowed Rommel's buildup. Malta recovered from Kesselring's aerial offensive with remarkable speed. The 10th Submarine Flotilla returned to the island almost as soon as Luftwaffe pressure lessened, and began to play havoc with Rommel's shipping lanes once again. They were followed by the RAF, now the most dangerous of all Rommel's enemies. The British pilots initially attacked Italian naval convoys, but soon expanded their operations to include long-range bombing of the Cyrenaican ports. Other RAF units based behind the Alamein front pounded Mersa Matruh and Bardia. On August 8 they bombed Tobruk in a devastating raid. Even after much of the damage was repaired the capacity of the port was reduced by another 20 percent.

To make a gloomy picture even worse, Rommel's health finally failed him. Not even an iron constitution can endure prolonged physical strain for months and months on end, and Rommel had fought in the harsh desert environment for more than 18 months. On August 23 he was so sick he could not leave his bed. When Hitler was informed of this development, he sent Professor Horster from Wurzburg University to treat the ill field marshal. The noted doctor found Rommel had a bad cold, digestive disturbances, and symptoms of exhaustion. The professor's report concluded: "Field Marshal Rommel [is] suffering from chronic stomach and intestinal catarrh, nasal diphtheria and considerable circulation trouble. He is not in a fit condition to command the forthcoming offensive."[10]

After the medical examination, Rommel agreed to relinqush command of the Panzer Army, but only if Colonel General Heinz Guderian, the inventor of the Blitzkrieg and the hero of the French campaign, would be named his successor. This request no doubt irritated Hitler, for Guderian had been in disgrace at Fuehrer Headquarters since his defeat before Moscow in the winter of 1941. "Guderian unacceptable" was the High Command's curt reply to Rommel's request. The sick Swabian's stubborn streak showed itself again after he received this dispatch, for he announced that he would command the coming attack on the Alamein line despite his poor physical condition.[11]

During the next few days Rommel's health improved slightly. Professor Horster telegraphed back to Berlin: "C-in-C's condition so far improved that he can command the battle under constant medical attention. Nevertheless, essential to have a replacement on the spot."[12]

This replacement, presumably, would be Walter Nehring. The entire German leadership in North Africa was in shaky physical health. Major General Gause had returned to the front, but was experiencing constant headaches and apparently had not fully recovered from his head wound at Gazala. Major General Gustav von Vaerst was back, and resumed command on the 15th Panzer Division. However, Westphal remained unfit for duty, and Colonel von Mellenthin contracted amebic dysentery, a disease that soon forced him to leave North Africa forever;[13] he was evacuated to Austria.

Disease and exhaustion also took its toll among the rank and file. In August, 9,418 of Rommel's men reported sick.[14] Some 17,000 Germans who had been with Rommel since the beginning of the Desert War were sent home to avoid serious and permanent damage to their health.[15] This represented a large part of Rommel's total force. Worse still, they were all veteran desert warriors, and included many of Rommel's best men.

While Rommel's physical and military strength deteriorated to a dangerous level, the Eighth Army flourished. In August, von Mellenthin estimated that it would be too strong to attack by mid-September.[16] Accordingly, the field marshal set about planning for a major offensive before then.

During this period, General Walter Warlimont, the deputy chief of operations for the Wehrmacht, visited Rommel's Headquarters, now located eight to twelve miles west of El Alamein. Here he found no defeatism, no talk of retreat. Rommel spoke only of resuming the offensive as soon as possible. However, Warlimont was no fool either. Later he wrote that he "... received a lasting impression of the intensity of the fighting on land and in the air, fighting which in the exposed desert now showed all signs of developing into a battle of material."[17]

Of his situation at this time, Rommel said, "When we advanced at Alamein at the beginning of July, against all reason and despite our exhaustion, I wanted to prevent the British from consolidating before Alexandria and to prevent them from bringing up their new material from

America. I wanted to prevent the war from becoming static with a fixed front line. The British troops, both officers and men, have been trained for such a war. The stubbornness of the Tommy bears fruit in such a position where his chronic rigidity works for him."[18]

The field marshal recognized that he was on the verge of failing. The battlefield had become static. Soon it would be like World War I all over again. Something had to be done immediately to break the deadlock or the Desert War was lost. Rommel summoned his top commanders and staff officers. He told them: "The successes of our Panzer Army in the last weeks have spread gloom and panic in Washington and London. It is quite clear that this alarm will encourage the Allies to make even greater efforts to prevent the loss of the Nile Delta and the Middle East." He struck the table with his fist. "Vast convoys are sailing with powerful escort round the Cape. Already the first of these are in the Red Sea, but that is only a beginning. More and more will arrive. Churchill and Roosevelt both know what is at stake in North Africa. It is obvious that by the middle of September the British 8th Army will be so strong that we shall not be able to deal with it."[19] He set the attack date for August 30. The stage for one of the decisive battles of modern warfare was set.

This time Rommel would be facing a new opponent. Prime Minister Churchill had visited Egypt in late July and inspected the Eighth Army. He did not like what he saw. On July 25 he relieved Sir Claude Auchinleck and replaced him with General (later Field Marshal) Sir Harold Alexander. This new commander-in-chief, Middle East named General Gott commander of the Eight Army.

Gott's tenure as Eighth Army commander was destined to be extremely short. The day after his appointment he decided to fly to Cairo via transport aircraft. Due to the recent lack of Luftwaffe activity and the short distance of the flight, he did not request RAF fighter escort. This proved to be a fatal mistake, because the transport was jumped by a pair of Messerschmitt fighters, probably of the fast Me109 variety. They quickly shot down the unarmed transport plane. Gott survived the crash, but while he was trying to rescue some wounded passengers from the wreckage the German pilots made a second pass. They strafed and killed the commander of the Eighth Army.[20] Churchill replaced him with Lieutenant General Bernard Law Montgomery.

When Rommel heard of this appointment, he ordered all intelligence files on Montgomery sent to him at once. As he read them he was heard to mutter, more to himself than to anyone else, "This is a dangerous man."[21]

As if to underline Rommel's fears, one of Monty's first orders to his divisional commanders was to stop attacking piecemeal. "We are finished with this splitting up of our forces which has enabled Rommel to win his victories," he said. "In the future, tanks and artillery will only be used en masse." He sent a report to the Cabinet in London, listing his minimum requirements for the offensive he was planning. "I shan't attack until they are fulfilled, but I will hold Alamein until you have fulfilled them," he wrote.[22] Of course, Nazi military intelligence brought these words back to Rommel, but what could he do? He now knew that Montgomery would wait until he could launch his offensive with overwhelming strength. Only one hope remained for the Axis cause in North Africa: Rommel's offensive of August 30.

Since April 1941, Rommel had defeated Neame, Wavell, Beresford-Peirse, Cunningham, Ritchie, and Auchinleck. Now, at last, he had met his match. This is not to say that Montgomery was a better commander than Rommel, any more than Schwarzenberg was superior to Napoleon, Grant to Lee, or Scipio to Hannibal. However, each of these victorious commanders took advantage of superior numbers and resources to defeat his more skillful antagonist. This is what Montgomery prepared to do in Egypt. Like Schwarzenberg, Grant, and Scipio, he set about using his superior resources to offset the brilliance of the enemy commander. In doing so, he turned the tide of the war on the Western Front and, along with Yeremenko at Stalingrad, sent Nazi Germany down the road toward final defeat.

Many Americans today refuse to credit Montgomery's accomplishments, or tend to minimize them. This trend is largely due to one of Montgomery's character flaws: He lacked tact, particularly in dealing with Americans; indeed, he showed little inclination toward getting along with them. His feud with U.S. General George S. Patton (also a fine, though tactless, leader) is well known and beyond the scope of this book. Suffice it to say that, in all justice, Montgomery was a good commander and an excellent leader of non-American men. If he did not equal Rommel in raw ability, he more than made up for this deficiency by using the resources at his disposal to stem the Nazi tide in the West. He should be given credit for this accomplishment, even by those many Americans who cordially despise him.

In mid-August, the British made the move that proved to be decisive in the Battle of the Central Mediterranean. Even while Rommel was grouping for his attack Malta had 250 British aircraft on it. The island-fortress also had submarines and assorted other naval vessels operating out of its harbor. Nevertheless, the German ring around the island, although weakened, remained unbroken. The garrison and people of Malta were still seriously short of food and other essential items. The Royal Navy decided to remedy this situation once and for all by dispatching a huge supply convoy to the island. It consisted of 16 merchant cargo ships, escorted by no less than two battleships, three aircraft carriers, seven cruisers, and 24 destroyers. This force paid a heavy toll to the German U-boats, and only five of the 16 merchant vessels reached Malta. One of these was damaged and another had to be lashed between two destroyers to finish the trip. One aircraft carrier was sunk and the other two were severely damaged. Two cruisers went down, and two others were hit by torpedoes and narrowly avoided the same fate. However, 47,000 tons of supplies and dozens of new aircraft were off-loaded at Malta.[23] The island had enough food to continue its operations until December. The ring was effectively broken after two years; the Allies had at last won the Battle of the Central Mediterranean.

Elsewhere, other British and American naval units were also busy. In the last half of August 1942, the Allies unloaded 500,000 tons of supplies on North African shores, against 13,000 tons for the Axis, which meant the supply imbalance stood at 38 to 1. The actual imbalance was much higher than this, particularly when one considers the distances Rommel's supplies had to be trucked, the effect of the RAF attacks on these vehicular convoys, the amount of petroleum consumed on these trips, and the precarious state of Rommel's motorized transport.

On the eve of the offensive, Rommel had only enough gasoline for each panzer to advance 80 miles. On August 27 he met with Cavallero and Kesselring at Panzer Army Headquarters. Rommel demanded a minimum fuel reserve of 6,000 tons before launching his attack. "The outcome of the battle depends on the punctual delivery of this fuel," he said, emphatically. "You can start your battle, Field Marshal," Cavallero replied. "The fuel is already on the way."[24]

Kesselring backed up Cavallero and said that the Luftwaffe would fly the necessary petroleum to North Africa if the Italians failed.[25] On the strength of these two promises Rommel began his offensive, which has since become known in German circles as the "Six Days' Race."

According to the Panzer Army General Staff, Erwin Rommel would be outnumbered three to one in tank strength and five to one in aircraft when the battle started. These figures were worse than Rommel expected. After reviewing this report and his adverse fuel situation, Rommel considered giving up the offensive altogether. However, in the end he accepted Kesselring's assurance that he could deliver 90,000 gallons of fuel per day. As it turned out, the Luftwaffe field marshal did supply the promised amount, but only to North Africa, not to the front. Most of the gasoline was consumed on the long journey from Tripoli or Benghazi to Alamein.[26]

Cavallero also tried to make good his promise, but, like Kesselring, he let Rommel down. A large tanker, loaded with thousands of gallons of fuel, was due in Tobruk on August 31. The Royal Navy sank it just a few miles from the harbor. With it sank the Axis' chance for victory in the battle that was by then already in progress.

In actuality, the Panzer Army intelligence estimates were very nearly 100 percent correct. The British had over 700 tanks, compared to 259 panzers and 243 nearly useless Italian tanks.[27] This gave the British a 2.7 to 1 tank superiority over the Germans. The British also had a definite and growing superiority in infantry strength. To make up for part of this, Rommel swept the Libyan countryside bare to send as many men as possible to the front. Support units operated on a bare minimum of manpower.[28] Despite these emergency measures, Montgomery maintained a sizeable edge in men, tanks, armored cars, artillery, aircraft, antitank guns, and every other category of military strength.

To meet the main Axis attack, which he was sure would come against his southern flank, Montgomery assembled an overwhelming force. It was under the Headquarters of the XIII Corps and included the 1st, 7th, and 10th Armoured divisions. The newly arrived 10th Armoured Division held the Alam Halfa Ridge, which Montgomery judged to be the critical terrain feature and the key to holding the El Alamein line. Map 9 shows Montgomery's dispositions and the Axis attack.

Rommel's proposed attack followed the same general pattern he had used successfully so many times before. While the Italian infantry, interlaced with some German units from the 164th Light, pinned down Allied forces to the north, Rommel would attack to the south with all available armored and motorized forces.

The young field marshal planned to assemble the Afrika Korps, XX Italian Motorized Corps, and the 90th Light Division in camouflaged assembly areas in the southern part of the Axis front. He did this over a period of several days. The initial assault was scheduled to gain a penetration of 25 to 30 miles. While the Italian Motorized corps held the gate open

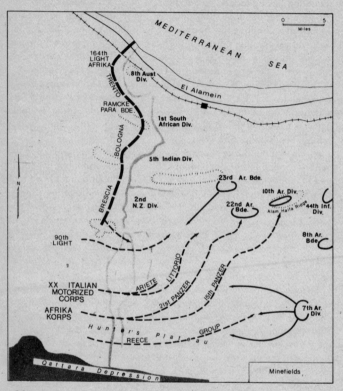

Map 9. The Battle of Alam Halfa Ridge, August 30–September 2, 1942

against a counterattack from the north, the Afrika Korps would break for the sea and either force a reatreat or surround the Eighth Army. It is notable that Rommel's plan called for a sweep east of the Alam Halfa Ridge. He did not consider its capture essential for victory.[29]

The entire plan depended on speed. "The decisive battle was on no account to become static," Rommel wrote later.[30]

The plan was good, but it had two major flaws. First, the Panzer Army no longer had enough fuel to carry it out. Second, General Montgomery expected just such an attack, so there was no surprise in it.

On the morning of August 30, despite the fact that ammunition stockpiles were low and the promised gasoline had not yet arrived, Rommel decided to go ahead with his attack as originally planned. The full moon, which the engineers needed to breach the minefield, was already on the wane. To wait three weeks for another was, of course, out of the question. That morning Professor Horster visited the field marshal and found him very troubled. He said: "Professor, the decision to attack today is the hardest I have ever taken. Either the army in Russia succeeds in getting through to Grozny and we in Africa manage to reach the Suez Canal, or . . ." and he made a gesture of defeat.[31]

His pessimistic thoughts did not find their way into his order of the day. It read:

Soldiers,

Today the Army, strengthened by new divisions, is embarking on the final destruction of the enemy in a renewed attack.

I expect every soldier under my command during these decisive hours to give of his utmost.

Signed: ROMMEL, Field Marshal
Commander-in-Chief[32]

For Rommel's army things went wrong almost immediately. The opening attack was a nightmare. It started on schedule, and the front line of the XIII Corps was overcome quickly enough, but then the panzers ran into a dense minefield, the existence of which had been kept secret from the German Army. An amazing total of 150,000 mines had been laid in this sector.[33] The 7th Armoured Division covered the minefield and resisted fiercely, instead of retreating as Rommel expected. As the Axis attack stalled in open terrain, the RAF appeared and shot up the motorized columns. They lit up the battlefield with a device called the Christmas tree, a new type of magnesium flare. The entire area was soon as bright as day. Stuck in the minefield with no place to hide, the Germans were sitting ducks. Panzers and other vehicles were shot up and set afire. Hundreds of veterans died that night, including one of Rommel's best generals.

At the head of his division, Major General Georg von Bismarck personally led the 21st Panzer forward toward the eastern edge of the minefield. He never reached it, however. Some sources claim his command vehicle struck a mine and exploded.[34] Others say an antitank gun or British tank drew a bead on him and scored a direct hit.[35] One thing is certain: One of Rommel's most valuable subordinates was incinerated.

General Walter Nehring, the commander of the Afrika Korps and Rommel's second-in-command, was also in serious trouble. A British pilot spotted his command vehicle, which was exposed by a Christmas tree. Despite German machine-gun fire the pilot dived and at low level dropped a bomb right beside Nehring's car. Several officers of the Afrika Korps were killed and others were seriously wounded by the blast.[36] Among those still alive was Walter Nehring, but he was so badly wounded that he had to be evacuated to Europe. Colonel Bayerlein, Nehring's chief of staff, assumed temporary command of the Afrika Korps. He would eventually be replaced by Major General von Vaerst, the senior surviving officer in the Korps.

Elsewhere on the battlefield, medics attended the wounds of Major General Ulrich Kleeman. Like Nehring, he survived his injuries, but the 90th Light Division would need yet another commander.[37] Within hours of the start of his offensive, Rommel had lost three of his four senior general field commanders, as well as several important staff officers. Of the original divisional commanders, only von Vaerst remained.

The battle raged on all night. Finally, after dawn, the Afrika Korps succeeded in breaching the minefield. Rommel had suffered tremendous casualties, done little damage to the enemy, and had gained only eight to 10 miles, instead of the 20 the original plan called for. Discouraged and desperately short of fuel, Rommel considered breaking off the battle.

"It was I who persuaded him to let me continue," the honest Colonel Bayerlein revealed later. "The strength of the defenses of the Alam el Halfa

Ridge came as a complete surprise to me. I was sure I could take it and went on attacking it much too long."[38]

The major difference in this battle and the dozens of others already fought in North Africa was apparent not only on the battlefield but behind it as well. In strange contrast to "Crusader," "Battleaxe," Cyrenacia, Knightsbridge, or Bir Hacheim, calm reigned at Eighth Army Headquarters. Montgomery never doubted for a moment that Rommel would attack in the south. The German-Italian attack on the north and center of the line was immediately dismissed as a feint, and not a single tank or field piece was released from the reserve to counter them. General Horrocks, to whom Monty had entrusted the XIII Corps and who therefore was the commander directly responsible for halting Rommel, was the coolest of them all. After the attack began he went to bed. He was not going to let anything as trivial as a major Nazi offensive disturb his sleep! The Eighth Army definitely had a new brand of leader.

The battle in the minefield and the soft sand had cost Rommel dearly in fuel. No new stocks arrived, despite the personal guarantees of Kesselring and Cavallero. The Italian commander-in-chief had tried his best. He had dispatched four huge tankers for North Africa. If only one of them made it through, Rommel would have the needed gasoline. The British sank all four.[39] Malta was making its recovery felt in a decisive manner. In June British pilots and seamen sank six Axis ships; in July, seven; and in the critical month of August a dozen Axis ships, including all of the vital tankers, went down.[40] The offensive was in serious jeopardy from the very start.

On the battlefield, Rommel had to revise his plan. He calculated that he did not have the fuel to make the wide swing he originally planned, so he decided to pivot northeast almost immediately. The Axis route of advance now carried them over Alam Halfa Ridge. The decisive clash of the war in North Africa was now imminent.

It was 1:00 P.M. on August 31 before Rommel could get his few remaining gasoline trucks through the gaps in the minefield to refuel the Afrika Korps. By then a sandstorm sprang up. The dust and heat made life almost unbearable, but at least the RAF was grounded, and the Germans made progress, despite the soft sand. The Littorio Armored Division also stayed on schedule, but Ariete and Trieste continued to be delayed by minefields, and lagged far behind and to the left of the main Axis advance. To the east the Reece battalions covered Rommel's right flank and made good time. When the sandstorm finally abated, the Allied Air Force apparently mistook this group for the main body of the Afrika Korps. The reconnaissance units were heavily bombed, and the RAF continued its attacks on them throughout the night,[41] even after the main German force revealed itself.

On the evening of August 31, the Afrika Korps struck its first blow at Alam Halfa. They attacked with PzKw IV (Specials) in front, and their high-velocity 75-millimeter guns caused heavy casualties among the defenders. However, they were met by the entire 44th Infantry Division and the 22nd Armoured Brigade, with dug-in tanks and very heavy artillery support.[42] At least one British tank squadron was wiped out, but the line held.[43] The Germans fell back to positions just south of the critical heights to regroup. The decisive attack would be launched the next day.

During the night the Afrika Korps was again mercilessly bombed by the Desert Air Force. The Luftwaffe was nowhere to be seen. It had been spread far too thin. German pilots had been committed from London to Stalingrad, from the Arctic Ocean to Egypt. There were simply not enough of them to go around. There would be fewer still in the days ahead.

Montgomery also made some moves on the night of August 31-September 1. He released strong elements of the 8th Armoured Division to Horrocks and ordered him to be prepared to close in on Rommel with a pincers movement. The 2nd New Zealand would form the northern jaw, while the 7th Armoured Division closed in from the south.[44] In the center of this semicircle lay the forces now defending Alam Halfa Ridge: the 10th Armoured and 44th Infantry divisions, plus assorted attached units and strong artillery forces. In case of an Axis collapse, which Monty seems to have hoped for, the X Corps (now under Lumsden) would pursue toward Fuka.[45] This, however, was wishful thinking on Montgomery's part. The Afrika Korps might be overwhelmed someday; it would never collapse.

Rommel was so ill during this offensive that he could not get out of his cot much of the time. Nevertheless, he remained in command (he had lost too many generals not to) and directed operations from the back of his truck.[46] In the early morning of September 1, he sent the 15th Panzer Division into action. The 21st Panzer had so little fuel left that it was practically out of gasoline, and could not be used against the British. The 15th Panzer had only 70 tanks when the offensive began.[47] Now it had even less. Horrocks had at least 400 tanks at Alam Halfa. Despite these odds, the first round went to the Germans. The antitank gunners closed with the inexperienced 8th Armoured Brigade and shot up a number of British tanks.[48] Unfortunately for Rommel, it was the pilot and the artilleryman who would decide this battle, not the antitank gunner. Colonel Eduard Crasemann led the 15th Panzer to within striking distance of the ridge, but as he charged forward the 7th Armoured Division caught him in the flank, and a fierce tank battle developed on the forward face of the high ground. Meanwhile, strong British artillery batteries and antitank units fired round after round into German ranks. The RAF was everywhere, and struck again and again. Panzer Army support vehicles were easy targets for the fast Hurricane and Spitfire fighters. Crasemann was soon pinned down.[49] Rommel himself dived for a slit trench a split second before a bomb exploded. Seven staff officers were too slow and were torn to shreds. A shovel lying beside the trench was pierced clean through by an eight-inch splinter, which fell into the foxhole beside the dirty field marshal.[50] By late afternoon the whole battlefield was littered with burning vehicles, most of them German. The attack had failed. Reluctantly, Rommel ordered a halt. The Panzer Army had suffered its "Stalingrad of the Desert." Rommel had reached his high-water mark. Now, inevitably, all roads led backward, to ultimate defeat.

Rommel's withdrawal of September 1 could be measured in yards. He simply did not have the fuel to go much farther, even if he wanted to. He had only one issue of gasoline left. This would carry one panzer 100 kilometers (62½ miles) over reasonably good terrain. The terrain here, as we have seen, was anything but good. Of the 6,000 tons of fuel Cavallero and Kesselring promised to deliver, 2,600 tons had already been sunk, and 1,500 tons were still in Italy. None had arrived at the front, and the Afrika Korps was left in the lurch, unable to maneuver in open terrain.[51] The night of September 1-2 was the worst yet experienced by the Panzer Army. The bombing continued all night long. By dawn even Rommel had had enough.[52] He ordered a general retreat sometime around sunrise.

The misery of the battered Afrika Korps continued throughout September 2, as relay bombing continued. If Montgomery had been Rommel, the Eighth Army would undoubtedly have launched a massive counterattack that day. However, Monty played it safe and confined himself to bombings and a few local attacks, which were easily driven off.

Rommel had yet another brush with death on that day when a vehicle blew apart within 10 yards of him. He again managed to dive into a foxhole (the men of the Afrika Korps dug a lot of foxholes in those days) and emerged unhurt.[53]

Kesselring showed up at Rommel's command vehicle at 5:30 that evening. He reprimanded Rommel for wrecking Hitler's grand strategy, as if there were anything Rommel could do that he had not already done. Rommel, who had had about enough of Kesselring since he had failed to produce the promised gasoline, emphatically explained why he had ordered a retreat. He demanded a "fundamental improvement of the supply situation." Kesselring thought this was an excuse to cover up his own demoralization, but was wise enough to refrain from saying so out loud. The Luftwaffe commander also felt that Rommel's illness played a part in the defeat. "I was convinced at the time that this battle would have been no problem for the 'old' Rommel . . ." he wrote later.[54]

On the night of September 2-3, the Royal Air Force appeared in strength for the fourth consecutive night. This time they seemed to concentrate on the 88-millimeter anti-aircraft guns, which had inflicted some casualties on their bombers in the previous days. Many of these guns and their irreplaceable crews, one of the few mainstays left in the Afrika Korps, were knocked out.[55]

The next day the German retreat continued. As on the day before, Montgomery launched a few local counterattacks but gained nothing from them. That night the RAF attacks finally lessened. Kesselring picked this moment to appear with the few bombers his Luftwaffe could still muster. Reconnaissance reports had indicated that the 10th Indian and 2nd New Zealand divisions were preparing to attack the Italians north of the salient created by Rommel's Alam Halfa offensive. To break up this potentially dangerous thrust before it could begin, Kesselring bombed the 10th Indian in its assembly areas. The raid completely disrupted the Indians' preparations and forced them to cancel the attack.[56] The New Zealanders did attack, but were not strong enough to do much alone, and were repulsed.[57]

That night the X Italian Corps surprised Freyberg's division with a rare night attack. The corps defeated the 6th New Zealand Brigade and took its commander, Brigadier G. H. Clinton, prisoner. Clinton was a resourceful man and a cunning warrior. He informed his captors that strong armored formations were on the way and that things would be rough for them unless they surrendered to him immediately. The Italians were in the process of bolting their rifles to surrender when a German officer appeared. He quickly put an end to this nonsense and led the disgusted Clinton into captivity.[58]

A few hours later Clinton met Rommel, and described him as "a short, stocky figure, running to waistline and obviously rather sensitive about it."[59] He later spoke of his meetings with Rommel to Brigadier Young:

Speaking in German, although he evidently understood English, he proceeded to harangue me about the "gangster" methods of the New Zealanders. It appeared that we had bayoneted the German wounded at Minqarqaim in the night battle behind Matruh and he was very much annoyed about it. He said that if we wanted to fight rough, so could they, and that any further action of this sort on our part would be answered by immediate reprisals.

As the nearest New Zealander available for such reprisals, it became rather a personal matter to me. I was, however, able to explain our point of view over the occurrences of that famous night attack. Our first wave, going through in the dark, caught the Germans by surprise. Some of them, lying on the ground, had fired or thrown bombs after the first company had passed. As a result, the supports following on simply struck every man who failed to stand up and surrender. . . . [Rommel accepted this as a sufficiently valid explanation, considering the confusion inherent in night battles.]

After some discussion . . . he asked "Why are you New Zealanders fighting? This is a European war, not yours. Are you here for the sport?" Realizing that he really meant this . . . I held up my hands with the fingers closed and said "The British Commonwealth fights together. If you attack England you attack Australia and New Zealand too. . . .

Rommel did not comment on this, wished me luck and off he went into battle. . . . [60]

Rommel said later that Clinton was "a brave man and very likeable."[61] However, he had not seen the last of the gallant Clinton. The New Zealander escaped through a lavatory window and headed for the open desert. He was at large for five days before being picked up by some young German officers who were out hunting gazelles. Again he found himself in the presence of Rommel.

The field marshal said to Clinton, "I do not blame you for attempting to escape, it is your duty and I would have done the same if I were in your position."

Clinton later told a friend, "Appreciating his increasing waistline and tight boots and breeches, I replied: 'I am quite sure you would try, sir, but I do not think you could have walked as far as I did' (more than 100 miles in less than five days on one can of water). Rommel came back very quickly with, 'No, I would have had more sense and borrowed a motor-car.' Trick to him . . . He then added I was a nuisance and that any further attempt to break would finish by my being shot while escaping. However, he decided to get rid of me quickly by plane from Daba early next morning directly to Rome."[62]

Clinton's adventures were certainly not over when he landed in Italy. He eventually managed to escape to Switzerland on his ninth attempt, despite having been seriously wounded on his eighth attempt.[63]

During the decisive battle of Alam Halfa, Rommel lost 570 men killed, 1,800 wounded, and 570 captured or missing, or 2,940 total casualties.[64] Two thirds of these were Germans. Montgomery lost 1,750 men killed, wounded, or captured.[65] The overall balance sheet was about even, as Table 7 indicates. However, this is not the real measure of the battle because, for

Table 7

Losses at Alam Halfa Ridge, August 30–September 4, 1942

	Allies	Axis
Casualties	1,750	2,940
Tanks	67	49
Aircraft	68	41
Antitank Guns	18	35
Field Guns	10	15
Trucks	*	400

Source: Jackson, p. 274; Rommel, p. 283.

---

*Unknown, but almost certainly less than 50.

the first time, Rommel had lost a battle before it had begun. The RAF had gained absolute air superiority in the desert. In the first four days of the battle their 500 aircraft flew 2,500 sorties in direct support of ground units, and a good number of others in raids against Axis rear areas. The United States Army Air Corps made its debut on the North African front, and flew another 180 sorties.[66] Luftwaffe aerial support had been largely nonexistent. The Allied air forces dropped an estimated 1,300 tons of bombs on Axis positions from August 30 to September 4, 1942.[67] The Royal Navy and RAF had also won the Battle of the Central Mediterranean, and with it the war for supplies. These two Allied victories had placed Rommel in a must-win situation against Montgomery. When the Eighth Army turned back Rommel's last bid for victory at Alam Halfa, the battle of attrition had set in for good. This meant dark days ahead for Erwin Rommel and his men.

From September 4 to 6 the Panzer Army's assault forces withdrew by stages with little interference from Allied ground forces. On September 6 the withdrawal was complete. Rommel took off his boots for the first time in a week, took a bath, and began to organize for Montgomery's eventual counteroffensive.[68] Of his defeat Rommel wrote: "With the failure of this offensive our last chance of gaining the Suez Canal had gone. We could now expect that the full production of British industry and, more important, the enormous potential of America . . . would finally turn the tide against us."[69]

It already had. The days of the Afrika Korps were numbered.

9

Disaster

Following Rommel's defeat at Alam Halfa Ridge, another lull descended on the North African desert. Rommel's veteran infantry, ill supplied and nearly exhausted, dug in with stubborn determination to await the inevitable counteroffensive. The static front, always Rommel's greatest fear, was a reality.

Montgomery attempted no immediate counterattacks. This leader would take no chances at all against Erwin Rommel. Slowly, deliberately, and despite pressure for speed from London, Montgomery began systematically building up his forces to an overwhelming level. Monty might be overcautious, but he was not going to give the Desert Fox the opportunity to pull off another one of his miracles, even if it meant bypassing a potentially decisive victory himself.

What Montgomery did attempt was a raid on Tobruk. The plan was originated by Colonel John Haselden, the commander of the Long Range Desert Group. This force spent most of its time raiding Rommel's supply line and shooting up transport columns, but now they became more ambitious. Haselden's scheme called for a massive bombing raid on the city and harbor, followed by ground and amphibious attacks by his commandos and British marines. They had three targets to destroy: Rommel's oil storage tanks, the harbor facilities, and the 548th (Panzer) Recovery Regiment, which had been one of the keys to many of Rommel's victories. Its crews were unexcelled experts at repairing damaged panzers, even under enemy fire. Their skill gave Rommel a decided advantage over the Allies, whose tank recovery techniques were still in their infancy. The elimination of the 548th could not help but weaken the Panzer Army's power to offer prolonged resistance in the coming offensive.[1]

Beginning at 8:00 P.M. on September 13, over 200 Wellington bombers pounded the city with tons of high explosives. Wave after wave came over, opposed by the 114th Heavy Flak and 46th Flak regiments. At least 23 aircraft were shot down. The Luftwaffe was nowhere to be seen.[2]

Under the cover of the noise and confusion caused by the air attack, Colonel Haselden divided his force into two units. His deputy, Major Campbell, overran an Italian battery and captured the eastern side of the harbor. At 1:30 A.M. the other commando group, under Colonel Haselden's personal direction, wiped out an Italian battery with their knives. However, the portable signal lights of both units were broken in the attacks. The commandos had no other way to guide the marines into the harbor entrance.[3] The raid was in serious trouble, and should have been called off at this point. However, tactical judgments are always easy in retrospect.

At 4:00 A.M. the Royal Navy destroyers *Sikl* and *Zulu* sailed closer to the harbor, and a searchlight from the 46th Flak Regiment pinpointed the *Sikl*. The vessel soon suffered a direct hit and steered off, burning. The *Zulu* rushed to its aid, but was blown apart. Both destroyers sank, while several other ships also took hits.[4] The anti-aircraft cruiser *Coventry* and five support vessels went down.[5]

It was daylight before the British marines could attempt their landings. Three large amphibious landing craft entered the harbor at full speed. At that moment the Allies paid dearly for their failure to neutralize the nearby airfields. A single Italian fighter flew over at just the right minute and sank all three assault vessels.[6]

Meanwhile, Major General Deindl, the German garrison commander, took notice of the commandos. Haselden and Campbell had failed to draw the proper conclusions and melt away during the darkness. Now it was too late. Colonel Haselden and his men died in a hail of machine-gun fire. Campbell's group was also overrun; its leader was mortally wounded. Only seven commandos escaped into the desert. The Long Range Desert Group was crippled, and the raid on Tobruk was a total failure.[7]

As the British naval assault force retreated that morning, the Luftwaffe finally arrived. It sank a cruiser, a fourth destroyer, and several more escort vessels. Like the ground forces, the Royal Navy paid a heavy price for the failure of the raid.[8]

Later in the morning Field Marshal Rommel flew to Tobruk, congratulated Deindl on his victory, and returned to the front.[9]

As gratifying as the elimination of the Long Range Desert Group must have been to Rommel, it settled no strategic questions, and did little to improve the situation at Alamein. Hitler absolutely forbade a retreat, although it is very unlikely that Rommel would have wanted to withdraw in any case, since he did not have enough fuel to conduct a retreat or wage mobile warfare. The El Alamein position was the only one in the Western Desert short of Gabes (in Tripolitania) that could not be outflanked. The desert in which the Panzer Army was operating was barren and rocky, like most of the Sahara. Forty miles south of the El Alamein station and the Mediterranean Sea lay the impassable Qattara Depression, a mass of salt marshes and quicksand. The 40 miles of wasteland between the depression and the sea would have to be held, or the Axis Empire in Africa would be threatened with extinction.

Rommel's first step in organizing the defense after Alam Halfa was fairly obvious: He incorporated the captured Allied minefields into his own defensive line. The six Italian infantry divisions manned the front, along with the 164th Light Afrika, which anchored Rommel's northern flank. The field marshal backed the front line with his three best German divisions: The 90th Light formed the reserve for the northern sector, the 15th Panzer for the center, and the 21st Panzer for the southern sector. Major General von Vaerst commanded the Afrika Korps, and Major General Heinz von Randow arrived from Germany to replace the late Georg von Bismarck as leader of the 21st Panzer Division.

Rommel labored under no illusions. He recognized the ever-growing might of the Eighth Army, and he realized that the British, trained for years in static, positional warfare, had a decided advantage over his own troops. Since he lacked the men, panzers, and fuel to carry out a successful mobile defense, he decided to rely on the land mine. Rommel's engineers dug up the captured Allied minefields at Gazala, Trobuk, and Mersa Matruh, and transported them east. Here they constructed huge defensive networks of interconnecting minefields, covered by antitank and machine guns, and often extending over a mile in depth. The soldiers called each cluster of minefields a "Devil's Garden." If the Axis could prevent a British penetration through these, the Alamein line could be held as long as Rommel cared to unless the Allies could starve the Panzer Army into submission.

This possibility was not farfetched in September 1942. The supply and material balance had swung heavily in favor of the Allies, never to return. The RAF grew even stronger and mauled Rommel's rear with even greater regularity. Rommel's men barely had enough to eat, and their food was universally bad. Also, ammunition was in short supply, and fuel reserves remained dangerously low. In addition, British aerial interdiction made reconnaissance flights behind Allied lines even more hazardous; soon they would be nearly impossible, and an important intelligence source would be denied to the Panzer Army Afrika.

On the Suez Canal, the first 100,000-ton convoy arrived safely from the United States. In Libya, the Panzer Army had received only 40 percent of its minimum supply requirements for the past eight months. It sustained itself on Allied stockpiles captured at Gazala and Tobruk, but these were now all but gone. So far, 1,300,000 tons of Axis shipping lay on the bottom of the Mediterranean. Between July 31 and October 15, twenty more Axis ships were sunk.[10]

In his *Papers*, Rommel listed four reasons for the loss of the supply war. First, it was never possible to get the Italian Navy to protect the convoys properly or to transport urgently needed supplies. "Of course, the fuel could then not have been used for the Rome taxis," Rommel added, bitterly.[11]

The second reason for the supply failure was the inability of the Axis to take Malta. Rommel must assume some degree of blame for this himself, but even with his full support, it is very doubtful that the Italians would have ever stormed the British naval base without massive German aid, which Hitler was loath to provide.

Rommel's third explanation for the supply crisis was laid at the door of Italian industry, which never managed to get quantity production of supply ships started. Fourth, the Italian support command could never be induced to construct docking facilities near the Panzer Army, or increase the unloading capacity of those installations that did exist.[12] When convoy ships finally did arrive in North Africa, a logistical bottleneck was formed that the Panzer Army could hardly afford. A ship might arrive at port and be sunk days later by the RAF with much of its cargo still on board.

Rommel hoped to wake up the German High Command and the Italian Commando Supremo with an extremely blunt dispatch. It read in part:

> The German troops of the Panzer Army Afrika, who are bearing the brunt of the war in Africa against the British Empire, must be provided with an uninterrupted flow of supplies essential for life and battle, and every available ship and transport aircraft should be employed for this purpose. Failing this, the continued successful maintenance of the African theatre of war will be impossible. . . .[13]

To add to his mounting problems, the bad rations and constant physical strain of their African service forced many of Rommel's best officers and men to report sick. Major General Gause, who had never completely recovered from his wound at Gazala, left for a cure in Europe. Colonel Westphal fell sick with jaundice, and von Mellenthin, as we have already noted, had to be evacuated to Austria with amebic dysentery. Rommel's own health continued to deteriorate to the point where Berlin decided it was necessary to have a potential replacement for him on the spot.

On September 16 General Georg Stumme arrived in Africa to become Rommel's deputy commander, a post left vacant since the capture of General Cruewell during the Gazala battles. Stumme was a man of action and an outstanding panzer leader. He had been Rommel's predecessor as commander of the 7th Panzer Division. Later Stumme had commanded the XXXX Panzer Corps in the Balkans and in Russia before he was arrested for a security violation, relieved of his command, and court-martialed, along with Lieutenant Colonel Gustav Franz, his chief of staff. Both received five-year prison sentences from Reichsmarshal Hermann Goering, the presiding officer of the court. However, Goering was impressed by Stumme's toughness and honesty. Along with Field Marshal von Bock, Goering made a personal appeal to Adolf Hitler for the commutation of Stumme's sentence, along with that of his chief of staff. Who recommended that the pair be sent to Africa is not clear, but General Stumme and Colonel Franz were soon out of prison and on their way to Egypt. When Bayerlein again moved up to chief of staff of the Panzer Army a few months later, Franz became chief of staff of the Afrika Korps.[14]

Rommel and Stumme worked in harness for a week. Then the field marshal, sick and exhausted by months of continuous physical and mental strain, left for Italy. Before he boarded the aircraft, Rommel told Stumme to signal for his return as soon as the Allied offensive began. Naturally, Stumme resented this remark, for it implied that he could not handle the situation.

Under normal circumstances, Georg Stumme would have been as good a choice as any to replace Erwin Rommel. However, circumstances were not normal. Like Rommel, Stumme had just endured months of hard campaigning. Like Rommel, his health was impaired. Unlike Rommel, it did not show on this vigorous, robust leader. Although he probably did not know it, General Stumme was not a well man.

Rommel landed in Rome on September 24 and went to visit Mussolini at his summer residence of Forbi. The interview centered around the all-important issue of supplies. "I left him in no doubt [that] unless supplies were sent to us at least on the scale I demanded we should have to get out of North Africa," he wrote later.[15]

As he was leaving the Duce's residence, Marshal Cavallero stopped him. "Can Italy count upon your immediate return if Montgomery attacks?" Cavallero asked. Rommel replied that it could. Cavallero said "Thank you," and shook the Swabian with both hands.[16]

The next day Rommel arrived at Fuehrer Headquarters in East Prussia, where Hitler publicly awarded him his marshal's baton. Then the private conferences began. Rommel and Goering clashed when the Reichsmarshal tried to minimize the Panzer Army's supply difficulties. When Rommel complained that the RAF was shooting up Axis tanks with 40-millimeter shells, Hitler's deputy denounced his statement as "completely impossible." Rommel, who did not like being called a liar, continued criticizing the Luftwaffe, and the argument became heated. Hitler finally intervened with a whole series of unrealistic promises. He would increase African supply shipments, send more anti-aircraft guns, a Nebelwerfer (multiple rocket-launcher) brigade, self-propelled guns, and 40 PzKw VI (Tiger) tanks to North Africa in the immediate future.[17] At this stage of the war Rommel was still politically naïve and took Hitler at his word. Rommel would get an education within two months.

Hitler shook hands with Rommel and sent him off to Berlin, where the field marshal spent several days with Dr. Goebbels and his family. They soon melted his reserve and had him talking well into the night. He horrified Goebbels with story after story of Italian incompetence, and told tale after tale of fierce battles and brushes with death. Goebbels, in turn, showed him newsreel footage of the battles of the Gazala line, the fall of Tobruk, and the pursuit into Egypt. The films greatly excited Rommel, who seemed to take a new lease on life.[18]

Goebbels was also working for Rommel behind the scenes. Goebbels knew that Hitler was considering making Rommel commander-in-chief of the Army after the war, and Goebbels was for this 100 percent. "A man like that certainly has what that job would take," he remarked.[19]

Despite his fame and the flattery of some of the most powerful men in Germany, he was still the same old Rommel. Many men have been spoiled by fewer successes than those Rommel had experienced since 1939, but not he. Perhaps this is best illustrated by the story of what happened at a party held for him by his friend General Rudolf Schmundt. Naturally, many

Nazi bigwigs were present, since Rommel was still in favor with Hitler. When Rommel knocked on the door, Schmundt's young son opened it. Rommel loved children and remembered that the boy had just had a birthday, so he asked him what presents he had received. The child told him he had gotten a train set. Then the two of them—child and field marshal— went upstairs and played with it the rest of the evening. Rommel never came down to meet the guests at all.[20]

The Desert Fox did make one mistake while in Berlin, and that was to attend a press reception at the Ministry of Propaganda. At one point they filmed Rommel with his hand on the auditorium doorknob. He stopped, faced them, and said, "Today we stand just fifty miles from Alexandria and Cairo, and we have the door to all Egypt in our hands. And we mean to do something with it, too! We haven't gone all that way just to get thrown back again. You can take that from me. What we have, we hang onto."[21] He would live to regret these words.

Later that day he left for Semmering, a mountain resort near Vienna, to clear up his liver and blood-pressure trouble. Apparently Hitler planned to let him recover and then give him command of an army group on the Eastern Front, probably in southern Russia. However, Rommel was unable to rest completely. He was still very much concerned about the desperate situation of his former command. This concern was increased by intelligence reports he had received since his arrival in Europe. Other secret dispatches, dealing with American industrial output and capacity, disturbed him even more. He soon became an avid follower of the Battle of the Atlantic. He was one of the few German leaders to understand that if the Anglo-American navies broke the U-boat screen "there would be little hope for us."[22]

At the front, things grew even worse. On October 9, the Allies began the systematic bombing of supply bases, harbors, and airfields in southern Italy and Cyrenaica, in preparation for their coming offensive. About 500 heavy bombers participated in these raids, which primarily originated from Malta.[23] The day after the Allied air offensive began, Kesselring responded with another all-out attempt to neutralize the base. This time, however, his fighters and bombers were defeated outright. All he could do now was strengthen the fighter escorts to North Africa.[24] The RAF and naval forces at Malta could no longer even be restrained.

During the next 13 days, Stumme and Montgomery completed the marshaling of their forces. Table 8 shows the relative strengths. However, Table 9 following is much more revealing, for it compares the German

Table 8

Opposing Strengths at El Alamein

Category	Panzer Army Afrika	Eighth Army
Men	104,000	195,000
Tanks*	489	1,029
Artillery	475	908
Antitank guns	744	1,403
Aircraft	675	750
Serviceable Aircraft	350	530

Sources: Kershaw, p. 42; Playfair and Molony, p. 2–30.

---
*Excluding light tanks.

Table 9

Allied vs. German Strength at El Alamein

Category	Germans	Allies	Ratio of Allied Superiority*
Men	50,000	195,000	4 to 1
Tanks	211†	1,029‡	5 to 1
Artillery	200	908§	5 to 1
Antitank guns	444	1,403	3 to 1
Aircraft	275	750	3 to 1
Serviceable aircraft	150	530	4 to 1

Sources: Kershaw, p. 42; Playfair and Molony, p. 2–30.

---
*To the nearest whole number.
†Including 85 PzKw III's, 88 PzKw III Specials, 8 PzKw IV's, and 30 PzKw IV Specials, but excluding light tanks, such as the PzKw II.
‡Excluding light tanks
§Excluding heavy artillery.

combat power to that of the Eighth Army. It also gives the odds more realistically, because, as we have seen, the Italian contingent could no longer be depended on to make a determined stand. Who won the war was of little concern to them. Their equipment was of the lowest quality, their political and military leadership corrupt, and their interest in expanding Fascist Italy's empire was nil. Why should they risk their lives against the British? Stumme knew he could not count on them, any more than Rommel could in Auchinleck's July offensive, when the Italians were frequently routed by smaller elements of the Eighth Army.

The odds against the Panzer Army became even greater when one considers the dangerously low fuel supplies that Stumme possessed. In mid-October he had only three issues of fuel per tank (one issue equaled the amount of fuel required to move one panzer 62½ miles under normal, not battle, conditions). Ten times this amount was considered the minimum requirement for such a battle.[25] The Army had enough ammunition for only nine days of fighting. This would be what Strawson called "the antithesis of the blitzkrieg."[26] Rommel called it "a battle without hope."

Neither Rommel nor Stumme had much choice in their battle plan for El Alamein. Since they could not wage mobile warfare, and since the Alamein position could not be flanked, Rommel ordered the Panzer Army to dig in behind the minefields. After Stumme took over he continued this policy, arranged the detailed dispositions, and issued orders that the line was to be held at all costs.

The main defensive line was situated 1,000 to 2,000 yards behind the first minebelt and extended 2,000 to 3,000 yards in depth. These positions were held by the Italian infantry, which was interlaced with German infantry to give them moral support. Behind the mine positions lay the armored and motorized forces, ready to launch immediate counterattacks if the front line wavered. Unfortunately, circumstances forced Stumme to divide the panzer divisions into smaller combat groups. This had the advantage of placing the tanks closer to where they would be needed, thus saving precious fuel. It also allowed for the interlacing of German and Italian mobile units, and made the reserves more dispersed and less subsceptible to concentrated aerial attacks. However, it also reduced the number of tanks available for the immediate counterstroke. The success of the vital counterattacks would have to depend on speed and shock action rather than mass. Due to the shortage of petroleum, the Panzer Army could no longer have both speed and mass.

Table 10.

Allied Order of Battle,
Second Battle of El Alamein

British Eighth Army: Lieutenant General Bernard Montgomery

  XXX Corps: Lieutenant General Sir Oliver Leese
    51st Infantry (Highlander) Division
    4th Indian Infantry Division
    9th Australian Infantry Division
    2nd New Zealand Infantry Divison
    1st South African Infantry Division
    23rd Armoured Brigade
    9th Armoured Brigade

  XIII Corps: Lieutenant General Sir Brian Horrocks
    7th Armoured Division
    50th Infantry (Northumbrian) Division
    44th Infantry Division
    1st Free French Infantry Brigade
    2nd Free French Infantry Brigade
    1st Greek Infantry Brigade

  X Corps: Lieutenant General Herbert Lumsden
    1st Armoured Division
    8th Armoured Division*
    10th Armoured Division

*Divisional Headquarters only; the 8th had no subordinate troop units present on
October 23.

Rommel's men depended mainly on the "Devil's Gardens" to hold off
the enemy. They planted over half a million mines, some of them in huge
clusters. Antitank and antipersonnel mines were intermixed to stop
combined-arms assaults, and all the minefields were protected by infantrymen and their close support weapons, backed up by the Panzer Army
Artillery and the tanks of the Afrika Korps and the XX Italian Motorized
Corps. In front of the minefields Stumme ran an outpost line, complete
with dogs, to provide early warning of an enemy attack and to prevent
British infiltration. However, all this preparation did not fool the expe-

rienced officers of the Afrika Korps. Johann Kramer, for instance, said later: "Alamein was lost before it was fought. We had not the petrol."[27] Rommel would have agreed. He wrote, ". . . victory was simply impossible under the terms on which we entered the battle."[28]

Montgomery's plan for the giant offensive differed from the usual desert attack in that the main blow would fall to the north, not to the south. The XXX Corps, with its four infantry divisions, was to cut two lanes in the minefields and break the Axis front line. Then the X Corps would pour through the hole with all its armor, occupy positions in the Axis deep left rear, and thus dominate Stumme's line of supply and communications. The panzer divisions would be forced to attack the bulk of Lumsden's armor under most unfavorable circumstances. Meanwhile, the British XIII Corps would launch heavy attacks to the south to pin down the 21st Panzer Division and thus prevent the Germans from concentrating to the north. Table 10 shows the Eighth Army's order of battle, and Table 11 shows the same thing for Panzer Army Afrika.

Montgomery faced the coming battle with confident determination. He

Table 11.

Axis Order of Battle,
Second Battle of El Alamein

Panzer Army Afrika
   General Georg Stumme*
   Lieutenant General Ritter von Thoma†
   Field Marshal Erwin Rommel

Northern Flank
   164th Light Afrika Division
   15th Panzer Division‡
   Littorio Armored Division‡
   Trento Infantry Division

Center
   21st Panzer Division‡

Brescia Infantry Division
Bologna Infantry Division
Ramcke Parachute Brigade

Southern Flank
   Ariete Armored Division‡
   Pavia Infantry Division
   Folgore Parachute Division

General Reserve
   90th Light Division
   Trieste Motorized Division
   19th Luftwaffe Flak Division§

*Died in action, October 24, 1942.
†Superseded by Field Marshal Rommel, evening of October 25.
‡In sector reserve.
§Dispersed throughout the area of operations.

entered a World War I-type battle with the mental attitude necessary to win it. Whatever it cost in men and material was the price he would pay for victory. The bill would be higher than even he expected, but he would pay it just the same.

Monty set the attack date for October 23. He and Alexander, his commander-in-chief, resisted all pressure from London to make it sooner. Even the grumblings of Prime Minister Churchill were firmly, though diplomatically, rebuffed. The soldiers of the Eighth Army were thoroughly trained and rehearsed for their missions, and were as well prepared for the offensive as was humanly possible. Montgomery's demands for men, equipment, and supplies were satisfied in every particular. When his men attacked, they were ready.

On October 23 Montgomery issued his order of the day. In it he told his soldiers: "The battle which is about to begin will be one of the decisive battles of history. It will be the turning point of the war."[29]

At 9:40 that night the Allies opened the battle with a massive artillery bombardment. Fifteen artillery regiments, over 1,200 guns, pounded Axis positions on a five-mile sector of the front. Over 500 of these guns had a caliber of over 105 millimeters.[30] The density of 1,200 guns for five miles is 240 guns per mile, or one cannon for every 7.3 yards of frontage! The main concentration was between Hill 35 and Deir el Shein, against Major General Karl Hans Lungershausen's 164th Light Afrika Division, a force still relatively inexperienced in desert warfare. The shelling lasted five hours. They were five hours of uninterrupted fury. The bombardment was on a scale seldom seen since 1918. The 164th was pulverized. Command posts were eliminated, and entire units were buried alive. Communications totally ceased to exist in many sectors. The barrage had a particularly bad effect on the Italians, many of whom ran away in terror. The entire 62nd Italian Infantry Regiment of the Trento Division fled to the rear.[31] Many of the heavy shells landed in the minefields, and the concussion from their blasts detonated thousands of Rommel's "Devil's Gardens." The breaching of the minefields was well under way before the first German rifleman shot down the first Allied engineer. Rommel had not counted on this possibility.[32]

At 1:00 A.M. on October 24 the British shifted their massive artillery fire to the rear areas of the 164th Light, and simultaneously began their ground attack against the Axis front. The New Zealanders and South Africans led the advance on the northern sector, where they did not expect to find a single German soldier left alive. Instead, they met the remains of the 125th Panzer Grenadier Regiment of the 164th Light. Despite their damaged communications and disrupted chain of command, the individual infantrymen dug themselves out, quickly pulled themselves together, and made a determined stand. Unbelievably, these battered remnants turned back the initial attack of two Allied divisions.[33]

South of the 125th, the Italians broke and ran. This left the remains of the 382nd Panzer Grenadier Regiment to face the 9th Australian and 51st Highlander divisions all by itself. The survivors of the grenadier regiment delayed the Allied breakthrough, but could not prevent it. Empire soldiers penetrated through the gap left by the rout of the 62nd Italian Infantry Regiment.[34] The Allied advance, however, was stopped by the 433rd Grenadier Regiment, which Lungershausen had held in reserve. Also, the 164th's Divisional Artillery poured shell after shell into Allied ranks. The German gunners had wisely held their fire against Montgomery's thousand-gun barrage and thus had not been destroyed by it. They denied Monty his initial victory, but costs were heavy on both sides.[35]

To the south, the XIII Corps also launched several attacks, but were repulsed by the German Ramcke Parachute Brigade and the Italian Ariete, Brescia, and Folgore divisions, supported by the Kiehl Combat Group, as Rommel's Kampfstaffel was now called.[36] The Italians were fighting well on the southern flank, at least.

The battle continued all night. By dawn the northern flank was on the verge of collapse. Four Allied infantry and two armored divisions—with an amazing total of 700 tanks—threatened to break out. General Stumme, who followed Rommel's tradition of leading from the front, drove toward the action. His eventual destination was the Headquarters of the 90th Light Division, but he never reached it. While observing the enemy's advance he came under machine-gun fire. Colonel Buechting, who had recently replaced von Mellenthin as chief intelligence officer, was hit in the head. He fell back into the car, dying. Stumme jumped on the running board of the car just as his driver sped away. In the excitement the general suffered a heart attack and fell off without being noticed. For several hours no one knew what had happened to him. Lieutenant General Ritter von Thoma, who had replaced the faithful von Vaerst as Afrika Korps commander after Rommel had left Egypt, reported Stumme's disappearance to Berlin and assumed command of the Panzer Army himself.

All during the day of October 24 Montgomery's attacks continued like

blows from a sledgehammer. He never let up, but constantly sent in new
infantry formations, supported by tanks, airplanes, and artillery. The main
assault that day was an infantry attack, supported by over 100 American
Grant and Sherman tanks from the 1st Armored Division. The Sherman, a
newcomer to the desert, was vastly superior to even the PzKw IV Special.
The blow fell on the Italians south of the 164th Light. The Italians panicked
and streamed to the rear, shouting "Front kaput, front kaput!" General von
Thoma threw in Colonel Willy Teege's tough 8th Panzer, the tank regiment of the 15th Panzer Division. Teege forced the Allied tanks back into
an intact sector of the minefield, where 35 Shermans were destroyed. The
rest retreated.[37] However, this setback bothered Montgomery only a little.
He simply called for massive RAF strikes against the 8th Panzer Regiment
and considered where to make his next effort.

To the south, the XIII Corps penetrated the first belt of minefields and
reached the second. This forced von Thoma to commit the 21st Panzer/Ar-
iete Combat groups to action on the southern flank. He still could not be
sure this was not the main attack. This move was exactly what Montgomery wanted him to do.[38]

During the afternoon of October 24, Montgomery's crumbling operations continued. Since he had been denied his quick victory called for in the
original plan, the British commander decided to wear down the Panzer
Army with unrelenting pressure. The X Corps railed against the northern
sector, gallantly defended by what was left of the 164th Light and combat
groups from the 15th Panzer and Littorio Armored divisions. The main
advance of the 51st (Highlander) Division and the 1st Armoured Division
was toward Kidney Ridge, but they were again repulsed with a loss of 31
more Shermans. During the day the RAF flew over 1,000 sorties against
Axis positions, and were supplemented by another 170 from the U.S. Army
Air Force.[39]

By the evening of October 24, Colonel Westphal had seen enough.
Despite the fact that no one yet knew Stumme's fate, Westphal signaled
Berlin: "Undoubtedly the long-expected full-scale offensive. Rommel's
return essential."[40]

Rommel was still in Austria, recovering from his illnesses. On the
afternoon of October 24, Field Marshal Keitel phoned him and asked if he
felt able to return to Africa. Rommel replied that he did. Keitel thanked
him and said that he would call back later if Hitler decided to send him back
to the front.

That evening Hitler personally called Rommel and asked him to start for Africa immediately. The field marshal left a short time later for the airfield at Wiener Neustadt. At 7:00 A.M. the next morning his airplane took off for Rome, where it landed four hours later. Rommel was met at the airport by Lieutenant General von Rintelen, the German military attaché to Italy. Von Rintelen informed him that part of the Axis line south of Hill 31 had been broken; several battalions of the 164th Light had been wiped out; Stumme was still missing; and only three issues of fuel remained in the entire African theater. Rommel was furious. Experience showed that one issue of fuel was necessary for each day of battle. Rommel had considered the minimum requirement for this battle to be 30 issues, and had built up a reserve of eight issues before he had left for his cure.[41] Now only three remained! At this rate, the Panzer Army would run out of gasoline by October 27 at the latest. Rommel asked von Rintelen what had happened to the other five issues, and why gasoline stockpiles had not been built up during his absence.

"You see," von Rintelen apologized, "I've been on leave until a few days ago. Insufficient attention was paid to the supply situation in my absence."

"Then the Italians must use every possible means, including their submarines and navy, to rush supplies to the Panzer Army," Rommel yelled at the attaché. "They'll have to start right now."[42]

As soon as he was through chewing out von Rintelen, Rommel departed for Crete. He landed at Herakleion Airfield at 2:45 P.M. Here General von Waldau, the commander of the X Air Corps, met him with a dispatch. General Stumme was dead, and British tanks were attacking in strength on both the northern and southern sectors. Rommel switched planes and took off immediately.[43]

Meanwhile, back in North Africa, the fighting continued at a brutal pace. After dark on October 24-25, Major General Gatehouse's 10th Armoured Division (8th, 9th, and 24th Armoured Brigades) attempted to break through in the Miteirya Ridge sector, south of Kidney Ridge. They captured the position, but suffered heavy losses to the 88-millimeter anti-aircraft guns and a rare Luftwaffe bombing raid. Under this pressure, the Allied tankers withdrew to positions east of the ridge as the dawn of October 25 broke.[44]

On October 25 Montgomery suspended the costly attacks in the Miteirya Ridge area, but stepped up operations against Hill 29, a critical position north of Kidney Ridge. Despite a massive artillery bombardment, the position continued to hold out against the 9th Australian and 10th

Armoured divisions for some time, but it was finally overwhelmed. The attacks by the 51st and 1st Armoured divisions against Kidney Ridge also met stiff resistance, and were unsuccessful.[45]

While von Thoma desperately tried to hold his line by throwing in almost all of his reserves, Rommel flew from Herakleion across the Mediterranean to Egypt, and landed at El Daba at 5:20 P.M. From this small base he hopped in a Storch and landed near his tactical headquarters about nightfall. Here he met with Ritter von Thoma, who turned the battle over to him shortly before midnight, probably with a great deal of relief. He informed Rommel that Stumme's body had finally been recovered, and that Axis losses were heavy, partially due to the necessity of launching several local counterattacks. Trento was smashed; the 164th Light Division was mauled, and other units badly hurt. He closed his report with these words: "The position, Herr Feldmarschall, has greatly deteriorated. The overwhelming enemy artillery has destroyed our Devil's Gardens. We have been able to halt the enemy but not repulse him. The fuel position is static. Artillery fire and repeated bombing attacks have decimated our troops. Only 31 panzers are battleworthy in the 15th Panzer Division."[46]

Rommel listened in silence to the gloomy but accurate report. "Rommel could do nothing," Colonel Bayerlein recalled later. "He took over a battle in which all reserves were already committed. No major decisions which could alter the course of events were possible."[47]

General Warlimont at OKW Headquarters in Berlin later agreed with this assessment. He wrote: ". . . El Alamein had developed into a typical battle of material in which no military genius on the part of the commander, and no amount of courage on the part of the men, could make up for the catastrophic situation brought about by the failure of the overseas supply lines."[48]

Conditions in the Afrika Korps were even worse than Rommel had been led to believe. He found that his Panzer Army had been hard hit by disease during his absence. The major cause of this high sickness rate was inadequate diet, a direct result of the pitifully inefficient supply efforts. Only 29,000 German soldiers were fit for combat; the all-important 15th Panzer Division had only 3,294 men, or about one third of its authorized level.[49] The Army was already on the brink of disaster, and Montgomery had only just begun his crumbling operations.

On October 26—his first day back in command—Rommel tried to organize a counterattack against Allied positions on Hill 29, which jeopardized the entire coastal sector. He brought the Kampfstaffel and the 90th Light up, but their attempts to regain the hill were nullified by the RAF and Allied artillery. By evening Rommel decided to reinforce the coastal sector further with the 21st Panzer and Trieste divisions. This meant that six Axis divisions—a full half of the Army—were posted in the northern sector. These were the 15th and 21st Panzers, Littorio, Trieste, the 90th Light, and the 164th Light, as well as the remnants of Trento, which really did not count, as it was no longer fit for action. Rommel knew he was taking a chance, especially in positioning both the Afrika Korps' divisions in one sector, but he concluded that this was the only way to muster enough armored strength for a successful counterattack.[50] Besides, he felt sure that Montgomery planned to break through to the sea between El Daba and Sidi Abd el Rahman, using Kidney Ridge to dominate the minefields. The concentration of all these divisions would delay, and perhaps even prevent, this breakthrough.

As if to confirm Rommel's suspicions, the British armored attacks grew more fierce as October 26 wore on. Finally, 160 British tanks succeeded in overrunning the ridge, wiping out a battalion from the 164th Light as they did so. They continued advancing to the southwest, but soon met a sharp counterattack from the Littorio Armored Division and some German panzer formations. In a bitter struggle the Allies were forced back, but the Italian tankers could not regain all the lost ground. Since its arrival after the fall of Tobruk, Littorio's men had shown as much courage as the soldiers of the Afrika Korps, but Littorio had lost 56 of its "self-propelled coffins" since October 24, and was no longer strong enough to recapture the vital ridge.[51]

In the air, October 26 was another disastrous day for the Luftwaffe. All day long the Desert Air Force sent 18 to 20 bombers per hour to pulverize the northern sector. The RAF suffered few losses, but smashed several Axis formations. Late in the afternoon a combined Luftwaffe-Italian squadron tried to retaliate by attacking the Eighth Army's forward positions. The raid was a catastrophe. The slow dive bombers were attacked by 60 fast Allied fighters. The German pilots pressed forward, despite heavy losses. The Italians, on the other hand, panicked. They jettisoned their bombs over Axis lines and fled to the west as rapidly as they could fly. The German Stuka element blew up several British supply vehicles and shot up a few positions, but their minor gains did not materially affect the situation, nor justify their heavy losses.[52]

As if to complete a perfectly horrible day, Rommel received a message stating that two more vital Axis tankers had been sunk in the Mediterranean.[53] The battle was going decidedly against him.

On October 27 the battle entered its fifth day, with no end in sight. Rommel took a few minutes off and wrote his wife, as was his custom. He told her, "Nobody can ever know the burden that lies on me. All the cards are stacked against us. Even so, I hope we can pull it off."[54] That morning, both Rommel and Montgomery withdrew forces from the southern sector in order to attack again in the north. Despite his tremendous handicaps, Rommel managed to strike first. He ordered Major General von Randow to take half of the 21st Panzer Division, along with half of the Panzer Army Artillery, and recapture Kidney Ridge. Meanwhile, the 90th Light, aided by

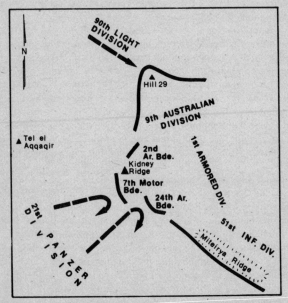

Map 10. The Battles for Hill 29 and Kidney Ridge, October 27, 1942. Rommel's attempts to retake these critical terrain features and force Montgomery to go on the defensive were unsuccessful.

elements of the 15th Panzer, were ordered to retake Hill 29. Kesselring was to give these attacks all the aerial support he could muster.[55] Map 10 shows this coordinated assault.

The thrust of the 21st Panzer, which Rommel hoped would be decisive, ended in failure. He described it this way:

> At 1500 hours [3:00 P.M.] our dive bombers swooped on British lines. Every artillery and anti-aircraft gun which we had in the northern sector concentrated a violent fire on the point of the intended attack. Then the armor moved forward. A murderous British fire struck into our ranks and our attack was soon brought to a halt by [an] immensely powerful anti-tank defence.... We suffered considerable losses and were obliged to withdraw....[56]

The 90th Light was also driven back with losses. It had been bombed three times by powerful RAF formations during the deployment phase alone.[57]

After the double repulse, Rommel admitted to himself that he would eventually be defeated. "Even the bravest soldier can be killed by a bomb," he said, with a note of resignation in his voice.[58]

The defeat of his attack was more critical than was immediately apparent, because Rommel's fuel shortage now became so acute that it dictated tactics, even at the battalion level. The 21st Panzer no longer had enough fuel to return to the southern sector, even though it was only a few miles away. Rommel's entire right flank was completely exposed. That night he was forced to commit most of his remaining tanks to the line to plug the gaps in the northern part of the front. Little was left of the old Afrika Korps to launch a counterattack, if one became necessary. The next day, localized Allied attacks forced the field marshal to denude the southern flank further and commit the entire combat force of the Afrika Korps to the front line.[59]

At 9:00 P.M. on the night of October 28-29 Montgomery reopened his drive for the coastal road. He sent Morshead's 9th Australian Division into an attack from Hill 29. The Aussies headed northward in an attempt to encircle the 125th Infantry Regiment of the 164th Light Division, which was still holding its positions. The Australians were supported by the 23rd Armoured Brigade, which had been largely rebuilt since its disaster in July.[60]

Morshead's attack failed because it struck a point on the line that the 90th

Light Division had just reinforced. The veteran antitank gunners from the 90th shot up a number of British tanks and forced the rest to retreat. Still, the Allied effort worried Rommel. If the main blow had fallen just a few hundred yards to the south, it might well have unglued the entire front, since no significant reserves remained in the whole Panzer Army. It was obvious that Montgomery's methods were working: The front was crumbling. "The battle is going against us," Rommel admitted. "We're simply being crushed by the enemy's weight."[61]

That night Rommel seriously considered retreating. He discussed the idea with Bayerlein and Westphal, his two most trusted staff officers, but decided not to withdraw because a retreat would inevitably lead to mobile warfare, which Rommel now found impossible to wage. Nevertheless he ordered some of his officers to reconnoiter the Fuka positions, 60 miles west of Alamein.[62]

Undoubtedly to Rommel's great relief, Montgomery launched no major attacks on October 29. That was all that relieved the Desert Fox, for at 11:30 A.M. he received word that the *Louisiana*, a tanker on which he was counting, had been sunk by an aerial torpedo. A few minutes later General Barbassetti, Cavallero's deputy, appeared at Panzer Army Headquarters. He promptly got a harsh tongue-lashing from the angry field marshal. Rommel wrote later: "What riled me most was that heavily armed Italian auxiliary cruisers and other vessels, carrying cargoes intended for the front, were still being sent to Benghazi in order to keep them out of range of the torpedo-carrying British aircraft."[63]

Perhaps Rommel's bitter words at last had their effect, because the rose-colored glasses suddenly came off in Rome and Berlin. Up until that time OKW was of the opinion that the position would be held. Even Kesselring stated that the British offensive was launched more for political than military reasons, and that there was little chance it would bring about a fundamental change in the overall situation. Not until October 30 did misgivings arise. "Suddenly, all the disadvantages of taking up a position too far forward became alarmingly clear," Keitel's deputy recorded.[64] Rommel reported all his reserves were committed, and if his front gave way there was nothing left to prevent the Allies from driving as far west as they wanted to go. Cavallero echoed Rommel's opinion that the only possible course of action was to hang on, despite all the dangers involved. Only Kesselring remained optimistic. He inspected the front on November 1 and reported that the danger had passed.[65]

On the panic in the councils of the Italian High Command, Rommel wrote with bitter irony:

> ... it now dawned on them even in Rome that the Army was facing annihilation unless its mobile formations could immediately be supplied with sufficient petrol. All at once it was decided to press submarines, warships, civilian aircraft and additional shipping space into service. If only this had been done after the fall of Tobruk, we would not have been sitting in front of El Alamein at the end of October. But now it was becoming steadily clearer that it was too late.[66]

Too late it was. Montgomery had pulled his main armored forces out of the battle and was massing them for one all-out assault. He gave it the appropriate code name of "Supercharge." It called for an initial, very strong diversionary attack by the Australian Division from Hill 29 north to the Coastal Road. This would begin on the night of October 30-31. The main blow would fall on November 1-2. In the first phase of the main attack, the 2nd New Zealand Division, reinforced by two British infantry brigades and the 23rd Armoured Brigade, would penetrate the center of Rommel's front just west of Kidney Ridge. Then the armored attack would follow. Four hundred British tanks were to pour through the gap at dawn on November 2 and destroy the remains of the Afrika Korps.[67] Map 11 shows the Allies' attack plans.

During the daylight hours of October 30, a deceptive quiet reigned on the North African Front. The lull was interrupted only by occasional shelling and a few minor air raids. Behind the lines an Italian tanker finally reached North Africa safely. Rommel received 600 tons of fuel.[68] "It's a tragedy that this sort of support only starts when things are virtually hopeless," Rommel wrote Lucie.[69] Nevertheless, the fuel crisis had changed from disastrous to merely dangerous.

Rommel also managed to scrape up a mobile reserve. He put the Trieste Motorized Division (which was now hardly motorized at all) into the line and withdrew the 21st Panzer Division a short distance behind the front. Thus a tactical reserve of sorts was created.

On the night of October 30-31 the Australians began their major diversionary attack. Supported by heavy artillery, they broke through the remnants of the 125th Infantry, cut the Coastal Road, and surrounded the already decimated regiment. Since the 21st Panzer Division was not yet

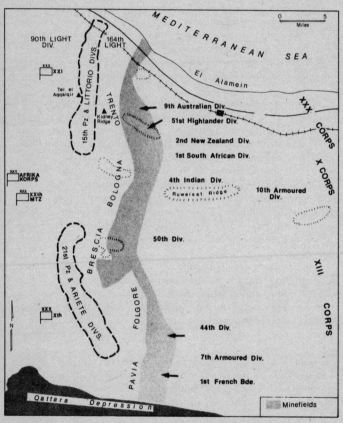

Map 11. Operation "Supercharge," November 2, 1942. Montgomery breaks the stalemate.

reassembled following its withdrawal from the front, Lieutenant General von Thoma led an immediate counterattack with all the forces he could lay his hands on. These included the 580th Reconnaissance Battalion and elements of the 361st Grenadier Regiment of the 164th Light. The counterattack was unsuccessful.[70]

The next day, November 1, Rommel took a personal hand in the rescue of the trapped 125th Grenadier. He sent elements of the 21st Panzer and 90th Light divisions down the Coastal Road. General von Thoma led the actual assault and drove the Australians south of the road, allowing the stubborn survivors of the 125th to escape. However, this move drew most of the German reserves into the northern sector—well away from Montgomery's intended point of attack.[71] The Allied diversion had succeeded; the battle was going roughly according to Montgomery's plan.

Rommel must have realized something was up, but he had no way of knowing what. He sorely missed Seebohm and his Wireless Intercept Service, but they had been dead since July. The Desert Fox was more worried than ever. "The fight is getting on my nerves," he wrote his wife.[72]

During the daylight hours of November 1, the German positions around Hill 29 were blasted 34 times by British bomber formations of 18 to 20 aircraft each. German ammunition was nearing exhaustion. Only 40 tons of ammunition had arrived since the offensive began, while Rommel's men had used up 450 tons.[73] In addition, Field Marshal Rommel had only 90 panzers and 140 nearly useless Italian tanks left to face over 800 tanks still operational in the Eighth Army.

Early on the evening of November 1, 87 British airplanes laid a carpet of bombs along the proposed route of advance for "Supercharge." They destroyed the Panzer Army communications and wiped out or neutralized several Axis positions. Thoma's Headquarters was among the targets. His telephone network was knocked out, and the general himself was wounded, though not seriously.[74]

During the night of November 1-2, Montgomery's two-pronged attack gained ground on both sides of Kidney Ridge. The northern prong penetrated the front of the 15th Panzer Division but ran into elements of the 90th Light and was checked. Farther south, 400 to 500 tanks from Lumsden's X Corps overran a regiment of Trieste and a German panzer grenadier battalion. Isolated groups of British tanks and armored cars broke completely through the Axis line and began shooting up the rear areas of Rommel's army. However, British losses were also quite heavy. The 9th

Armoured Brigade, for instance, lost 70 out of its 94 tanks against tenacious resistance. The Panzer Army was dying hard. The 15th Panzer Division was the unit directly in front of Montgomery's path, and it suffered the highest rate of casualties. Colonel Teege's 8th Panzer Regiment lost 35 of its precious tanks. In the end, Montgomery's persistence paid off. His southern prong tore a 4,000-yard hole in Rommel's front line. The German leader knew that he would have to eradicate this penetration or all was lost.[75]

As November 2 dawned, Erwin Rommel grabbed a quick breakfast of chicken fricassee with rice (probably left over from supper) and rushed off to join the fighting. His interpreter watched him go with great emotion, and confided to his diary, "Today will probably decide the outcome. Poor Rommel, he has to shoulder too much responsibility and there's so little he can do. Accursed gang in Rome! Pray God we pull it off." Rommel himself had written Lucie a frank note just before leaving. It read: "Things are not going well for us. The enemy is gradually battering us out of our position by sheer brute force. This means the end. You can imagine the mood I'm in. Air raids and still more air raids."[76]

The battle entered its eleventh day like an enraged bull. Almost all the Devil's Gardens were in Allied hands by now, and Rommel's front was threatened with total collapse. Harassed by the RAF and British artillery, he transferred his remaining panzer strength to the central sector and ordered von Thoma to counterattack the Allied "Supercharge" forces. At 11:00 A.M. and 2:00 P.M. the commander of the Afrika Korps led two attacks in a desperate and violent attempt to restore the line. Of these charges, Montgomery later commented, "The enemy fought with all the certain knowledge that all was at stake, and with all the skill of his long experience in armored fighting."[77]

After Thoma was thrown back, Lumsden's tanks surged forward again. The 15th Panzer Division quickly rallied and made a last-ditch stand that has since been known as the Battle of Tel el Aqqaqir, one of the toughest and most bitter tank clashes in the history of warfare. It was the death ride of the 8th Panzer Regiment. Colonel Teege's 35 remaining tanks (all that were left in the division) faced over 400 British tanks, with another 400 in reserve. Rommel's "Africans" charged forward with reckless abandon. Soon the battlefield was littered with burning British tanks, but there is a limit to what human skill and courage can accomplish. The elite 8th Panzer was completely wiped out, except for rear-area service support units. Not a single panzer that entered the Battle of Tel el Aqqaqir survived it. Colonel Teege died with his men. The 33rd Panzer Artillery Regiment fought with equal courage and skill, and almost suffered the same fate as the men of the 8th Panzer. A few members of this unit did manage to escape, but only enough to bring off seven guns.[78] The once-mighty 15th Panzer Division—a full half of the Afrika Korps—was reduced to zero tanks and seven guns! Surely the end had come.

Disaster overtook the Panzer Army all along the line. Toward the end of the morning the Littorio and Trieste divisions finally broke under the strain and streamed to the rear. In response to this latest disaster Rommel brought up the Ariete Division from the south, thus entirely denuding that flank of armored protection. Rommel knew that the Italians in their "mobile coffins" had little chance against Grants, Lees, and Shermans, but he threw them into battle anyway. By this time he had no choice.[79]

At midday seven 18-plane formations of British bombers dropped their loads on the Panzer Army. Their main targets were Rommel's 88-millimeter anti-aircraft batteries, which had been so effective against Allied armor. By the end of the day only 24 of the vital 88s were left in action. ". . . final destruction was on us," Rommel wrote. The Afrika Korps had only 35 tanks left in operation,[80] despite the superhuman efforts of the tank recovery teams.

Rommel ordered his aide, Reserve Captain Ingmar Berndt, to prepare to go to Fuehrer Headquarters. This action showed that Rommel was beginning to understand Hitler, because Berndt was a Nazi, a political officer, a former high-ranking employee of Goebbels' Ministry of Propaganda, and a man the Fuehrer personally liked. When Colonel Westphal, a professional and non-political soldier, volunteered for the mission, Rommel snapped, "He [Hitler] won't listen to any of your arguments." Rommel's instructions to Berndt were: "Make our position quite clear to the Fuehrer and suggest that the African theater of war is lost for us. . . ." He told Berndt to get freedom of maneuver (that is, permission to retreat) for the Panzer Army.[81]

During the night of November 2-3, the Battle of Tel el Aqqaqir continued. Now the burden of the fight was on the 21st Panzer Division, in actuality the only one left in the Afrika Korps, and it was only of battalion strength. That night Rommel received a call from von Thoma. "We have done what we can do to string together some kind of defense," the Korps commander reported. "The line is intact again, but thin. And tomorrow we'll have only 30 or at the most 35 tanks fit for action."[82] Still, the remnants of the Afrika Korps continued to put up a spirited fight, in spite of their reduced numbers. The British noted no slackening of German resistance.[83]

This resistance was deceptive. On the morning of November 3 Rommel began a general retreat on both the central and southern flanks. Covered by the Afrika Korps, which still held off Montgomery's armor, the withdrawal went unnoticed by the British, even though the Axis infantrymen had to push their field guns across the desert manually, toward the rear.

For the first time in his life, Erwin Rommel watched his men fall back in absolute defeat. This time he knew there would be no miraculous turn-abouts. The war in North Africa would be decided by material strength and industrial output; it would no longer be a reflection of his iron will and dynamic personality. "The dead are lucky," he wrote his wife in bitter despair. Then he bade farewell to Berndt and returned to the Afrika Korps.[84]

The Afrika Korps may have been broken, but it was not routed. Colonel Teege and his men had sold their lives for a high price. The Allies spent the morning of November 3 licking their wounds, repairing damaged tanks, and trying to get the attack back on track. General Montgomery decided not to launch a major tank attack this day, but he did order the RAF to bomb the Afrika Korps time and time again with massive formations. In addition, he finally discovered that the Italians south of Tel el Aqqaqir were retreating. He had them strafed by 200 fighter-bombers.[85]

It must have looked to Rommel as if his retreat would be successful. Time would be allowed at least to get the motorized formations back to Tripolitania, where they could be evacuated to Italy and form the core of a new army. However, it was not to be. At 1:00 P.M. Captain von Helldorf of the Panzer Army Operations Staff arrived with an order from Adolf Hitler. He approached Westphal. "An order from the Fuehrer, Herr Oberst," he said.

"What does it say, von Helldorf?" the colonel asked.

"It is the death warrant of the Army, Herr Oberst," von Helldorf replied, simply.

"What?" growled the astonished Westphal. He read it and flung it on the table. "Now they've gone completely mad back there," he said, probably more to himself than to von Helldorf.

Rommel returned to Headquarters at almost the same minute. He found his operations officer completely disgusted. "An order from the Fuehrer," Westphal snapped without preamble. Rommel raised an eyebrow.[86] He was not accustomed to being addressed in this manner by a subordinate, even one who had been with him as long as Westphal. Nevertheless he picked up the message and read it. It said:

November 3, 1942

TO FIELD MARSHAL ROMMEL:

It is with trusting confidence in your leadership and the courage of the German-Italian troops under your command that the German people and I are following the heroic struggle in Egypt. In this situation in which you find yourself there can be no other thought but to stand fast, yield not a yard of ground, and throw every gun and every man into the battle. Considerable Air Force reinforcements are being sent to the C-in-C South. The Duce and the Commando Supremo are also making the utmost efforts to send you the means to continue the fight. Your enemy, despite his superiority, must also be at the end of his strength. It would not be the first time in history that a strong will has triumphed over bigger battalions. As to your troops, you can show them no other road than that to victory or death.

(signed) ADOLF HITLER[87]

Rommel finished reading, sat down, and simply stared out the window. The sound of artillery fire was distinctly audible.[88]

Rommel was flabbergasted. For perhaps the first time in his life he did not know what to do. Finally he said, "So far I have always insisted upon unqualified obedience from my men . . . even if they do not understand my orders or consider them wrong. Personally I cannot depart from this principle and I must submit to it."

"That means the end of the army," Westphal replied.

"I am a soldier," Rommel answered.[89] He would live to regret this decision to obey his commander-in-chief.

Rommel ordered the retreat halted. He commanded the Army to "fight to the last shot," and had hand grenades and machine guns issued to the members of his staff.[90] "You are to fight on to the very utmost," Rommel signaled von Thoma. "You have got to instill this order into your troops—they are to fight to the very limit."[91]

Hitler's order greatly affected the German soldiers, who, by and large, still believed in the Fuehrer. "At the Fuehrer's command they were ready to sacrifice themselves to the last man," Rommel wrote later.[92]

It was too late to do much about the retreat on the southern flank. The British had spent all morning shelling the positions the Italian X Infantry Corps had evacuated, but in the afternoon the British noticed their mistake and occupied the vacant positions. It would be unthinkable to order the Italians to try to retake them. On the northern flank the British attacks were local in nature and easily beaten off. However, in the center, the Royal Dragoons' armored car units and the 4th South African Armoured Car Regiment got through and went on a spree in Rommel's rear. They destroyed supply columns, transport, and shot up whatever rear-echelon units they could find. They also cut off supplies to the front-line soldiers south of them. Now the exhausted Axis veterans faced food and water shortages in the hot desert sun, in addition to everything else.[93]

That night Rommel could see no escape for any part of the Panzer Army. "I can no longer, or scarcely any longer, believe in a successful outcome," he wrote his wife. "What will become of us is in God's hands. Farewell, you and the lad. . . ."[94]

That night Major Elmar Warning of Westphal's staff section sat up with Rommel. The field marshal was still arguing with his conscience. "If we stay put here, then the army won't last three days," he said. "But do I have the right as C-in-C, or even as a soldier, to disobey an order?" He brooded a while longer, and then continued: "If I *do* obey the Fuehrer's order, then there's the danger that my troops won't obey me." Then suddenly he dismissed this thought, and made his decision. "My men's lives come first!" he snapped. "The Fuehrer is crazy. . . ."[95] Rommel had reached the turning point of his life.

Still, old habits are hard to break. He decided to try to hold on a little while longer, until he got the chance to speak to Kesselring the following morning. Perhaps they could get the order reversed, Rommel thought.

On the morning of November 4 the Axis line (if it could still be called that) ran north to south, roughly as follows: The 90th Light Division, now under Major General Theodor von Sponeck, held the coastal sector with 1,000 men, exclusive of the remnants of the 164th Light Afrika Division, which was intermixed with them. Immediately south of them lay the Afrika Korps, with only 24 battleworthy tanks left. The Korps consisted of the 21st Panzer Division and the Kampfstaffel, since the 15th Panzer had virtually ceased to exist. South of this battered force lay the XX Italian Motorized Corps, with only Ariete still in fighting shape. The remains of the Littorio and Trieste divisions formed up south of Ariete. Littorio had only 17 tanks left; Trieste was a total write-off.[96] On the southern flank the XXI Italian Infantry Corps, the Ramcke Parachute Brigade, and the X Italian Infantry Corps (Folgore Parachute and Pavia divisions) lay stranded in the desert. They were under attack from hundreds of British tanks, supported by all arms. The Italian and German paratroopers resisted courageously. Unfortunately, courage was about all they had left.

At 8:00 A.M. on November 4 the first Allied attack against the central sector began. It was spearheaded by 200 tanks. Lieutenant General von Thoma met it with 20 panzers of inferior quality. Nevertheless he turned it back, despite odds of 10 to 1 against him. This fight ran the Eighth Army's tank losses to over 500, or roughtly three times the number lost by Rommel.[97] The difference was that Montgomery could afford it. Rommel could not.

While this battle was in progress, Field Marshal Kesselring arrived at Rommel's headquarters. He received an extremely cold reception. Rommel suspected that Kesselring had been sent by Hitler to see if the Fuehrer's order was being carried out. Rommel berated the commander-in-chief South and denounced Hitler's order as "crazy." To Rommel's surprise, the Luftwaffe commander agreed with the sentiment, if not the wording, of Rommel's remarks. He announced that the Fuehrer's order could not be carried out and must be revoked.

"I would be inclined to regard Hitler's order as an appeal, rather than a binding order," he said to Rommel.

"I regard the Fuehrer's directive as absolutely binding," the Desert Fox replied.

"You must act as the situation demands," Kesselring stated emphatically. "The Fuehrer certainly cannot have intended for your army to perish here."

"It came just like a bolt from the blue," Rommel remarked, with great bitterness. "And I always thought that the Fuehrer trusted me. . . ." He obviously felt betrayed.

Kesselring told Rommel to radio Hitler. "Say that with your forces decimated and vastly outnumbered, the line cannot be held and the only chance of retaining at least a part of Africa lies in a fighting retreat." Kesselring agreed to add his influence to the proposal.[98] Both marshals sent messages to Hitler, demanding that the order be withdrawn.[99]

Meanwhile, another drama was being played out on another part of the battlefield. The setting was a 16-foot-high sand dune on the central sector, almost due west of Kidney Ridge. Here, at a spot on the map called Tel el Mampsra, stood the remaining survivors of the once-proud Afrika Korps and the 90th Light Division. Ritter von Thoma ordered them away, to establish a thin front on either side of the dune. He would personally take the Kampfstaffel and hold the vital position at all costs. The commander of the Afrika Korps had chosen the ground for his last stand.

When Colonel Bayerlein reported to his chief, he found the general wearing all of his many decorations, something no one ever did in Africa. "Bayerlein," von Thoma said to his chief of staff, "the Fuehrer's order is madness. It's the death warrant of the Army. How can I explain it to my men?" He then ordered the valuable Bayerlein to establish a Korps Head-quarters at El Daba, far to the rear, an order that had the effect of sending the colonel to a place of safety. "I shall remain here and conduct the defense of Tel el Mampsra in person, as Rastenburg [that is, Fuehrer Headquarters] orders," concluded the general, with harsh irony. Does the general want to die? Bayerlein asked himself as he departed for El Daba.[100]

Lieutenant General Ritter von Thoma was every inch the fighting soldier Erwin Rommel was. Von Thoma had fought in two world wars and led German armor in the Spanish Civil War. He had been wounded 20 times and held the highest decorations that Germany could give. Now he fought his last battle.[101]

At 11:00 A.M. Thoma's aide arrived at the new Afrika Korps Head-quarters that Bayerlein was in the process of establishing at El Daba. He too had been sent off the battlefield on a pretext. He reported to Bayerlein that von Thoma's force was almost destroyed: tanks, antitank guns, flak, everything. Bayerlein jumped into a small "reece" [reconnaissance] vehicle and raced back to the front. British tank fire forced him to abandon the car, but he proceeded on foot until he came to a crest of sand dunes about 200 yards away from Tel el Mampsra. From here he could see the von Thoma command. As the aide said, it was practically wiped out. Only a few badly wounded men survived. Like some sort of weird ghost the general stood beside a burning panzer in the middle of a hail of machine-gun fire. It was a minor miracle that he was alive at all, but not a bullet touched him. As Bayerlein watched, the firing suddenly stopped. Several Shermans and a Jeep approached. The general walked toward the Jeep and got in without saying a word. The Battle of Tel el Mampsra was over. The dust-covered Bayerlein ran westward, on foot, and finally reached safety.[102] When he told the story to Rommel and Westphal, the chief of operations exclaimed, "For God's sake, Bayerlein, keep it to yourself—otherwise Thoma's entire family will have to suffer for it."[103]

Lieutenant General Thoma dined that night with General Bernard Montgomery, who respected him and treated him with the greatest courtesy. Thoma returned his kindness by inviting the Eighth Army commander to visit him in Germany after the war. This mutual admiration by two opposing soldiers who did not hate each other was the subject of considerable criticism in England and the United States; however, it was not criticized in North Africa by either side.[104]

The destruction of the Kampfstaffel meant that the northern half of the front, like the south, was on the verge of collapse. Despite this development the XX Italian Motorized Corps fought on with their "mobile coffins" against over a hundred British heavy tanks. Major von Luck, one of the German battalion commanders supporting the XX, signaled Rommel that the Italians were resisting "with exemplary courage,"[105] but their low-caliber shells could not penetrate the armor on most points of the Allied tanks.

After leaving Kesselring, Rommel drove to the new Afrika Korps Headquarters at El Daba. He had done considerable soul-searching in the past two days, and had come to a conclusion of momentous importance. He would defy the Fuehrer and order a retreat on his own initiative. It had been the hardest decision of his life. He had decided to break the principle of unconditional obedience for the first time. In doing so, he underwent a "sea change," and would never be the same again. Erwin Rommel had begun to question. Inevitably he would find the answers that would turn him into an enemy of the Nazi regime.

The initial step in Rommel's break with Hitler might be dated from his conversation with Major Warning, or from the remarks Rommel made to Colonel Bayerlein on the afternoon of November 4. He said, "Our front is broken, and the enemy is pouring through to our rear. The Fuehrer's order has become meaningless. We'll fall back on the Fuka position and save what we can. Colonel Bayerlein, I hand over the command of the Afrika Korps to you. If we have to face a court-martial for disobedience we must stand by our decision. . . . All orders to the troops are to be issued in my name. . . ."[106]

At Fuehrer Headquarters, no one appreciated the gravity of the situation at El Alamein for some time. Rommel's dispatch of November 2, in which he reported the initial British breakthrough and requested permission to withdraw 60 miles to Fuka, did not reach Colonel General Jodl until midday on November 3. The duty officer, a reservist major, had received it the night before, but had not seen fit to awaken either Hitler or Jodl. Therefore it reached Hitler's operations officer's desk with the routine correspondence.

Jodl knew that the Fuehrer's order of November 2 had been drafted several days before. Its purpose was to stimulate morale and was based on the assumption that the situation was bad but not catastrophic. Jodl grasped the implications immediately. He rushed into Hitler's private quarters.

"What's the trouble?" Hitler snapped as soon as he saw the look on Jodl's face.

"Bad news from Rommel," was the reply. Jodl handed Rommel's message to Hitler.

Hitler read it and stared into space: always a dangerous sign! "This on top of everything else," he muttered. "Was my special order sent off to Rommel?" he asked quietly.

"Yes, mein Fuehrer, it went off last night."

This answer touched off an explosion. "Why have I only just received Rommel's report on the situation?" he screamed. "Why was it not shown to me last night? Why wasn't I woken? Why?!?" The dictator was roaring at the top of his lungs.

"The major on duty thought—"

"The major thought!" Hitler cut in, having partially regained control of his temper. "Who is the fellow? Couldn't he see that the order I had just sent put me in the wrong on the African position?" A moment later came another violent eruption. "Another instance of stupidity and indifference! I'll make an example of him! The major is to be court-martialed!"[107]

Before the day was out the disgraced major—now a private—was on his way to a labor battalion. However, Rommel did not receive notification that the order was revoked until the morning of November 5. It was a sour note at that. It read: "In view of the way things have gone, I approve your request [to abandon the El Alamein line]. . . ."[108] It was really a superfluous gesture, because the retreat was already well under way by then.

Meanwhile, the men of Ariete had been needlessly sacrificed. They had fought like lions, but could not withstand the weight of numbers that were thrown against them. At 3:30 P.M. on November 4 the division's last signal came in: "Enemy tanks penetrated south of Ariete. Ariete now encircled." Rommel and these men had had their differences, but in their moment of tragedy his heart went out to them. By the evening of November 4 the entire XX Italian Motorized Corps, including Ariete and Littorio Armored divisions and the Trieste Motorized Division, had been destroyed,[109] and all because of an order issued by a Supreme Commander hundreds of miles away from the battlefield!

On October 23 the Panzer Army reported a strength of 293 tanks.[110] After blowing up over 40 tanks in repair shops that they could not take with them, Rommel's army had only 12 tanks left. One dozen tanks in the whole Army! A far cry from the proud legions that had so confidently overrun Tobruk and invaded Egypt just 4½ months before.

10

The Battle of the Tunisian Bridgehead: A Second Front in Africa

During the night of November 4 the remnants of Panzer Army Afrika retreated toward Fuka. The Coastal Road was under constant RAF attack, so most of the Army fell back across the desert. The retreat degenerated into a race with the British armor for the Fuka position, 60 miles west of Alamein. The 1st and 10th Armoured divisions rolled across the desert, and then swung northwest in an attempt to cut the Coastal Road west of El Daba. In a converging move, the 7th Armoured Division headed straight for Fuka. Rommel's veterans eluded this trap, partially due to unnecessary caution on the part of Montgomery, who was not about to take any chances. The Desert Fox had slipped through the noose again.

Although Rommel tried desperately to get the survivors back to Tripolitania, he saw little hope for rebuilding the Panzer Army. During the two-day delay caused by Hitler's order, Rommel lost 200 tanks and armored vehicles.[1] The Italian infantry had been virtually wiped out or taken prisoner, simply because no transportation was available to haul them away. If they had been allowed to march off two days earlier, they might well have escaped. Now they trekked across the desert, isolated from the German contingent at Fuka, and their chances of escaping to the west were just about nil. Miles to the northwest, Rommel had only a few hundred exhausted infantry, a dozen panzers, and a handful of artillery with which to fight.

Rommel did have one advantage for the retreat, and this was the Coastal Road. If he could get his mobile forces out of RAF range and receive sufficient gasoline, he could delay the Allies long enough to get out of Cyrenaica. On the other hand, if Montgomery could reach Mersa el Brega before Rommel, the Axis army would be hopelessly trapped in the Cyrenaican bulge.

The night of November 4 was pitch black, except for when the RAF dropped their magnesium flares. Rommel was in a bitter mood, but the morale of his soldiers remained good, in spite of all they had been through.

On November 5 most of the Afrika Korps, the 90th Light, and a few Italians reached Fuka. Here Rommel made a brief stand in an attempt to rally his army. Soon 200 British tanks and 200 armored cars clashed with his rear guard.[2] Rommel hoped to delay at Fuka long enough to allow part of the X Italian Infantry Corps and the Ramcke Parachute Brigade to link up with the main body. Their escape depended on whether or not Rommel could hold Fuka long enough for them to reach it.

He could not. About noon the British attacked Fuka in a blinding sandstorm. With Rommel's visibility obscured, they soon found their way around his southern flank and threatened his only escape route. Then the sandstorm abated and the RAF reappeared. Their squadrons, unopposed by the Luftwaffe, shot up German motor columns that crowded the Coastal Road, spreading panic and confusion in the Axis rear. Panzer Army Headquarters was bombed twice. Seeing that a decisive engagement was about to develop and knowing that he could not fight one, Rommel ordered a retreat toward Mersa Matruh. This sealed the fate of the Italian infantry to the south.

At dawn on November 6 Rommel tried to reassemble his army, which was scattered all over the desert. The remainders reached the rally points southwest of Mersa Matruh, but the 21st Panzer Division ran out of gasoline and was forced to hedgehog well east of the town. With this force were the last tanks left in Afrika Korps. They were screened by the rear guard, which consisted of what was left of the 580th Reconnaissance Battalion. Captain Voss, one of Rommel's former aides, now commanded this unit. On the afternoon of November 5 he tried to trick the British by deploying for battle, in hopes that they would do the same. The feint did not work, and Allied pursuit columns outflanked him during the night. At 10:00 A.M. the next day 60 Allied tanks attacked the immobilized 21st Panzer. The remnants of the division came very close to being overwhelmed before Voss, on his way back from Fuka, struck the British vanguard in the rear with his entire command. Fortunately for him, the

British did not realize how weak their opponents were. They broke off their attack and withdrew in confusion. Voss joined forces with the panzer unit, and together they repulsed several more attacks before finally being forced to retreat. All immobilized tanks were destroyed,[3] and this meant the loss of most of the panzers left in the Army. Even these ran out of gasoline before reaching Mersa Matruh, but the British did not follow them because it was raining. When the 21st Panzer Division camped for the night it had only four tanks left.[4]

The torrential rains of November 6-7 slowed down the movement of both sides, but they benefited Rommel more. The RAF was temporarily grounded, Montgomery's pursuit efforts were crippled, and the 1st Armoured Division was marooned. It had been in the process of rounding Rommel's right flank when the heavens opened up. Since the division's supply units had wheeled, rather than tracked vehicles, they were stuck in the mud and could not reach the tanks to refuel them. Rommel had gained some breathing space, and a small fuel consignment at last reached him. The 21st Panzer was rescued, while Rommel reorganized the rest of his forces. He sent the Italians to Capuzzo, on the Libyan side of the wire, where General Stefanis, the former commander of the now-defunct XX Motorized Corps, rallied the survivors and formed a new combat group. Soon he had a force of about battalion strength, including 10 tanks.[5]

In the afternoon General Gandin arrived at Rommel's headquarters. he had been sent by the Commando Supremo to assess the situation and ask Rommel what his plans were. Gandin was in no way prepared for what he found. With brutal frankness the German field marshal told him that the Axis forces no longer had a chance of winning a major battle, and would do well to escape at all. Montgomery could go right into Tripolitania if he chose, for there was no one left to stop him. Gandin was visibly shaken when he left Panzer Army Headquarters.

The next day Rommel had another surprise, and a pleasant one, for a change. The Ramcke Parachute Brigade re-established contact with the Army, long after it had been written off as captured. Its escape reminds one of a Greek odyssey. The credit for this daring feat rests solely with its commander, Major General Hermann Bernard Ramcke. This tough warrior had served in the German Marines during World War I, and won a battlefield commission. Later he fought with the Freikorps in the Baltic States from 1918 to 1919. In 1941 he completed jump school (at the age of 51!) and commanded a parachute group in the invasion of Crete, where he took the vital Maleme Airfield. On November 2, 1942, he was cut off when Montgomery penetrated Rommel's center at El Alamein. Ramcke led his brigade through the desert on foot for three days, but refused to surrender, even after news arrived that Rommel had lost Fuka. By now Ramcke's unit was the only Axis force on the former southern flank that was still at large, for the X Italian Infantry Corps had already capitulated. Ramcke, on the other hand, ambushed a British pursuit column, took its trucks, and made good his escape in captured vehicles. After traveling 185 miles through the desert, he reached safety near Mersa Matruh on November 7.[6] Rommel must have felt much younger as he went forward to congratulate the paratroopers.

The rest of Ramcke's career turned out to be as exciting as his escape. After leaving Africa in early 1943, he led the 2nd Parachute Division in the Italian campaign of 1943, and later on the Russian Front. He was transferred to France in 1944 and conducted a brilliant but hopeless defense at Brest later that year. Germany's highest decoration, the Knights Cross with Oak Leaves, Swords, and Diamonds, was parachuted in to him just before the fortress fell.[7] He had received the Oak Leaves to his Knights Cross for his escape from El Alamein.[8]

Rommel had little time to celebrate Ramcke's exploit, for the British attacked again shortly afterward. The 90th Light Division, now the rear guard of the Army, beat off three attacks by the 2nd New Zealand and 7th Armoured divisions. Meanwhile, the Allies flanked the Mersa Matruh positions. They cut the Coastal Road west of Matruh the next day (November 8), but were too late: Rommel had escaped again.

Following his fruitless victory at Mersa Matruh, Montgomery accepted the fact that the pursuit would be a long one, and ordered his main force to halt so that it could rest and reorganize. The pursuit continued under General Lumsden, whose X Corps (now consisting of the 2nd New Zealand and 7th Armoured divisions) was ordered to take the frontier positions and continue on to Tobruk.

Meanwhile, Rommel moved his Army Headquarters to Sidi Barrani, only 60 miles from the Libyan border. Here he worked on military traffic control, because of the large number of traffic jams on the Coastal Road. He also positioned his few remaining anti-aircraft guns along the road, in the vain hope of discouraging the RAF.

Meanwhile, events elsewhere took the African situation even farther out

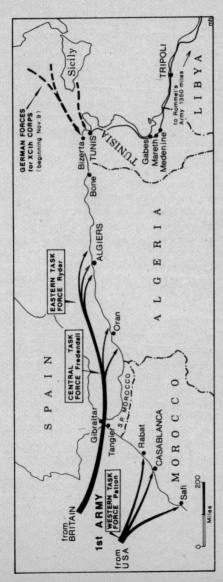

Map 12. The Invasion of French North Africa, November 7, 1942. This surprise Allied move induced Hitler to occupy Vichy France and send 130,000 soldiers to Tunisia, in spite of Rommel's protests that the Axis Empire in Africa was already doomed. This disagreement led to their first serious confrontation.

of Rommel's control. An entire new Allied Army (the First Army) landed in French North Africa. This force, under the overall command of General Eisenhower, waded ashore on November 8 in three widely separated strikes. General Ryder's task force took Algiers, General Fredendall took Oran, and General Patton seized Casablanca. French resistance, which Hitler expected to be formidable, collapsed almost immediately. At best the Vichy forces put up a token defense; at places they surrendered without firing a shot. Algiers capitulated almost immediately; Oran surrendered on November 9; and Patton encountered sporadic firing until November 11. By November 12 the Allied vanguard was within 150 miles of Tunis, and Rommel was caught between two flames. Map 12 shows the Allied landings.

Eisenhower landed in Morocco and Algeria with 80,000 Americans and 25,000 Britons. Panzer Army Afrika was cornered between two strong armies, with the sea to the north and the desert to the south. Rommel barely had enough men left to delay even one of these armies; his rear was completely undefended, for there were no German or Italian military units in Tunisia. Of the Allied landings and the fall of French North Africa, Rommel wrote: "This spelt the end of the Army in Africa."[9] That night, in a state of great bitterness, he voiced his fears to Major General Lunger-shausen. "The campaign in Africa is lost," Rommel said. "If Rome and Rastenburg don't realize it and take measures in time to rescue my soldiers, then one of the bravest German armies ever will take the long road to the P.O.W. camps. Who will then defend Italy against the threatened invasion?"[10]

Rommel's suggested plan of reaction called for an African Dunkirk. Every possible man must be evacuated to defend Italy and southern France from the forces of Eisenhower and Montgomery. Hitler's reaction was very much different, and only compounded the ultimate disaster. He ordered the occupation of Vichy France, and earmarked three German and two Italian divisions for Tunisia. By the end of November, 15,000 men were already in the country. The II Air Corps moved even faster. By midmonth it had 81 fighters (including some of the new FW-190 aircraft) and 28 dive bombers in Tunisia.[11]

For the Allies, Operation "Torch" was almost a total success. Now they had only one strategic objective left before effectively finishing off the Axis Empire in Africa. This was the capture of Tunis, the capital of the French colony of Tunisia. However, the terrain between there and the British vanguard at Algiers was difficult, and much different from that of the Western Desert. The Atlas Mountains and their subsidiary ranges stretch from Morocco to Tunis. Between Algiers and Bizerta the mountains run close to the coast itself. The land is broken, rugged, and occasionally forested. The passes between the mountains are few, and easy to defend; the heavily cultivated coastal valleys become impassable to vehicles in times of rain.[12]

As previously mentioned, the Allied forces in "Torch" belonged to their First Army. They were commanded by British Lieutenant General Kenneth A. N. Anderson and, together with the Eighth Army, made up the Eighteenth Army Group under General Dwight D. Eisenhower. While Patton's Western Task Force remained in Morocco (to guard against a possible Nazi thrust through Spain into Eisenhower's rear), Anderson headed for Tunis with the rest of the Army. He had the 78th (Br.) Infantry, 6th (Br.) Armoured, and 1st (U.S.)* Armored divisions at his immediate disposal. On the other side, Hitler sent every unit he could lay his hands on straight into the bridgehead. On the day of the landings he phoned Kesselring. "What can you send to Tunis?" he asked.

"A handful of paratroops and my staff company," was the reply.

"Send everything you can across," ordered the Fuehrer.[13]

On November 11 the elite 5th Parachute Regiment under the young but battle-hardened Lieutenant Colonel Walter Koch landed in Tunisia. This regiment, nicknamed the "Green Devils," was a tough assortment of veterans, led by an officer of ruthless determination. Koch was a former Prussian police officer who joined the paratroopers in 1935. He had already fought in France, Russia, and Crete, and had won the Knights Cross in the daring glider assault on the Belgian fortress of Eban Emael in 1940.[14] However, not even a veteran regiment like Koch's could do much against two armored divisions. Eisenhower considered the fall of Tunis only a matter of days. Unfortunately, he reckoned without the weather. The heavens opened up and, since western Tunisia was devoid of hard-surfaced roads, Anderson's assault forces were soon literally stuck in the mud.

Eisenhower soon had other problems, which began to mount with alarming frequency. German submarines attacked his supply convoys with

---

*Throughout the remainder of this book, American units will be identified by the symbol (U.S.) and the British by (Br.) when the author believes there is a possibility that the reader might become confused as to the nationality of a particular Allied unit.

Map 13. The Tunisian Theater of Operations

reckless abandon. German pilots were also active, and another fact became painfully apparent: Many of the Allied pilots were still green and were no match for the veteran Luftwaffe aviators, who soon established a limited air superiority for the German forces in Tunisia.

While the Allied advance stalled, General Walter Nehring returned to Africa. He assumed command of the provisional XC Corps, which was given the mission of defending Tunisia. Nehring had no staff, except for his aide. He had only the "Green Devils," an engineer (parachute) battalion, a panzer reconnaissance battalion, and a single 88-millimeter flak battery. His chief of staff, Colonel Pomtow, was with the 3rd Panzer Division in Russia, where his airplane was grounded by snowstorms. Nehring had almost no service support units at all; his transport, for example, consisted mainly of impressed Tunisian taxicabs.[15]

The first major battle of the race for Tunis was fought at Medjez el Bab, south of Jefna and Mateur, between elements of Koch's regiment and a combined force of French, British, and American units (see Map 13). British Major General Evelegh of the 78th Division led the Allied attack. He was supported by parts of the 1st (U.S.) Armored Division and the 6th (Br.) Armoured Division, as well as a French division under General Barré.[16]

Koch was defeated at Medjez el Bab. His regiment was too small to defend such a large sector, and the Allies attacked in overpowering force. One advancing American column overran the vital Djedeida Airfield, and 39 German aircraft were destroyed on the ground. A second American column penetrated to within sight of Tunis itself. Nehring beat them back with the flak battery: his last reserve. Once again the 88-millimeter anti-aircraft gun proved to be the decisive factor in a tank battle. The Americans lost 20 tanks and retreated to Djedeida.[17]

Meanwhile, new German and Italian forces arrived in Tunisia. These included the improvised Barenthin Parachute Regiment, under Colonel Walter Barenthin. By November 22 Nehring had established a thin front on the line Mateur-Tebourba-Massicault.[18] Supported by around-the-clock Luftwaffe air raids from bases in Tunisia and Sicily, he began to solidify his position. Table 12 shows the figures for the aerial support missions and air raids flown by both sides, November 22 - 30. However, this table can be highly misleading if it is interpreted too literally. The Allied air forces had several missions. They concentrated on protecting their shipping routes from Axis air and naval attack, on protecting their recently captured ports

Table 12

**Air Sorties Flown in Support of the First Army and XC Corps,
November 22–30, 1942**

Unit	Sorties Flown	Aircraft Lost
Royal Air Force	1,720	45
Twelfth (U.S.) Air Force	180	7
II Luftwaffe Corps	1,084	63
Italian Air Force	*	?

Source: Jackson, p. 321.

---

*Unknown, but believed to be about 500.

and on bombing Axis shipping and airfields. Kesselring's men concentrated on only one mission: attacking Anderson's strike forces. They killed as many of his men and destroyed as many of his tanks as they could. All other aerial missions received the bare minimum of support, or were canceled altogether. As a result, the Allied advance was slowed and eventually halted.

From November 26 to 29 Anderson again tried to take Mateur and break Nehring's line, but Anderson failed in the face of determined opposition. Colonel Barenthin's paratroopers were primarily responsible for holding the line and saving Tunis.[19]

Meanwhile, an American amphibious force landed behind German lines. Nehring rushed newly landed infantrymen to the threatened sector at once. Of the 500 men in the amphibious task force, most were killed or captured. The rest escaped via naval vessels. The Allied beachhead was wiped out. In a supporting move an American parachute battalion landed north of Zaghouan. It suffered the same fate as the amphibious unit. Of its 500 men, 400 were killed or captured by Nehring's reconnaissance units. Despite their superb training, the immobilized paratroopers were no match for experienced German mobile forces.[20]

By the end of November, most of Major General Wolfgang Fischer's 10th Panzer Division had arrived in Tunisia. This veteran formation had fought in Poland under General Schaal, and was with Guderian in the French campaign. Under Fischer, it had been part of the Second Panzer Army in Russia, where it had distinguished itself at Minsk, Kiev, Smolensk, and the Dneiper crossings. In the summer of 1942 the High Command sent it to France to rest and refit. These processes were largely completed when Eisenhower landed; Hitler promptly threw it into the Tunisian cauldron, where it became the backbone of Nehring's ad hoc XC Corps. The 10th Panzer Division consisted of Major Luder's 501st Panzer Detachment, the 7th Panzer Regiment, the 86th Panzer Grenadier Regiment, the 69th Panzer Grenadier Regiment, and the 90th Panzer Artillery Regiment.[21] The 501st Detachment was equipped with the newly manufactured PzKw VI "Tiger" tank. They were superior to any armored vehicle yet seen in Africa. They weighed over 50 tons and had a long-barreled 88-millimeter gun. No Allied tank yet manufactured could defeat it in a one-on-one situation. In fact, the inferiority of the American tanks was a major reason Anderson lost the race for Tunis, because they were no match even for the PzKw III's. The Allied armored divisions advancing against Nehring consisted mainly of M-3 Stuart (Honey) tanks, not the dependable Sherman. In his book *The Battle for North Africa,* John Strawson described a fire fight in which an M-3 scored 18 hits on a PzKw IV at ranges of 75 to 150 yards without effect. The panzer then destroyed the Stuart at its leisure with a single shell at almost point-blank range. Only one dazed crewman survived.[22] Incidents of this kind occurred all along the Tunisian Front in November and December 1942.

On December 1, Major General Fischer launched a brilliant counterattack in the Djedeida area. The British and American forces barely escaped encirclement. Despite their superior numbers, they were decisively defeated. Eisenhower lost 1,000 to 1,100 men captured, 29 guns and 40 mortars captured, 55 tanks destroyed, and 300 other motor vehicles captured or destroyed.[23] The Anglo-American retreat could not be halted until after the Germans had retaken the critical Djebel el Ahmera position, commonly known and now famous as "Longstop Hill," located about five miles northeast of Medjez el Bab. Eisenhower tried to get the offensive going again by launching another attack with new, better-equipped forces, but was unsuccessful because of stiffening German resistance and the onset of the Tunisian rainy season. He later wrote:

Rain fell constantly. We went out personally to inspect the countryside over which the troops would have to advance and while doing so I observed an incident which, as much as anything else, I think convinced me of the hopelessness of an attack. About thirty feet off the road, in a field that appeared to be covered with winter wheat, a motorcycle had become stuck in the mud. Four soldiers were struggling to extricate it but in spite of their most strenuous efforts succeeded only in getting themselves mired in the sticky clay. . . . We went back to headquarters and I directed the attack to be indefinitely postponed. It was a bitter decision.[24]

Rommel's back door was saved. Eisenhower and Anderson would not join hands with Montgomery and crush the Afrika Korps, at least not in the immediate future. However, it also meant that the Nazis would be pouring thousands more of Germany's first-rate combat soldiers into North Africa, and Erwin Rommel did not like this prospect at all.

A Doomed Empire

While the battles of the Tunisian bridgehead were beginning, Erwin Rommel was still desperately trying to get out of Egypt. He knew that he must reach Mersa el Brega on the Gulf of Sirte before Montgomery; otherwise, Rommel's army would be trapped in the Cyrenaican bulge. This fate had overtaken Graziani in the winter campaign of 1940-41, when Wavell and O'Connor annihilated the Italian First Army in North Africa, and Rommel was afraid history might repeat itself in the winter of 1942–43.

Despite the realities of the situation, Mussolini ordered the Sollum line held at all costs. Rommel considered this impossible. He continued to advocate the total abandonment of North Africa so his army could be saved to defend southern Europe. However, like Hitler, the Duce could not be restrained from pouring new divisions into the area. Elements of the Pistoia Infantry Division arrived on the Libyan-Egyptian frontier, and the Young Fascists Division began to assemble at Mersa el Brega, south of Benghazi, on the Coastal Road. Rommel, still angry with the Commando Supremo, refused to take command of these static units, because he could neither transport nor supply them.[1]

On November 9 Rommel assessed his strength as follows: At Sollum he had 2,000 Italians and 2,000 German soldiers fit for combat. The German contingent had 15 antitank and 40 field guns, while the Italians had several of each. In his mobile reserve, some miles to the rear, Rommel had 3,000 Germans and 500 Italians. They had 11 panzers, 10 Italian tanks, 20 German antitank guns, 24 flak guns, and 25 German field pieces.[2] Despite the quality of the individual soldiers, it was a pitiful force indeed to send against Montgomery's Eighth Army, now the pride of the British Empire.

Winston Churchill recognized the importance of Rommel's defeat at El Alamein. A few months before, at the Cairo conference, he had cried:

"Rommel! Rommel! What else matters but beating him?" Now, on November 10, with the Desert Fox in full retreat, he told the House of Commons, "This is not the end. It is not even the beginning of the end. But it is, perhaps, the end of the beginning."[3] He continued to flood the desert with replacements and reinforcements for the Eighth Army.

For Rommel and his men, it was the beginning of the end. Exhausted soldiers pressed rearward, trying to escape the Allied onslaught. They ate half rations, dove into ditches to escape RAF fighter-bombers, and engaged in bitter rear-guard skirmishes with British pursuit columns. Familiar names and places were passed: Mersa Matruh, Sidi Barrani, Sollum, Capuzzo, and Barbia were all abandoned, never to be retaken. Back they continued, always back. At Halfaya Pass they almost lost the 90th Light. A British armored brigade got behind the gallant little division and headed for the pass, where a small Italian garrison surrendered without a fight. Major General Count von Sponeck narrowly managed to avoid permanent encirclement by turning south, into the desert.[4] However, the vital pass was forever lost to Germany.

The agony continued for weeks. Major General Karl Buelowius, who had replaced the wounded Hecker as chief of Rommel's engineers, made things as difficult as possible for the pursuers. He blew up the Coastal Road wherever it crossed difficult terrain, and set up mines and numerous booby traps all along the route. Allied vanguards moved into new areas with justifiable caution, for there was no way of telling what kind of reception Buelowius and his men had in store for them.

Although he did not show it to his men, Erwin Rommel was almost on the verge of despair. He was still quite sick, and suffered several fainting spells. He did not write Lucie for a whole week—an unprecedented occurrence, even in war. Finally, on November 9, he sent her a four-word, typed letter. "I am all right," was all it said. When he finally did get around to writing he was hardly cheerful. "When an army gets broken through, it gets a raw deal," he said. "You've got to fight your way out, and you lose the rest of your fighting power in the process. Things can't go on like this much longer, because we're being pursued by a superior enemy."[5]

Rommel's frustration was compounded by the fact that he could not get anyone in Rome or Berlin to see things his way. On November 11, he requested that Kesselring and Cavallero come to North Africa to discuss the possibility of evacuating the Panzer Army to Italy via Tunis. Neither the Luftwaffe commander nor the Italian field marshal would come.[6] The decision had been made: Hitler would not voluntarily give up North Africa. Rommel, of course, realized that he would have to give it up, voluntarily or otherwise, in the near future. This knowledge did not make his job in Cyrenaica any easier.

The next day, November 12, Captain Berndt returned to the front. He had been told at Fuehrer Headquarters to inform Rommel that the Tunisian Bridgehead would be held, despite his opinions on the subject. He was to leave Tunisia out of his calculations. Mersa el Brega was to be held at all costs.[7] The order did not take into consideration the very real possibility that the Panzer Army would be destroyed before it could even reach this position.

"All our work in this theater has been for nothing," the Swabian wrote his wife that day. "I've made a superhuman effort, that's true enough. But for it all to end like this is very bitter."[8] "I wish I were just a newspaper vendor in Berlin," he confided to Lieutenant Armbruster about the same time. "Then I could sleep nights without the responsibility I have now."[9]

Meanwhile, the main body of the Panzer Army reached the Gazala line. Rommel ordered von Sponeck to hold Tobruk until nightfall, so he could get the retreating columns safely behind the minefields. Von Sponeck obeyed, and the fortress was abandoned during the night of November 12-13. Rommel had held his great prize less than five months.

On November 13 German intelligence reported another giant British flanking movement. Over 1,000 vehicles were spotted south of the 90th Light. Rommel wasted no time in ordering the evacuation of all of Cyrenaica at full speed.

The next day Rommel ran out of gasoline. The Luftwaffe had flown only 60 tons of fuel over the Mediterranean in the previous month, instead of the 250 tons Rommel demanded. The Army was unable to reach its daily objectives, and the British were not far behind.

On November 15 the fuel crisis reached its peak, when all German combat divisions except the 90th Light ran out of gasoline. "Overzealous people" blew up Rommel's ammunition dump at Barce. The Panzer Army was now in danger of running out of ammunition as well as gas. To add insult to injury, an Italian naval convoy loaded with fuel turned back instead of entering the endangered harbor of Benghazi.[10]

On that same day General Ritter von Pohl, the Luftwaffe liaison officer to Rome, was unfortunate enough to be on a visit to Rommel's headquarters. It was the field marshal's 51st birthday, and von Pohl brought him a large cake from Kesselring and a box of chocolate and almond macaroons from Lucie. Although these were his favorite candies, they did nothing to sweeten his attitude, because von Pohl also brought a message from Commando Supremo: "Mussolini wants you to know that massive reinforcements are already flowing into Tunis and Tripoli, but they will take time to reach the front line. The fate of the Axis presence in Africa depends on your holding the new line at Agheila."[11]

The discussion quickly turned to supplies. Rommel needed 400 tons of gasoline a day, he said, but some days he got none at all. If things continued like this, the Panzer Army Afrika was doomed.

Pohl tried to defend the Luftwaffe, and thus incurred Rommel's wrath. "Stop fobbing me with your phony figures," he snapped at the unhappy general. "What I need is gasoline by the shipload. If your Luftwaffe offers to airlift certain quantities to me, then I must expect you to keep your word. I need 175 tons to enable my army to move at all. You can't even give me 40!" The interview ended unsatisfactorily for all concerned. "It's enough to make you scream," Rommel wrote to his wife.[12]

The Afrika Korps remained immobile throughout November 16. The only thing that prevented the Eighth Army from completing the destruction of the Panzer Army was Rommel's reputation. If his power was gone, his spell was not. His mystique alone caused his thousands of enemies to advance on his shattered little army as if it were still capable of offering serious resistance. As a result, the Afrika Korps survived two consecutive days of total isolation in the face of an overwhelming enemy.

While the main German forces lay immobilized, the Italian Supply Headquarters panicked. They were seized by what Rommel described as "a perfect frenzy of destruction." Vitally needed supply and ammunition dumps, and even water points, were destroyed.[13]

The British grew somewhat more aggressive on November 17. They appeared on Rommel's right flank, at Msus. This meant that Benghazi was effectively outflanked, and the British were driving on Agedabia, south of the Cyrenaican bulge. Rommel would have to reach this position on the Gulf of Sirte first, or the Army would be cut off. Fortunately for the Desert Fox, the torrential rains of November 6-7 had caused flooding in the Msus area. The wet ground delayed the British flanking column, while the Germans, at last refueled, could move much more rapidly along the Coastal Road. Also, Monty still advanced with great timidity.[14] He continued to act as if he halfway expected Rommel to create another army out of thin air.

On November 17 Rommel sent the 33rd Reconnaissance Battalion to cover his flank, which the British column at Msus had put in such serious jeopardy. This move provoked a small battle west of the ruined village at dawn the next day. The British forces were beaten back by the reconnaissance unit. Meanwhile, Rommel hastily prepared for the evacuation of Benghazi. Several supply barges were lost in heavy seas when Rommel tried to ship them out. As this evacuation continued, Major General Buelowius prepared to blow up harbor and dock installations. These operations were completed by the morning of the 19th. Before noon von Sponeck's division passed through the city, the tattered rear guard of a once-powerful army. The capital of Cyrenaica changed hands for the fifth and final time in the war. That evening the German contingent reached Agedabia, where the gasoline and diesel again ran out. Although 500 tons of fuel had been accumulated at Tripoli, and a tanker carrying 1,200 tons had just arrived, the Commando Supremo could not get it to the front. Even the 10 tons at Buerat were 250 miles away. Rommel ordered every available supply vehicle in the army to bring up fuel so he could become mobile again. Fortunately for him the British remained relatively inactive. The risky but expedient measure eased the situation. However, Rommel's army was rescued by an occurrence that must have seemed like a miracle to the men involved. On the morning of November 21 the field marshal was sitting in his staff car, listening to the rain, apparently lost in thought. At that moment Luftwaffe General Hans Seidemann ran up to the car in a state of great excitement. The entire coastline from Agheil to Mersa el Brega was littered with thousands of oildrums! They were the cargo of the Italian tanker sunk on the 17th.[15] Quickly Rommel sent detachments out to salvage them. This piece of luck and the emergency resupply effort saved Panzer Army Afrika. By November 23 the Army was safely installed in the Mersa el Brega line, south of Agedabia. This excellent position lay behind a 10-mile salt marsh that Montgomery would find very difficult to outflank.[16] The race had been won, and the Panzer Army was out of danger, at least for the moment.

The respite gained by the successful withdrawal to Mersa el Brega gave Rommel time to reorganize and count his losses. The force that assembled behind the salt marsh was equal to about a third the strength of the Army that defended El Alamein. Table 13 shows the losses Rommel suffered between October 23 and November 21. Only one conclusion is possible from an examination of these figures: The Army was crippled.

As of November 21, Rommel had four German divisions at his disposal: the 15th and 21st Panzer, the 90th Light, and the 164th Light Afrika, reinforced by the Ramcke Parachute Brigade. Not a single division was at anything approaching 50 percent of its authorized strength. The Italian forces at Mersa el Brega were in somewhat better shape, especially the reconstituted XXI Italian Infantry Corps, now under General Navarrani. However, all three of his divisions (Pistoia, Spezia, and Young Fascists) were new to the North African Theater, and were still quite green.[17]

Table 13

Casualties Suffered by Panzer Army Afrika, October 23–November 22, 1942

	Killed	Wounded	Captured*	Total
Germans	1,100	3,900	7,900	12,900
Italians	1,200	1,600	20,000	22,800
Totals	2,300	5,500	27,900	35,700

Source: Rommel, p. 358.

---

*Includes missing.

While Rommel's men improved their positions, Marshal Bastico visited their leader at Mersa el Brega. He urged Rommel to hold the line here at all costs. Rommel refused to adopt this shortsighted course of action. He tried to convert the Italian to his way of thinking, but Bastico remained unconvinced. As a result another conference was called, for November 24.

On that day Marshals Cavallero and Kesselring finally came to Africa for the meeting Rommel had been demanding for some time. It took place in a small village on the Cyrenaica-Tripolitanja border. Bastico also was present.

Rommel felt that Kesselring and Cavallero were far too optimistic about the general situation, so he painted as gloomy a picture as possible concerning the Army's condition. He stated that the whole Panzer Army's resources equaled the strength of one weak division. He said that he would not allow the new and inexperienced Italian divisions to do battle with the veteran British under any circumstances. With such reduced forces, the Mersa el Brega line could not be held. He proposed that Tripolitania be evacuated as soon as possible. As usual, Kesselring and Cavallero opposed a retreat. Kesselring tried to flatter Rommel into attempting a stand. "We're all full of admiration for your retreat from El Alamein," he said. "To have brought back a major army over 800 miles along one highway, without the enemy being able to prevent you, is surely unique in the history of this war!"

"What am I supposed to do if the enemy ties into my army in the next day or two on the front and then outflanks me with stronger forces?" Rommel interrupted.[18]

Kesselring could not answer this question. However, he expressed the view that if the British were allowed to capture the air bases in Tripolitania, the Luftwaffe's position in Africa would be greatly jeopardized. To this Rommel replied that if they really wanted to hold the Mersa el Brega line, they must supply him with at least 4,000 tons of gasoline and 4,000 tons of ammunition. He also requested 50 PzKw IV's, 50 75-millimeter antitank guns, and 78 field guns of over 100 millimeters in caliber. The other three marshals remained silent while Rommel presented his requirements. They all knew perfectly well that these requirements could not be met. At the time Rommel spoke he was receiving less than 13 percent of his supply needs each day.[19]

Rommel summed up the overall military situation this way: "We either lose the position four days earlier and save the army, or lose both the position and the army four days later."[20]

No agreement could be reached with such diametrically opposing views. The decision was left to Mussolini. While Rommel awaited the Duce's reply, Rommel decided to take a break, and went to see a movie on the evening of November 25. The newsreel came on. There was Rommel at the Berlin press reception. "We have the door to Egypt in our hands . . ." he said. The troops roared with laughter. This was probably the most embarrassing moment in Rommel's life. Erwin Rommel laughed at by his own soldiers! His depression deepened. Was he now the laughingstock of the Third Reich?[21]

Rommel's mood was not improved the next day, when a dispatch reached him from the Italian dictator. Rommel did not have the authority to order a retreat, it said. Only Bastico had that right. The Duce even expected Rommel to launch limited counterattacks![22] As one might expect, the field marshal's already frayed temper flared into anger. He decided to go over Mussolini's head, and personally fly to Rastenburg and appeal directly to Hitler. Rommel placed General Gustav Fehn in temporary command of the Panzer Army.[23] This decision indicates how critical Rommel considered the situation. The new general had just arrived to replace the captured Ritter von Thoma. Rommel had probably never served with Fehn before, and apparently had little confidence in him. Nevertheless, Rommel considered it imperative that he fly to East Prussia, so he swallowed the pill and left Fehn in charge.

Rommel was convinced that overly optimistic reports from the Italians and Kesselring lay behind Hitler's failure to understand the actual situation in North Africa. Rommel believed that once he briefed the Fuehrer on the true state of affairs, the leader would draw the necessary conclusions and accept Rommel's views as long-range policy. Little did Rommel know how much times had changed; he was no longer a favorite of the Nazi dictator, as he had been in the days of Cherbourg, "Battleaxe," and Knightsbridge. Now he was just another professional soldier who had been defeated and had thus let the Fuehrer down.

Rommel arrived at Rastenburg at 4:00 P.M. and immediately went to see Jodl, Keitel, and his friend Schmundt. He found Jodl and Keitel "wary and reserved."[24] A man with more political understanding would have grasped the full significance of their attitude immediately, but Rommel was never politically adroit. At 5:00 P.M. he was ushered into Hitler's presence.

"There was a noticeable chill in the atmosphere from the outset,"[25] Rommel commented later. Hitler's first words were harsh. "How dare you leave your theater of command without my permission!" he exclaimed.[26] Nevertheless, Rommel ignored the warning signs and spoke his mind, and again made the mistake of being too blunt. He said that the situation in North Africa was hopeless and that the abandonment of that zone of operations should be accepted as long-term strategic policy.

Hitler exploded. For the first time Rommel was treated to one of his famous scenes. The field marshal remembered: "I had expected a rational discussion of my arguments. . . . But I did not get very far, for the mere mention of the strategic question worked like a spark in a powder barrel. The Fuehrer flew into a fury and directed a stream of completely unfounded attacks upon us."[27]

Hitler called Rommel a defeatist and accused his men of being cowards.

Generals who had made the same sort of suggestions in Russia had been shot, he bellowed. He would not yet do this to Rommel, but the field marshal had better be careful. Never afraid, Rommel began to explain the reasons for his defeat at El Alamein and the reasons why he felt North Africa was a lost cause. He was continually interrupted by Reichsmarshall Goering, who was playing the role of Hitler's mouthpiece. The conversation went something like this:

ROMMEL: "We had not enough fuel."

GOERING: "But your trucks fled back in their hundreds along the coastal road. There was fuel enough for that."

ROMMEL: "We also had no ammunition."

GOERING: "Nevertheless, you left 10,000 artillery shells behind in Tobruk and Benghazi."

ROMMEL (flushing): "We also had not enough weapons" (emphatically).

GOERING: "And what happened to the weapons? The weapons were thrown away on your flight."

HITLER (breaking in): "But anyone who throws away his weapons deserves to rot."

ROMMEL (jumping to his feet, scarlet with rage): "Mein Fuehrer . . ."

HITLER (banging his fist on the table and screaming): "Anyone who throws his weapons away and has no gun left to defend himself with must be left to rot. Withdraw from Africa? Never!" he roared. "What arms have we in Naples?" he asked the chief of OKW.

KEITEL: "Six thousand rifles lie there ready to be transported, mein Fuehrer."

HITLER: "Send them all over at once."

ROMMEL (not satisfied with 6,000 rifles): "Of what use would they be, mein Fuhrer?" Then, despite Hitler's close-minded and violent attitude, he continued to evaluate the North African situation. He concluded that the region could not be held, and said: "Let me withdraw the Panzer Army to Italy so that it can defend the Continent against Eisenhower's anticipated invasion."

HITLER (very coldly): "I no longer want to hear such rubbish from your lips. North Africa will be defended as Stalingrad will. Eisenhower's invading army must be defeated at the Italian front door and not in the Sicilian parlor." Rommel tried to continue, but Hitler cut him off again. "North Africa will be defended and not evacuated. That is an order, Herr Feldmarschall!"

Hitler was beyond control. He raved on and on about how his decision to hold on at all costs had saved the Eastern Front in the winter of 1941-42. He expected his orders to be ruthlessly obeyed in Africa as well.

Rommel interrupted, and asked him whether it was better to lose Tripoli or the Afrika Korps.

Hitler replied that the Afrika Korps did not matter. It would have to fight to the bitter end.

Rommel, also very angry now and totally uncowed by Hitler's tantrum, asked if Hitler or some of his entourage would come to Africa and show them how to do it.

At this, Hitler became completely unglued. "Go!" he screamed. "I have other things to do than to talk to you!"

Rommel saluted, turned on his heel, and walked out. After he had shut the door, Hitler came running after him. He put his arm around Rommel's shoulder and said, "You must excuse me. I'm in a very nervous state. But everything's going to be all right. Come and see me tomorrow and we will talk about it calmly. It is impossible to think of the Afrika Korps being destroyed."[28]

The next day, November 29, Rommel reported to Hitler as ordered. As promised, the Fuehrer was in a calm mood. He said to Goering, "Do anything you like, but see the Afrika Korps is supplied with all Rommel needs." "You can build houses on me," the Reichsmarshall replied, using an old German adage. "I am going to attend to it myself."

The Luftwaffe chief took Rommel with him on his special train to Rome, and Frau Rommel was invited to travel with them. In the train Goering talked of nothing but diamonds and pictures. He described how Balbo sent him a statue of Aphrodite from Cirene, but otherwise North Africa was not mentioned. Goering did award Rommel the Air Force Pilot's Cross in Diamonds, apparently thinking this should satisfy the Desert Fox. To Frau Rommel, who received Goering's assurances that he would look after her husband, it seemed as if Goering were on the verge of megalomania. She recalled later: "My husband was quite shattered. 'They just can't and won't see the danger,' he said. 'But it is coming at us with giant strides. The danger is—defeat.' "[29]

Rommel commented later that "Goering did nothing but look for pictures and sculpture. He was planning how to fill his train with them. He never tried to see anyone on business or do anything for me." This went on for three days. Finally Rommel gave up and said, "I'm doing no good over here—only losing my temper. I'd better get back to the Afrika Korps." He decided to fly back to Libya on December 2, convinced that Goering was mad.[30] However, Rommel was to be twice humiliated before he got to make the trip.

Rommel did make one attempt to convert Goering to his view of the African situation before he left. With Captain Berndt he tried to make the proposed retreat acceptable to the Reichsmarshall. The persuasive Nazi captain succeeded, but only until they reached Rome. There Kesselring broke the spell created by Berndt and again infected Goering with false optimism. The Reichsmarshall soon announced that further retreats were out of the question.

In the Italian capital Rommel and Goering met with Mussolini. Hitler's second-in-command informed the dictator that Rommel had left the Italians in the lurch at El Alamein. Before the Desert Fox had recovered from his outrage enough to speak, the Duce replied, "That's news to me! Your retreat was a masterpiece, Marshal Rommel."

Despite Mussolini's words of praise, Rommel finally broke down later that day. He had luncheon at the luxurious Hotel Excelsior, with Goering, Milch, and other German and Italian officers. "During the lunch," Luftwaffe Field Marshal Erhard Milch later wrote in his private papers, "Goering savagely insulted Rommel, which cut him to the quick. Rommel asked me up to his room afterward, and for several hours I tried to console him. But he was such a nervous wreck deep down inside that he finally buried his head in my right shoulder and wept for some time. He just couldn't get over Hitler's lack of trust in his leadership."[31]

Rommel must have been relieved to return to the front, if for no other reason than to escape the Roman circus in which he found himself. He rejoined the army at Mersa el Brega, whence he had launched his daring drive on Cairo just eleven months before. In that short period he had retaken Benghazi, overrun the Galaza line, stormed Tobruk, invaded Egypt, penetrated almost to the gates of Alexandria and the Nile, and caused panic in the most powerful capitals in the world. He had won great victories against overwhelming odds, and was a legend in his own time. His name would live on after his death in the annals of warfare as one of the most cunning warriors in all history. His reputation alone was enough to cause greatly superior forces to advance against his pitifully small army with the utmost timidity. Now, however, most of the men with whom he had left Mersa el Brega were in European hospitals, Canadian prison camps, or lying dead in unmarked graves somewhere in the Sahara Desert. The Panzer Army was now a shell, the Afrika Korps a broken reed, too weak now to throw itself at the throats of the masses that would soon overwhelm it. Still, they had been men; they had advanced boldly, attacked recklessly, and defended stubbornly; they had been something to reckon with in their time. Rommel knew all this as he walked through their camps, watching the young men carefully tending their faithful but worn-out panzers as if they were sick old friends. They were getting ready for their next encounter just as if they were sure they were going to win it, when both he and they knew they would not. That they would surely face the inevitable defeat with the spirit and courage the world had come to expect from the Afrika Korps did not make Rommel feel any better. They had been betrayed and were being sacrificed. The Afrika Korps was doomed.

Epitaph

The end came six months later. Hitler continued to pour soldiers into his Tunisian house of cards until it collapsed. Germany lost 130,000 men it could not afford to lose. The Afrika Korps died hard, as Rommel knew it would. After firing their last rounds into the advancing enemy, the survivors of a hundred fire fights smashed their rifles, blew up their panzers, and marched off to prison camps. As Rommel predicted, there was nothing left with which to defend Italy. Sicily fell in July 1943, and by September Mussolini was overthrown, to be replaced by an anti-Nazi government. Meanwhile, the German Sixth Army was annihilated at Stalingrad, because Hitler again had refused to consider a timely evacuation. Germany was now retreating on all fronts, and the days of the Third Reich and a unified Germany were numbered.

Erwin Rommel was recalled from Africa in March 1943. He soldiered on, with increasing misgivings about Hitler and a deep and growing distrust for the Nazis. Finally he became convinced that they were betraying the German people, as they had betrayed the Afrika Korps. He then took what was for him a characteristic step: He joined the conspiracy to dispose of the dictator and stop the slaughter, despite the risk of his own life.

On July 17, 1944, Field Marshal Erwin Rommel was commanding German forces in Normandy when bullets from an enemy aircraft shattered his skull. Three days later, while the Desert Fox lay in a coma in a French hospital, Colonel Count Claus von Stauffenberg planted a bomb under Adolf Hitler's feet. The mass murderer was wounded in the subsequent explosion, but survived. Enraged and almost out of control, he ordered the Gestapo to track down everyone associated with the plot, along with their families. The conspirators were to be hung with piano wire; their loved ones were to be sent to concentration camps. Soon Rommel's complicity was discovered, and on October 14, 1944, he was offered the choice of suicide or a trial by the People's Court, where the verdict was already decided. If he killed himself, Hitler's messengers said, none of the customary actions against his family would be taken. Rommel replied that he would be dead in 15 minutes. He is buried in the village of Herrlingen, not many miles from Heidenheim, where he was born.

Notes

1.

1. Desmond Young, *Rommel: The Desert Fox* (New York: Harper & Row, 1965), p. 90.
2. Erwin Rommel, *The Rommel Papers*, ed. B. H. Liddell Hart (New York; Harcourt, Brace & Company 1953), p. 170 (hereafter cited as "Rommel"); W. G. F. Jackson *The Battle for North Africa, 1940-43* (New York: Mason/Charter, 1975), p. 178.
3. Ronald Lewin, *Rommel as a Military Commander* (New York: Ballantine Books, 1970), p. 12 (originally published by D. Van Nostrand Company, Princeton, N.J., 1968).
4. Paul Carell, *The Foxes of the Desert* (New York: E. P. Dutton & Company, 1960), p. 93 (hereafter cited as "Carell").
5. David Irving, *The Trail of the Fox* (E. P. Dutton & Company, 1977), p. 150.
6. Frederick Wilhelm von Mellenthin, *Panzer Battles: A Study in the Employment of Armor in the Second World War* (Norman: University of Oklahoma Press, 1956), p. 86; Rommel, p. 177; Lewin put the British losses at 37 tanks against seven for the Germans (Lewin, p. 119).
7. Carell, p. 117.
8. Young, p. 14.
9. Charles Douglas-Home, *Rommel* (London: Excalibur, n.d.), p. 20 (originally published by Saturday Review Press, New York, 1973).
10. Young, pp. 13-16; Irving, pp. 12-13.
11. Young, pp. 15-16.
12. Ibid., pp. 16-17.
13. Irving, pp. 12-13.
14. Erwin Rommel, *Attacks* (Vienna, Virginia: Athena Press, 1979), p. 59. (originally published in Germany as *Infantry Greift An [Infantry in the Attack]*, 1936).
15. Irving, p. 14.

16. Lewin, pp. 5-6; Young, pp. 20-21.

17. Irving, p. 22; Young, pp. 30-31.

18. Ibid.

19. Young, p. 31.

20. Irving, p. 24.

21. Ibid., p. 29.

22. Young, pp. 40-41.

23. Irving, p. 32.

24. Young, p. 41.

25. Ibid.

26. Heinz Werner Schmidt, *With Rommel in the Desert* (London: G. Harrap and Company, 1951), p. 86.

27. Rommel, p. 4.

28. Heinz Guderian, *Panzer Leader* (New York: Ballantine Books, 1967), p. 18 (originally published by E. P. Dutton & Company, New York, 1957).

29. Irving, pp. 40-42.

30. Ibid.

31. Ibid.

32. Rommel, pp. 82-84; Young, p. 54.

33. United States National Archives Microfilm T-84, Roll 276; Rommel, p. 84.

34. Rommel, pp. 94-95.

35. Ibid., p. 9.

36. Ibid., p. 4.

37. Young, p. 104.

38. Ibid.

39. von Mellenthin, p. 63; the noted British military writer and historian, B. H. Liddell Hart, also concluded that the Allies had a qualitative superiority in armor (see Hart, *The Tanks: The History of the Royal Tank Regiment and Its Predecessors* [2 vol.] (London: Cassell & Company, 1959) Vol. II, pp. 92-98 and 154-56).

40. Ibid.

41. Young, pp. 103-4.

42. Ibid., p. 101.

43. Ibid., p. 101-3.

44. Schmidt, p. 88.

45. John Strawson, *The Battle for North Africa* (New York: Bonanza Books, 1969), p. 75.

2.

1. Young, p. 89.
2. Carell, pp. 108—9.
3. Ibid.
4. Walter Warlimont, "The Decision in the Mediterranean" in H. A. Jacobsen and J. Rohwer, eds., *Decisive Battles of World War II: The German View* (New York: G. P. Putnam's Sons, 1965), p. 187; also see Herbert A. Werner, *Iron Coffins* (New York: Bantam Books, 1978) (originally published by Holt, Rinehart & Winston, 1969) for an excellent account of the German U-boats in the war.
5. Warlimont, p. 187.
6. Rommel, p. 180; another 55 tanks dispatched to North Africa were sunk en route in late December (Lewin, pp. 118-19).
7. von Mellenthin, p. 87.
8. Ibid.
9. Irving, p. 154.
10. Carell, pp. 126-27.
11. Ibid., p. 129.
12. Rommel, p. 180.
13. B. H. Liddell Hart, *History of the Second World War* (2 vols.) (New York: G. P. Putnam's Sons, 1972); Vol. I, p. 266.
14. Ibid, p. 95.
15. Carell, p. 128.
16. Ibid., pp. 127-28.
17. Irving, p. 155.
18. Carell, p. 129.
19. Ibid.
20. Young, p. 91.
21. Rommel, p. 181.
22. Carell, p. 133.
23. Schmidt, pp. 125-26.
24. Strawson, p. 97.
25. Rommel, p. 182.
26. Irving, p. 156.
27. Ibid.
28. Carell, p. 133.

29. von Mellenthin, p. 104.

30. I. S. O. Playfair, *The Mediterranean and Middle East*, Vol. III, *British Fortunes Reach Their Low Ebb* (London: Her Majesty's Stationery Office, 1960), pp. 148-49; Carell, pp. 134-35.

31. Irving, p. 155; Playfair, pp. 227-28. Strictly speaking, some of the British Grant tanks were actually General Lee tanks, an earlier but almost identical model (Playfair, p. 214).

32. Playfair, pp. 148-49; Carell, pp. 132-34.

33. Carell, p. 135.

34. von Mellenthin, p. 105.

3.

1. Carell, pp. 155-56.

2. von Mellenthin, p. 92.

3. Roger Edwards, *German Airborne Troops, 1936-1945* (Garden City, N.Y.: Doubleday & Company, 1974), p. 109.

4. Irving, p. 156.

5. Ibid., p. 153.

6. Carell, p. 153.

7. von Mellenthin, pp. 92-93.

8. Irving, pp. 159-60.

9. Ibid., p. 160.

10. von Mellenthin, p. 93.

11. Jackson, p. 206.

12. von Mellenthin, p. 93.

13. Playfair, p. 220.

14. von Mellenthin, p. 94.

15. Ibid., p. 93.

16. Rommel, p. 197.

17. Warlimont, p. 190.

18. Rommel, p. 195.

19. Andrew Kershaw and Ian Close, eds., *The Desert War* (New York: Marshall Cavendish Promotions, 1975), p. 28.

20. Jackson, p. 205.

21. von Mellenthin, pp. 111-12.

22. Schmidt, p. 130.

23. Playfair, p. 218.

24. Irving, pp. 162-63.

25. Rommel, p. 187.

26. Irving, p. 160.

27. Ibid.

28. Carell, p. 160.

29. Ibid., p. 161.

30. Rommel, p. 206.

31. Jackson, p. 208; Playfair, p. 223.

32. Carell, p. 165.

33. von Mellenthin, p. 99.

34. Carell, pp. 164-65.

35. Ibid., p. 168.

36. Ibid.

37. von Mellenthin, p. 100.

38. Rommel, pp. 209-10.

39. Carell, p. 168.

40. Irving, p. 166. The South Africans took about 400 prisoners when they repulsed Sabratha's attack (Playfair, pp. 226-28).

41. Jackson, p. 214.

42. Ibid.

43. Carell, p. 170.

44. Rommel, pp. 211-12.

45. Carell, p. 170; von Mellenthin, p. 103.

46. Rommel, p. 211.

47. Jackson, pp. 215-16.

48. von Mellenthin, p. 103.

49. Young, pp. 94-95.

50. Carell, p. 172.

51. Young, p. 93.

52. Ibid.

53. Irving, pp. 171-72.

54. Jackson, pp. 216-17.

55. Carell, pp. 174-75.

56. Ibid., p. 176.

57. Ibid.

58. Ibid., p. 177.
59. Ibid.
60. von Mellenthin, p. 103.
61. Rommel, p. 214.
62. Ibid., p. 218.

4.

1. Jackson, p. 219.
2. Playfair, p. 232; von Mellenthin, p. 128.
3. Playfair, pp. 232-33.
4. von Mellenthin, p. 109; also see Playfair, p. 232.
5. von Mellenthin, p. 109.
6. Ibid. Curiously enough, Field Marshal Auchinleck later wrote: "The failure of
   the Eighth Army's counterattack on 5 June was probably the turning point of
   the battle" (Lewin, p. 149).
7. Carell, p. 179.
8. Jackson, pp. 206-21.
9. Carell, p. 179.
10. Ibid., p. 181.
11. Irving, p. 177.
12. Ibid.
13. Carell, p. 181.
14. Ibid. Hecker was promoted to Major General in the summer of 1944 and later
    commanded the 3rd Panzer Division on the Eastern Front. Baade later
    commanded the 90th Panzer Grenadier Division in Italy and was a lieutenant
    general when he was killed in action in April 1945.
15. Jackson, p. 222.
16. Carell, pp. 182-83.
17. Irving, p. 175. About 2,700 of the original 3,600-man garrison escaped (Play-
    fair, p. 237).
18. Jackson, p. 224; Playfair, p. 240.
19. Jackson, pp. 224-25.
20. Ibid., p. 225. When General Norrie, the XXX Corps commander, learned that
    Messervy was missing, he attached its 2nd and 4th Armoured brigades to the 1st

Armoured Division, but by then it was too late to affect the outcome of the battle.

5.

1. Jackson, p. 225.
2. Ibid.
3. Strawson, p. 106.
4. Playfair, p. 243.
5. The South Africans lost 27 killed and 366 wounded or missing and 13 guns captured in this retreat (Playfair, p. 116).
6. Alan Moorehead, *The March to Tunis* (New York: Dell Publishing Company, 1968), pp. 442-43 (originally published by Harper & Row, New York, 1943); Carell, p. 187.
7. Rommel, p. 224.
8. Young, p. 97.
9. Jackson, p. 231.
10. von Mellenthin, p. 50.
11. Ibid.
12. Ibid.
13. Ibid., pp. 50-51.
14. Ibid., p. 51.
15. Rommel, p. 225.
16. von Mellenthin, p. 53.
17. Rommel, p. 224.
18. Jackson, pp. 232-33.
19. Irving, p. 179.
20. Rommel, pp. 228-30.
21. Ibid., p. 228. Littorio was originally drawn from to create Ariete and Trieste in early 1941, and later supplied these divisions with equipment and replacements in 1942. It was not completely reformed in June, lacking transport and service units and having no engineers at all. Commando Supremo sent it to the front reluctantly, and only because Rommel insisted on having it (Playfair, p. 265).
22. Jackson, pp. 233-34.

23. Rommel, p. 228.
24. Ibid., p. 230.
25. von Mellenthin, p. 144.
26. Carell, p. 194.
27. Irving, p. 182.
28. Ibid.
29. Rommel, p. 231.
30. Ibid.
31. Irving, p. 185.
32. Ibid., p. 186.
33. Young, p. 100.
34. Ibid.

6.

1. Strawson, p. 109.
2. von Mellenthin, p. 122.
3. Warlimont, p. 192.
4. Ibid., p. 193.
5. Ibid.
6. Rommel, p. 232.
7. Jackson, p. 239.
8. Michael Carver, *El Alamein* (New York: The Macmillan Company, 1962), p. 25; Rommel, p. 236; Hart, *Second World War*, Vol. I, p. 277.
9. Rommel, p. 237.
10. Jackson, p. 240.
11. Rommel, p. 237.
12. von Mellenthin, p. 125.
13. Ibid., p. 126.
14. Ibid., pp. 124-26.
15. Rommel, p. 237.
16. von Mellenthin, p. 127.
17. Ibid., pp. 124-27.
18. Carell, p. 232.

19. von Mellenthin, pp. 127-28.
20. Jackson, p. 243.
21. von Mellenthin, p. 127.
22. Rommel, p. 238.
23. Hart, *Second World War*, Vol. I, p. 279.
24. von Mellenthin, p. 129. Most of these prisoners were members of the already decimated 29th Indian Brigade (Playfair, p. 294).
25. Carell, pp. 233-34.

7.

1. Rommel, p. 241.
2. Jackson, p. 243.
3. Ibid., p. 250.
4. Ibid.
5. Ibid.
6. Irving, pp. 190-91.
7. Carell, pp. 238-39.
8. Rommel, p. 243.
9. Ibid., pp. 243-44.
10. Ibid., p. 245.
11. Carell, p. 239.
12. Jackson, p. 253.
13. Rommel, p. 246.
14. von Mellenthin, p. 132.
15. Rommel, p. 249.
16. Ibid. The New Zealanders reported the capture of 44 field guns; some of these were probably taken from the Brescia Infantry Division (see Playfair, p. 343).
17. Jackson, pp. 255-56.
18. Ibid. p. 256.
19. Strawson, p. 125.
20. Rommel, p. 250.
21. Ibid., p. 251.
22. Ibid.

23. Ibid.
24. Ibid.
25. Playfair, pp. 344-45.
26. Rommel, pp. 250-51.
27. Irving, p. 194.
28. Carell, pp. 242-43.
29. Playfair, p. 246.
30. Rommel, p. 253.
31. Irving, p. 195.
32. Carell, p. 243.
33. Rommel, pp. 253-54.
34. Ibid., p. 254.
35. Ibid., p. 255.
36. Carell, p. 244.
37. Playfair, pp. 347-48.
38. Strawson, p. 117.
39. Carell, p. 244. According to the British Official History, the attack on the New
    Zealand antitank gunners was spearheaded by a detachment of eight to 10
    tanks from the 8th Panzer Regiment, which took 350 prisoners after the
    ambush (Playfair, p. 349).
40. Jackson, p. 258. A regiment of the 22nd Armoured Brigade was attached to the
    2nd Armoured Brigade in this battle (Playfair, p. 351).
41. Rommel, p. 256; Jackson, p. 258. Brigadier Barrows of the 4th New Zealand
    Brigade was captured in this action, but later escaped (Playfair, p. 351).
42. Carell, p. 244.
43. Ibid., p. 239.
44. Rommel, p. 259.
45. Ibid., p. 258.
46. Carell, pp. 244-47.
47. Jackson, p. 260.
48. Carell, p. 247.
49. Rommel, p. 258.
50. Ibid., p. 259.
51. See Jackson, pp. 260-61.
52. Ibid.
53. Rommel, p. 260.
54. Young, p. 130.

8.

1. Rommel, pp. 264-65.
2. Carell, p. 248; Rommel, p. 266.
3. Carell, pp. 248-49.
4. Irving, p. 201.
5. Carell, p. 249.
6. Rommel, p. 267.
7. Ibid.
8. Ibid., p. 269.
9. Ibid., pp. 251-69.
10. Ibid., p. 271.
11. Ibid.
12. Ibid.
13. von Mellenthin, p. 151.
14. Irving, p. 205.
15. Rommel, p. 266.
16. von Mellenthin, pp. 140-42.
17. Warlimont, p. 195.
18. Carell, p. 248.
19. Ibid., p. 249.
20. Carver, p. 32.
21. Carell, p. 250.
22. Ibid.
23. Warlimont, p. 200; Jackson, p. 269.
24. Carell, p. 256.
25. Ibid.
26. von Mellenthin, p. 142.
27. Carell, p. 249.
28. Warlimont, p. 200.
29. Rommel, p. 200.
30. Ibid., p. 274.
31. Rommel, p. 274; Carver, p. 128.
32. Carell, p. 251.
33. Rommel, p. 276.
34. Ibid., p. 277.

35. Carell, p. 258.
36. Ibid.
37. Ibid.
38. Young, p. 134.
39. Carell, p. 260.
40. Jackson, p. 269.
41. Rommel, p. 278.
42 von Mellenthin, pp. 144-45.
43. Carver, pp. 58-59.
44. Ibid.
45. Ibid.
46. J. F. C. Fuller, *A Military History of the Western World* (3 vols.) (Minerva Press, 1956); Vol. III, p. 488.
47. Carell, p. 257. This figure excludes the nearly useless PzKw I, II and former Czech tanks.
48. Jackson, p. 274.
49. Carell, p. 260.
50. Carver, p. 66.
51. Rommel, pp. 280-81.
52. Hart, *Second World War*, Vol. I, p. 295.
53. Rommel, p. 280.
54. Irving, pp. 210-11.
55. Rommel, p. 281.
56. Ibid.
57. Jackson, p. 274.
58. Rommel, p. 281; Young, p. 122.
59. Young, p. 126.
60. Ibid., pp. 126-27.
61. Rommel, p. 281.
62. Young, pp. 123-24.
63. Ibid., p. 121.
64. Rommel, p. 283.
65. Jackson, p. 274.
66. Ibid.
67. Rommel, p. 284.
68. Irving, p. 211.
69. Rommel, p. 287.

9.

1. Carell, p. 264.
2. Ibid., p. 267.
3. Ibid.
4. Ibid., p. 269.
5. I. S. O. Playfair and C. J. C. Molony, *The Mediterranean and Middle East*, Vol. IV, *The Destruction of the Axis Forces in Africa* (London: Her Majesty's Stationery Office, 1966), p. 23.
6. Carell, p. 269.
7. Ibid., pp. 268-69.
8. Rommel, p. 291.
9. Ibid.
10. Ibid., p. 287.
11. Ibid., p. 288.
12. Ibid.
13. Ibid. p. 289.
14. Paul Carell, *Hitler Moves East, 1941-1943* (New York: Bantam Books, 1966), pp. 512-19 (originally published by Little, Brown and Company, Boston, 1965). Field Marshal Wilhelm Keitel, the chief of the Armed Forces High Command (OKW), claims to have collaborated with Goering in acquiring a pardon for Stumme (see Wilhelm Keitel, *In the Service of the Reich* [Briarcliff Manor, N.Y.: Stein and Day Publishers, 1979], p. 178).
15. Rommel, p. 293.
16. Carell, p. 283.
17. Rommel, p. 295.
18. Irving, p. 213.
19. Ibid.
20. Ibid., pp. 215-16.
21. Ibid.
22. Rommel, p. 296.
23. Warlimont, p. 201.
24. Ibid., p. 200.
25. Strawson, p. 148.
26. Ibid., p. 132.
27. Young, p. 136.

28. Rommel, p. 300.
29. Field Marshal the Viscount Montgomery of El Alamein, *El Alamein to the River Sangro* (London: Hutchinson, 1956), p. 16.
30. Carell, p. 284.
31. Rommel, p. 303.
32. Carell, pp. 285-86.
33. Ibid., p. 286.
34. Rommel, p. 303.
35. Carell, pp. 285-86.
36. Carell, pp. 286-87; Playfair and Molony, pp. 42-43 and Map 6.
37. Carell, p. 288.
38. Jackson, p. 292.
39. Ibid., p. 293. The British reported dropping more than 135 tons of bombs on the 15th Panzer's sector on October 24 (Playfair, p. 47).
40. Carell, p. 287.
41. Rommel, pp. 304-5.
42. Irving, pp. 218-19.
43. Ibid., p. 219.
44. Jackson, pp. 293-94.
45. Ibid., p. 294. These attacks were turned back primarily by combined battle groups from the 15th Panzer and Littorio Armored divisions.
46. Carell, p. 289. Trento had already lost more than 50 percent of its infantry and most of its artillery (Playfair and Molony, p. 50)
47. Young, p. 136.
48. Warlimont, p. 203.
49. Irving, pp. 219-20.
50. Jackson, p. 295.
51. Rommel, p. 307.
52. Ibid.
53. Jackson, p. 295.
54. Irving, p. 222.
55. Carell, pp. 289-90; Jackson, p. 296.
56. Rommel, p. 310.
57. Ibid.
58. Carell, p. 290.
59. Rommel, p. 311.
60. Jackson, p. 297.
61. Strawson, p. 137.

62. Rommel, pp. 313-15. Rommel also asked OKW to send him the 47th Infantry Regiment from Crete as a reinforcement; Hitler replied that he could have men or supplies delivered by air, but not both. No reinforcements were forthcoming (Playfair and Molony, p. 55).

63. Rommel, p. 313.

64. Warlimont, p. 201.

65. Ibid.

66. Rommel, p. 313.

67. Jackson, p. 298.

68. Rommel, p. 314.

69. Irving, p. 225.

70. Rommel, pp. 314-15.

71. Montgomery, p. 23; Rommel, p. 315.

72. Irving, p. 226.

73. Rommel, pp. 315-16.

74. Irving, p. 226.

75. Playfair and Molony, p. 67; Jackson, p. 300; Rommel, p. 319.

76. Irving, p. 227.

77. Young, p. 138.

78. Carell, p. 292.

79. Rommel, p. 319.

80. Ibid.

81. Carell, p. 293.

82. Irving, p. 228.

83. Jackson, p. 301.

84. Rommel, p. 320; Carver, p. 173.

85. Ibid.

86. Carell, p. 294.

87. Carver, p. 177; Playfair and Molony, pp. 475-76.

88. Carell, p. 294.

89. Ibid., p. 295.

90. Ibid.

91. Irving, p. 232.

92. Rommel, p. 322.

93. Ibid., pp. 323-24.

94. Irving, p. 233.

95. Ibid.

96. Ibid., p. 232.

97. Carell, p. 295.

98. Irving, p. 234.

99. Carell, p. 297.

100. Ibid., 296.

101. Ibid.

102. Ibid., pp. 296-97. The normal establishment of the Kampfstaffel was about 700 men, but its strength on the morning of November 4 is unknown. It probably numbered 300 to 400 men.

103. Irving, p. 235.

104. Young, p. 139.

105. Rommel, p. 325.

106. Carell, p. 297.

107. Ibid., p. 299.

108. Irving, p. 235. The order was dated 8:50 P.M., November 4, 1942 (Playfair and Molony, p. 477).

109. Rommel, p. 325.

110. Carell, p. 301.

10.

1. Rommel, p. 336.

2. Ibid., pp. 338-39.

3. Ibid., pp. 340-41; Carver, p. 189.

4. Carell, p. 310.

5. Rommel, p. 343.

6. Edwards, pp. 151-52.

7. Ibid.

8. Ibid.

9. Rommel, p. 345.

10. Carell, p. 310.

11. Strawson, p. 163.

12. George F. Howe, *Northwest Africa: Seizing the Initiative in the West* in *Mediterranean Theater of Operations* (Washington, D.C.: Office of the Chief of Military History, U.S. Department of the Army, 1957), pp. 280-83.

13. Carell, p. 317.
14. Edwards, p. 159.
15. Carell, p. 319.
16. Jackson, pp. 319-20; Carell, p. 324.
17. Carell, pp. 324-25. The 88 millimeter guns were from the advanced element of the 29th Flak Division.
18. Ibid., pp. 322-24; Howe, pp. 288-90.
19. Carell, pp. 322-24.
20. Ibid., p. 326. The U.S. Army's Official History places the paratroopers' losses at 299, of which 266 were missing.
21. U.S. Army Military Intelligence Service, "Order of Battle of the German Army" (Washington, D.C.: Military Intelligence Service, April 1943), p. 202.
22. Strawson, pp. 160-62.
23. Howe, p. 320.
24. Dwight D. Eisenhower, *Crusade in Europe* (Garden City, N.Y.: Doubleday & Company, 1949), p. 124.

11.

1. Rommel, p. 347.
2. Ibid.
3. Strawson, p. 167.
4. Carell, p. 311.
5. Irving, p. 236.
6. Rommel, p. 348.
7. Ibid., pp. 348-51.
8. Irving, p. 237.
9. Ibid., p. 241.
10. Rommel, pp. 351-52.
11. Irving, p. 242.
12. Ibid.
13. Rommel, p. 354.
14. Ibid. Montgomery implies that the rains significantly delayed his pursuit of the Panzer Army, and this is why it escaped (see Montgomery, pp. 27-29; Playfair and Molony, p. 81-98).

15. Irving, p. 242.
16. Ibid., p. 355.
17. Ibid., p. 358.
18. Rommel, pp. 363-64; Irving, pp. 244-45.
19. Rommel, pp. 363-64.
20. Ibid., p. 362.
21. Irving, p. 245.
22. Ibid.
23. Ibid.
24. Rommel, p. 365.
25. Ibid.
26. Irving, p. 245.
27. Rommel, p. 365.
28. The transcript of this Fuehrer conference was apparently destroyed when the Third Reich fell, and the last known participant died (more exactly, was hanged) in 1947. The author consulted several sources concerning this conference, and none of them agreed exactly. My version is a composite of these, and may not be perfect in every detail. The most useful accounts of this historic meeting are found in Rommel, pp. 364-65; Carell, pp. 313-14; and Young, pp. 141-42.
29. Young, pp. 142-43; Irving, p. 247.
30. Young, p. 143.
31. Irving, p. 248.

Bibliography

Carell, Paul. *The Foxes of the Desert*. New York: E. P. Dutton, 1960.

———. *Hitler Moves East, 1941-43*. New York: Bantam Books, 1966 (originally published by Little, Brown and Company, Boston, 1965).

Carver, Michael. *El Alamein*. New York: The Macmillan Company, 1962.

Chant, Christopher; Humble, Richard; Fowler, William; and Shaw, Jenny. *Hitler's Generals and Their Battles*. New York: Chartwell Books, 1976.

Douglas-Home, Charles. *Rommel*. London: Excalibur, n.d. (originally published by Saturday Review Press, New York, 1973).

Edwards, Roger. *German Airborne Troops, 1936-1945*. Garden City, N.Y.: Doubleday & Company, 1974.

Eisenhower, Dwight D. *Crusade in Europe*. Garden City, N.Y.: Doubleday & Company, 1949.

Esposito, Vincent J., ed. *A Concise History of World War II*. New York: Frederick A. Praeger, 1964.

Forman, James. *Code Name Valkyrie: Count von Stauffenberg and the Plot to Kill Hitler*. New York: Dell Publishing Company, 1975.

Fuller, J. F. C. *A Military History of the Western World* (3 vols.). Minerva Press, 1956.

Goebbels, Joseph. *The Goebbels Dairies*. ed. Louis P. Lochner. Garden City, N.Y.: Doubleday & Company, 1948.

Guderian, Heinz. *Panzer Leader*. New York: Ballantine Books, 1967 (originally published by E. P. Dutton & Company, New York, 1957).

Hart, B. H. Liddell. *History of the Second World War* (2 vols.). New York: G. P. Putnam's Sons, 1972.

———. *The Tanks: The History of the Royal Tank Regiment and Its Predecessors* (2 vols.). London: Cassell & Company, Ltd., 1959.

Hartmann, Theodor. *Wehrmacht Divisional Signs, 1938-1945*. London: Almark Publications, 1970.

Howe, George F. *Northwest Africa: Seizing the Initiative in the West* in *Mediterranean Theater of Operations*. Washington, D.C.: Office of the Chief of Military History, Department of the Army, 1957.

Irving, David. *The Trail of the Fox.* New York: Thomas Congdon Books, E. P. Dutton & Company, 1977.

Jablonski, David. *The Desert Warriors.* New York: Lancer Books, 1972.

Jackson, W. G. F. *The Battle for North Africa, 1940-43.* New York: Mason/Charter, 1975.

Jacobsen, H. A., and Rohwer, J., eds. *Decisive Battles of World War II: The German View.* New York: G. P. Putnam's Sons, 1965.

Keitel, Wilhelm. *In the Service of the Reich.* Briarcliff Manor, N.Y.: Stein and Day Publishers, 1979.

Kennedy, Robert M. *The German Campaign in Poland (1939).* Washington, D.C.: U.S. Department of the Army Pamphlet No. 20-255, April 1956.

Kershaw, Andrew, and Close, Ian, eds. *The Desert War.* New York: Marshal Cavendish Promotions, 1975.

Lewin, Ronald. *Rommel as a Military Commander.* New York: Ballantine Books, 1970 (originally published by D. Van Nostrand Co., Princeton, N.J., 1968).

Montgomery, Field Marshal the Viscount of El Alamein. *El Alamein to the River Sangro.* London: Hutchinson, 1956.

Moorehead, Alan. *The March To Tunis: The North African War, 1940-1943.* New York: Dell Publishing Company, 1968 (originally published by Harper & Brothers, New York, 1943).

Mosley, Leonard. *The Reich Marshal: A Biography of Hermann Goering.* Garden City, N.Y.: Doubleday & Company, 1974.

Neumann, Peter. *The Black March: The Personal Story of an SS Man.* New York: Bantam Books, 1960 (originally published by Éditions France-Empire, Paris, under the title *SS!*, 1958).

Payne, Robert. *The Life and Death of Adolf Hitler.* New York: Praeger Publishers, 1973.

Playfair, I. S. O. *The Mediterranean and Middle East*, Vol. III, *British Fortunes Reach Their Lowest Ebb.* London: Her Majesty's Stationery Office, 1960.

_____. and C. J. C. Molony. *The Mediterranean and Middle East*, Vol. IV, *The Destruction of the Axis in Africa.* London: Her Majesty's Stationery Office, 1966.

Rommel, Erwin. *Attacks*. Vienna, Va.: Athena Press, 1979 (originally published in Germany as *Infantry Greift An [Infantry in the Attack]*, 1936).

———. *The Rommel Papers*. ed. B. H. Liddell Hart. New York: Harcourt, Brace & Company, 1953.

Schmidt, Heinz Werner. *With Rommel in the Desert*. London: G. Harrap and Company, Ldt., 1951.

Shirer, William L. *The Rise and Fall of the Third Reich*. New York: Simon & Schuster, 1960.

Speidel, Hans. *Invasion 1944*. New York: Paperback Library, 1950 (originally published as *Invasion 1944, Ein Beitrag zu Rommels und des Reiches Schicksal*. Tubingen and Stuttgart: Rainer Wunderlich Verlag Hermann Leins, 1949).

Strawson, John. *The Battle for North Africa*. New York: Bonanza Books, 1969.

United States Military Intelligence Service. "Order of Battle of the German Army." Washington, D.C.: Military Intelligence Service, October 1942 (on microfilm at U.S. National Archives, Washington, D.C.; a hard-cover copy may be found at the Library, Army War College, Carlisle Barracks, Pennsylvania).

———. "Order of Battle of the German Army." Washington D.C.: Military Intelligence Service, April 1943 (on microfilm at U.S. National Archives, Washington, D.C.; a hardcover copy may be found at the Library, Army War College, Carlisle Barracks, Pennsylvania).

United States National Archives. Untitled documents concerning the 7th Panzer Division in France, 1940, on Microfilm T-84, Roll 276. Washington, D.C., n.d.

von Mellenthin, Frederick Wilhelm. *Panzer Battles: A Study in the Employment of Armor in the Second World War*. Norman: University of Oklahoma Press, 1956.

Warlimont, Walter. "The Decision in the Mediterranean" in H. A. Jacobsen and J. Rohwer, eds., *Decisive Battles of World War II: The German View*. New York: G. P. Putnam's Sons, 1965.

Werner, Herbert A. *Iron Coffins*. New York: Bantam Books, 1978 (originally published by Holt, Rinehart and Winston, New York, 1969).

Young, Desmond. *Rommel: The Desert Fox*. New York: Harper & Row, Publishers, 1965.

APPENDIX 1

German Units, Ranks, and Strengths

Unit	Rank of Commander*	Strength†
Army Group	Field Marshal	2 or more armies
Army	Colonel General	2 or more corps
Corps	General	2 or more divisions
Division	Lieutenant General/ Major General	10,000–18,000 men 200–350 tanks (if panzer)
Brigade‡	Major General/ Colonel	2 or more regiments
Regiment	Colonel	2–7 battalions
Battalion	Lieutenant Colonel/ Major/Captain	2 or more companies (approximately 500 men per infantry battalion; usually 50–80 tanks per panzer battalion)
Company§	Captain/Lieutenant	3–5 platoons
Platoon	Lieutenant/ Sergeant Major	Infantry: 30–40 men Panzer: 4 or 5 tanks
Section	Warrant Officer/ Sergeant Major	2 squads (more or less)
Squad	Sergeant	Infantry: 7–10 men Armor: 1 tank

---

*Frequently, units were commanded by lower-ranking men as the war went on.

†As the war progressed, the number of men and tanks in most units declined accordingly. SS units usually had more men and tanks than Army units.

‡Rarely used in the German Army.

§Called batteries in the artillery (4 or 5 guns per battery).

APPENDIX 2

German Staff Abbreviations

Ia—Staff Officer, Operations
    (equivalent to S-3 in the U.S. Army)
Ib—Staff Officer, Supplies
    (equivalent to S-4 in the U.S. Army)
Ic—Staff Officer, Intelligence
    (equivalent to S-2 in the U.S. Army)
IIa—Staff Officer, Personnel
    (equivalent to S-1 in the U.S. Army)

The U.S. staff position S-5 (Civil Affairs Section) had no equivalent in the German Army during World War II.

General Index

211

Subject Index